In the COMPANY of FRIENDS

GROUP SUPPORT FOR PEOPLE WHO STUTTER

Dozens and Dozens of Ideas & Plans for Group Meetings

KENNETH O. ST. LOUIS, PHD

Populore
Populore Publishing Company
Morgantown, West Virginia

In the Company of Friends: Group Support for People Who Stutter
Kenneth O. St. Louis

Populore® Publishing Company
PO Box 4382
Morgantown, WV 26504
304-599-3830
stories@populore.com
www.populore.com

Copyright© 2021 Populore Publishing Company

Library of Congress Control Number: 2021913618
ISBN: 978-0-9652699-8-8

All rights reserved. No part of this publication may be reproduced, stored in a retrieval system, or transmitted in any form or by any means, electronic, mechanical, photocopying, recording, or otherwise without prior written permission from the author or publisher, except by a reviewer, who may quote brief passages in a review.

This book is available at www.amazon.com. An electronic version that can be printed, hole-punched, and used in a 3-ring binder is available at www.teacherspayteachers.com.

CONTENTS

Dear Reader ix
Acknowledgments xi

Getting Started

Introduction 1

On Leading a Support Group 5

Conducting a Support Group 9

Lesson Plans

Organization of Lesson Plan Entries:

Theme
Number, Title, (*sub-theme*), Level [L1 = Discussion; L2 = Speaking Activity in Group, L3 = Speaking Activity outside Group]

Support for Stuttering
1. Personalizing the Support Group (*enhancing support for stuttering*), L1 20
2. Identifying Support for Stuttering (*enhancing support for stuttering*), L1 22
3. Seeking the Support We Need (*enhancing listener support*), L1 26

Understanding Stuttering
4. The Stuttering and the Stutterer (*understanding stuttering in total*), L1 28
5. Individual and Situational Factors Affecting the Severity of Stuttering (*understanding the moment of stuttering*), L1 30
6. Understanding Accessory Behaviors (*understanding accessory behaviors*), L1 32
7. Defining Moments of Stuttering (*understanding stuttering in total*), L1 34
8. Nagging Problems Associated with Stuttering (*understanding associated problems*), L1 36
9. Keeping Up Morale in Difficult Circumstances (*understanding moods and stuttering*), L1 38
10. Understanding Thoughts and Emotions Associated with Stuttering (*understanding thoughts and feelings about stuttering*), L1 40

Stuttering in Life
11. Your Life Journey (*stuttering journey now and in the future*), L1 44
12. Telling Our "Story of Stuttering" (*stuttering journey now and in the future*), L1 48
13. Our Stuttering and Our Traits (*identifying assets and liabilities*), L1 50
14. Our Assets: Letting in the Good Stuff (*identifying assets and liabilities*), L1 52

15. Our Liabilities: Opening Up and Trusting (*identifying assets and liabilities*), L1 54
16. Our Self-Image and Our Stuttering (*stuttering and self-concept*), L1 56
17. Determination and Achievement (*following your dream in spite of stuttering*), L1 58
18. Contemplating the Future (*stuttering journey now and in the future*), L1 60
19. Preparing for Job Interviews (*stuttering and job interviews*), L2 or L3 62

Managing Emotions
20. Thoughts and Feelings before, during, and after Stuttering
    (*understanding thoughts and feelings about stuttering*), L1 64
21. The Relationship between Thoughts and Feelings
    (*managing thoughts and emotions related to stuttering*), L1... 66
22. Identifying Emotions Associated with Stuttering
    (*identifying emotions related to stuttering*), L1.. 70
23. Clarifying the Emotions of Stuttering
    (*managing emotions related to stuttering*), L1..72
24. Embarrassment and Shame in Stuttering
    (*managing emotions related to stuttering*), L1..74
25. Feeling Trapped by Stuttering (*feeling trapped by stuttering*), L1 76
26. Identifying Automatic Negative Thoughts
    (*dealing with anxious negative thoughts*), L1 78
27. Analyzing Automatic Negative Thoughts
    (*dealing with anxious negative thoughts*), L1 80
28. Dealing with Negative Thoughts and Emotions
    (*managing thoughts and emotions related to stuttering*), L1.. 82
29. Processing Negative Early Memories of Stuttering
    (*identifying early negative memories of stuttering*), L1... 84
30. Unburdening Negative Memories (*managing emotions related to stuttering*), L1 86
31. Understanding Why We Avoid (*reducing avoidance*), L1...90
32. Avoiding and Missing Opportunities (*reducing avoidance*), L1 92
33. Avoiding Avoidance (*reducing avoidance*), L1... 94
34. Confronting Avoidance (*reducing avoidance*), L1 98
35. Accepting What We Cannot Change (*accepting stuttering*), L1 100
36. Voluntary Stuttering: What Is It and Why Do It?
    (*using voluntary stuttering to reduce fear*), L3..102
37. Voluntary Stuttering to Weaken Fear of Phone Calls
    (*using voluntary stuttering to reduce fear of the telephone*), L3 104
38. Anticipating and Receiving Phone Calls
    (*managing emotions related to stuttering*), L3 108
39. Managing Stressors That Increase Stuttering
    (*managing emotions related to stuttering*), L1.. 112
40. Humor and Stuttering (*using humor in stuttering*), L1.. 114

Dealing with Nonstutterers
41. How Stutterers Are Seen by Nonstutterers
    (*effects of stuttering on listeners*), L1 118
42. Handling Unhelpful Advice (*dealing with negative reactions to stuttering*), L1...............120

43. Understanding and Dealing with Negative Reactions to Stuttering
    (*dealing with negative reactions to stuttering*), L2 124
44. Confronting Negative Personal Messages
    (*dealing with negative reactions to stuttering*), L1 126
45. Messages about Stuttering from Our Childhood
    (*dealing with negative reactions to stuttering*), L1 128
46. Compliments That Aren't (*managing stuttering in difficult situations*), L1 130
47. Understanding Our Reactions to Teasing (*understanding teasing*), L1 132
48. Understanding and Managing Listener Reactions
    (*dealing with negative reactions to stuttering*), L2 136
49. Managing Speaking Situations in Which We Are Judged
    (*dealing with negative reactions to stuttering*), L1 138

Dealing with Adversity
50. Identifying Our Personal Strengths
    (*using strengths to manage difficult situations*), L1... 140
51. Starting Over Successfully (*making a fresh start*), L1..142
52. Making Fresh Starts after Life Changes (*making a fresh start*), L1 144
53. Keeping and Disclosing Secrets (*understanding secrets*), L1 146
54. Being the Best You (*being authentic*), L1 148
55. Reducing the Baggage of Stuttering
    (*unburdening baggage related to stuttering*), L1...150
56. Success and Failure in Achieving Goals (*maintaining a positive attitude*), L1 154
57. Facing Phone Anxiety (*managing stuttering in difficult situations*), L3............................156
58. Overcoming Obstacles to Being Authentic (*being authentic*), L1 158

Goals and Change
59. Choosing or Not Choosing a New Path (*understanding change*), L1............................... 160
60. Understanding the Stages of Change (*understanding change*), L1...................................162
61. Making New Changes in Stuttering (*understanding change*), L1 164
62. Forming Long-Term Habits to Accomplish Goals (*setting realistic goals*), L1.................166
63. Setting Short-Term Goals (*setting realistic goals*), L1 168
64. Giving Up the Idea of Being "Normal" (*setting realistic goals*), L2 172
65. Life Priorities and Change (*understanding change*), L1..176
66. Stuttering Journeys of Change (*understanding change*), L1 178
67. Resisting Change (*resistance to changing stuttering behaviors*), L1...................................182
68. Cost Versus Benefit of Speech Therapy (*motivation for change*), L1 184

Understanding Therapeutic Change
69. Understanding "Comfort Zones" (*expanding comfort zones*), L1 186
70. Expanding Our "Comfort Zone" (*expanding comfort zones*), L1.......................................188
71. Practice and Comfort Zones (*expanding comfort zones*), L2..192

Managing Stuttering
72. Stuttering Behaviors and Stuttering Emotions: The Chicken or the Egg?
    (*managing emotions related to stuttering*), L1..194

73. Acknowledging a Problem (*acknowledging stuttering*), L1 198
74. Acknowledging the Elephant in the Room (*disclosing your stutter*), L2 200
75. Feeling Out of Control When Stuttering (*gaining and maintaining control*), L2 204
76. If You Really Knew Me (*disclosing your stutter*), L1 206
77. Disclosing Stuttering (*disclosing your stutter*), L2 208
78. Monitoring Accessory or Secondary Behaviors
    (*reducing accessory behaviors*), L2 212
79. Improving Eye Contact (*improving eye contact*), L2 216
80. Experimenting with Fluency Shaping (*speaking in a new way*), L2 218
81. Experimenting with Controlling or Changing Stuttering
    (*gaining and maintaining control*), L3 222
82. When a Loved One Does Not Understand
    (*discussing stuttering with significant others*), L1 226
83. Friends, Family, and Stuttering
    (*discussing stuttering with significant others*), L2 228
84. Handling New Situations and New People
    (*managing stuttering in different roles*), L1 230
85. "Speed Dating" and Stuttering (*managing difficult situations*), L2 232
86. Reducing Audience Pressure (*managing difficult situations*), L2 236
87. Managing Time Pressure (*dealing with time pressure*), L2 238
88. Building Confidence (*improving confidence*), L3 240
89. Handling Holiday Stress (*managing stuttering with significant others*), L1 242
90. Staying the Course to Maintain Gains in Stuttering
    (*gaining and maintaining control*), L1 244
91. Pros and Cons of "Quick Fixes" for Stuttering (*searching for a cure*), L2 248

Relapse
92. Understanding Relapse (*understanding relapse*), L1 252
93. Creating a "Return-from-Relapse" Plan (*overcoming relapse*), L1 256

Resilience
94. Being Realistic about Challenges (*enhancing courage and realism*), L1 260
95. Finding Resilience (*enhancing courage and realism*), L1 264

Social Interactions
96. Reducing Social Impediments from Stuttering
    (*effects of stuttering on relationships*), L1 264
97. Stuttering in Conversations When Being Evaluated
    (*managing stuttering in difficult situations*), L2 266

Public Attitudes toward Stuttering
98. Understanding Stuttering Stereotypes (*understanding public attitudes*), L1 268
99. Interacting with Nonstutterers
    (*educating friends and family about stuttering*), L1 270
100. Educating Others about Stuttering
    (*educating the public about stuttering*), L1 272

Stuttering in the Media
101. Stuttering in Movies and Television *(stuttering in the media)*, L1 274
102. Stuttering in the Media *(stuttering in the media)*, L1 276

Improving Communication
103. Identifying Better Communication Skills
    (conversation skills and stuttering), L1 278
104. Encouraging and Discouraging Social Interactions
    (conversation skills and stuttering), L1 280
105. Conversation Skills and Stuttering *(conversation skills and stuttering)*, L1 282
106. Gestures and Body Language *(understanding body language)*, L2 284
107. Communicating Nonverbally in Silence *(understanding body language)*, L2 288
108. Making Small Talk *(improving small talk)*, L2 290
109. Managing Unexpected Social Stress and Stuttering
    (improving small talk), L1 294
110. Becoming a Better Public Speaker *(improving public speaking)*, L2 296
111. Maximizing Enjoyment during Conversation
    (conversation skills and stuttering), L1 298

Appendices
A. Icebreakers 303
B. Brief Speaking or Role Playing Topics 311
C. Speaker/Listener Roles or Characteristics 317
D. Paired Role Playing Scenarios and Debate Topics 319
E. Welcoming Words and Closing Words 325
F. Instruments and Handouts 327
G. Session Goals for Participants 335
H. Glossary of Stuttering Words 337
I. Other Ideas for Support Group Sessions 343
J. Sample Descriptions of Actual Group Meetings 345
K. Benefits for Visitors 357

About the Author 363

DEAR READER

Let me introduce myself and tell you why and how I wrote this book.

In terms of training and career, I'm a recently retired speech-language pathologist who spent all but three years of his professional career at West Virginia University (WVU). As a professor there for 42 years, I did all the things professors do, which they like to classify as teaching, research, and service. I taught classes to undergraduate and graduate students training to become speech-language pathologists who would, for the most part, take jobs where they would provide speech therapy for the entire gamut of speech, language, and swallowing disorders. Although I taught, supervised clinical practica, and carried out research in most of those areas, the overwhelming amount of my effort was with stuttering. I taught the undergraduate and graduate courses in fluency disorders. I carried out many, many research projects in stuttering and its second cousin, cluttering, and I am still very much involved in research. However, the part of my work that is relevant to this book is the clinical supervision I did with stuttering individuals every single semester at WVU wherein graduate students would carry out speech therapy. For the first two decades, I did not arrange group therapy for our stuttering clients; all the work was in individual settings. Whereas this is no doubt the ideal setting in which to learn specific stutter-reducing skills, I always knew something was missing. Therefore, in the late 1990s, I arranged for a few stutterers to meet in groups and found that their shared experiences were enlightening, affirming, and highly useful to them as part of their individual therapy.

Fortuitously, in about 1999, a young man sought my help to start a chapter of the National Stuttering Association in Morgantown. We tried several different approaches in the support group and gradually settled on an overall plan that has not changed much in the past 23 years. Having been a member of the National Stuttering Association, and its predecessor, the National Stuttering Project, since its inception, I knew that our unique approach was more structured than most support group chapters. But it worked for us. I invited my graduate students to attend and found that, with this brief experience in the company of people who stutter, their comfort level, interest, and enthusiasm for treating stuttering increased dramatically. For that reason, I decided to organize a parallel group therapy setting for stuttering adults using the relatively structured scheme we had developed. I arranged for two graduate students to facilitate the group each week throughout the university semesters. Additionally, all of my graduate students in the fluency disorders courses visited the group, so we typically had at least one or two nonstuttering guests. I invited the stutterers in the NSA group to attend the group therapy if they wished and the stuttering clients in the group therapy to attend the NSA group if they wished. In this way, the two groups ran consecutively twice a month, with the NSA group following every other weekly group therapy for at least 10 years. I tried to keep the NSA group relatively unstructured, which was suggested by a few "veterans." Over time, however, lack of attendance at the NSA group increasingly occurred because the participants preferred the structure of the group therapy.

For this reason, I successfully petitioned the NSA Board to permit me to combine the groups. Thus, for the past ten years, the Morgantown Chapter of the NSA has meet weekly during the university semesters and only rarely in the summer. Our support group has intermittently had a sizeable attendance, but mostly the number of "regulars" is small, typically three to five, but sometimes a few as one or two. The written lesson plans and evaluations of more than 450 sessions were the raw material for this book.

Why have I persisted in leading these groups so long? My whole life, I have had an abiding interest in improving the lot of people who stutter. I stuttered myself as long as I can remember. It was in college that I finally gained control of my stuttering on any long-term basis, and, interestingly, this included a group therapy component. Although I am mostly recovered now, I still stutter from time to time, especially when I begin speaking Turkish (which I learned in a two-year stint in the Peace Corps after my undergraduate degree). I found the NSA group to be the best teaching tool I ever developed for students as well as the most effective way to provide insight and desensitization toward stuttering in clients. Probably the most important reason for my persistence, however, is that the support group became the highlight of my week in many ways. I always emerged from the group feeling lighter, more centered, and happier. What else could I wish for?

Not to be self-serving, but it might be useful to readers in other fields to know that I hold the Certificate of Clinical Competence in Speech-Language Pathology from the American Speech-Language-Hearing Association (ASHA) as well as having been recognized as a Board Certified Specialist in Fluency Disorders from the American Board of Fluency and Fluency Disorders. At West Virginia University, I have been recognized as a Benedum Distinguished Scholar and recipient of the Heebink Distinguished Service Award to the State of West Virginia, the latter for my efforts helping local citizens who stutter. Internationally, I was awarded the Deso Weiss Award for Excellence in Cluttering by the International Cluttering Association the Lifetime Achievement Award by the International Fluency Association and the Dave Rowley Award for International Initiatives from the British Stammering Association.

—Kenneth (Ken) O. St. Louis, PhD

ACKNOWLEDGMENTS

I wish to thank all of the people who stutter or clutter who attended our group for the past 23 years. I learned from every single one of the individuals listed below. It was their participation that made our support group a success.

This book could not have been done without the hours and hours of help by a host of graduate students in speech-language pathology at West Virginia University. Two at a time for an entire semester, they helped me develop plans, facilitate meetings, and write reports of their sessions. I acknowledge them below, many or most of the women by their maiden names when they were students.

STUTTERING OR CLUTTERING PARTICIPANTS

Abhinau, Adam, Adel, Adnan, Alana, Alden, Alan, Alta, Amin, Andrew, Asif, Asma, Austin, Becky, Ben, Beth, Bill, Brian, Brooke, Bryan, Charlene, Chris, Clay, Cody, Danielle, Danny, Dixie, Elias, Fred, Gemma, Gene, Gina, Ian, Joe, Joe, Joey, John, Kelly, Kevin, Kim, Kirk, Ksenia, Kunal, Larry, Maggie, Maroua, Mary, Matt, Matt, Matthew, Megan, Michael, Mike, Mike, Mike, Moriah, Natasha, Pavel, Ray, Ron, Ryan, Sam, Saurav, Scott, Seth, Tiffany, Tim, Tony, Undra, Vivash, 1 remote from Florida, 2 remote from Pennsylvania, and 13 remote from Wisconsin.

STUDENT FACILITATORS

Trish Adkins, Jennifer Asbury, Lindsey Ashworth, Paige Bankert, Alivia Bartifay, Olivia Bayer, Jesse Beaseley, Kaitlyn Bond, Ashley Boyle, Emily Brewer, Megan Burgess, Melissa Carr, Jessica Cartee, Casey Carter, Karli Casto, Megan Church, Sarah Cole, Jennifer Cruse, Linsey Cushing, Ashley Daniels, Vanessa DeCesare, Benjamin DeFazio, Angela Dixon, Dana Douglas, Mackenzie Dowdy, Katie Duffe, Jessica Fair, Christa Fisher, Carrie Fox, Seneca Fox, Katie Frazier, Emily Garnett, Erica Gorman, Jennifer Gregory, Jamie Griffith, Brittany Grove, Jenny Haines, Tess Halverson, Anne Hardy, Avery Harris, Carolyn Helenski, Erin Hicks, Crystal Hightower, Nicole Horne, Shaunda Isabelle, Emily Justice, Elisabeth Kee, Nikki Keefer, Rhea Lafferty, Jennifer Lawrence, Ryan Lee, Staci LeMasters, Kristen Mack, Natalie Miller, Victoria Molinaro, Amanda Morgan, Leah Muccioli, Lauren Myers, Elena Nicholl, Taylor Nichols, Sara Palmer, Amanda Payne, Desiree Phillips, Sandra Policicchio, Debi Rodeheaver, Jensen Scott, Max Shafer, Cindy Shaffer, Whitney Shannon, Lora Siers, Taylor Snodgrass, Heidi Solomon, Maggie Sphar, Alyssa Spielman, Ashley Suddath, Sarah Swoger, Sarah Teter, Tracy Toman, Katherine Valora, Brianne Worek, Amanda Worrell, Amy Wyatt, and Cynthia Zmroczek.

GETTING STARTED

INTRODUCTION

If this book achieves its purpose, it will no doubt have pages with corners turned down, pages with coffee stains, and pages with scribbled notes in the margins documenting comments that were made by various participants or new ideas for next time. The book aims to serve as a guide for leaders of self help or support groups for the slightly less than 1% of the population who have a chronic stutter after the age of about 16. Organized by themes, *In the Company of Friends: Group Support for People Who Stutter* presents specific plans for activities found to provide dynamic, meaningful, and healing group sessions for people who stutter and anyone who cares to attend who might not stutter.

These session descriptions were selected from more than 450 sessions individually planned and carried out in the Morgantown Chapter of the National Stuttering Association (NSA) or as part of group therapy for adults who stutter at West Virginia University (WVU) from 2001 to 2019. For virtually the entire period, two speech-language pathology master's level students were assigned by semester to alternate each week leading the NSA chapter support group. They met weekly with their supervisor, the author, for one hour each week to plan the upcoming session; carried out the plan in the group; and summarized the outcome of the session in writing. Those plans and evaluations served as the raw material for this book. Of course, no individual participants' comments or reactions are provided; the book only summarizes the goals, activities, and potential take-away lessons for each chosen idea and plan.

Covering 15 different themes and 63 sub-themes, each of the 111 plans in the book follows a predictable format. Every session begins with NSA's "Welcoming Words," read by anyone who volunteers or even read in unison. Immediately after that, all participants identify a goal they would like to work on during the session and evaluate at the end. Next, a short warm-up or icebreaker ensues that is designed to set the stage for a fun, even whimsical, interchange of ideas. Activities that are highly variable, from introspections to role plays to watching videos, have the purpose of getting beyond simply thinking or talking about stuttering. Instead they seek to connect with everyone's lived experience. After the activity, the session typically moves to a discussion of what might be learned or what lessons could be "take aways" from the session. Finally, everyone evaluates their performance, relative to their individual goals, on a scale from 1 to 10, and someone volunteers to read the "Closing Words."

As noted, *In the Company of Friends* is meant primarily to be a guide for group leaders. Obviously, it does not include a plan for every conceivable group. In such cases, the ideas and themes presented, along with a list of other ideas in an appendix, can be used as the raw material to generate novel plans that meet the needs of any particular group. Additionally, the book could and has been adapted for group therapy with adults who stutter carried out by speech-language pathologists (SLPs). It does not advocate any particular approach to becoming more fluent or stuttering less, which are best taught in individual therapy, but every session is designed to help enhance greater insight into one's stuttering and/or foster desensitization to the negative emotions that frequently accompany chronic stuttering.

The book will also be useful as a clinical resource for SLP graduate students and practicing SLPs for use with any speech-language disorder for which group therapy with clients can be beneficial. Clearly, some of the themes deal directly with stuttering, but most deal with feelings associated with any life-style change, and many deal with communication effectiveness in general. Whereas the ideas and plans are designed for adults, most of them could be adapted for adolescents or even elementary-school-aged children. Furthermore, many of the plans could easily be adapted for a group of parents of children in speech therapy, whether the children all have the same diagnosis or not.

The author has often told group participants that the groups are not so much about stuttering as they are about life. No one gets through life without dealing with hardships, injuries, shortcomings, or disabilities. Great healing for any of these unwanted or unwelcome circumstances can come from dealing with them in a gentle, sensitive, and even humorous way in a safe place with others doing the same thing. Therefore, *In the Company of Friends* can be adapted and used in many other settings, from support groups for other issues to intentional groups wishing only to experience more happiness.

DISCLOSURE ON TERMINOLOGY

I've been told that I'm a bit of a maverick. I'd like rather to think of myself as a person who follows rules that make sense but questions rules that are outdated or that create other problems, which are worse than the solutions they intend. In any event, I need to disclose that in this book, I do not follow the common "person-first terminology." The reader will immediately discover that the word "stutterer" appears in virtually every plan.

I am fully aware of the arguments for writing "person who stutters" or "people who stutter" rather than using the labels "stutterer" or "stutterers." The rationale is that we who stutter are much more than our stuttering, just as those with virtually any disability or difference are much more than the disability or difference. I, like many in the stuttering self-help movement, have chosen not to be obliged never to use the term "stutterer." My reasons are as follows:

First, strict person-first terminology has resulted in confusion. Because clinicians and researchers in the field of fluency disorders found "person/people who stutter" to be awkward, they immediately adopted the abbreviation "PWS." When they needed to make a distinction between adults and children, it split to "AWS" and "CWS." And when a distinction in research studies needed to differentiate stuttering and nonstuttering participants, those who did not stutter have been designated "PWNS" or "PWDS," and so on. In a recent study on cluttering, a "syntactic clutterer" was referred to as "PWSC," and a "phonological clutterer" as "PWPC." Furthermore, with these abbreviations, it becomes impossible to distinguish singular or plural in some contexts. These "letter salads" have, in my view, made our communication unclear and disjointed.

Second and more important, the above abbreviations trivialize the serious difference between pejorative versus non-pejorative labeling of someone who stutters. Although others feel differently, personally, I find it more pejorative to be labeled as a "PWS" than a "stutterer." In the end, however, it is how one regards a fellow human being with stuttering that indicates empathy and acceptance—not the word or letters one uses to label him or her.

My third reason is that there is virtually no evidence that the term "stutterer" is more pejorative than the term "person who stutters." I showed that clearly in a study published in the Journal of Fluency Disorders *in 1999. Since then, the findings of that study have been replicated or supported in a number of other research studies or Op Ed pieces by Brocklehust, Collier, and Dietrich, Jensen, and Williams.*

Of course, I could have used "spelled out" person-first terminology in this book, which I have done in numerous articles. Yet, in the lesson plans, it would be exceedingly awkward to do so consistently. For example, in one plan that highlights the difference between the behavior and the person, "The Stuttering and the Stutterer," an instruction reads, "4. Ask the participants to look at their ratings and think about the extent to which their ratings were on how the person likely perceived their stuttering ("the stutterER") versus how much the ratings were on the actual observable and/or audible symptoms ("the stutterING"). Invite them to share their insights." To try to make clear the distinction between the nonstutterers and the stutterers as well as between the stutterer's behavior and their thoughts and feelings toward their stuttering would be awkward indeed.

REFERENCES:

Brocklehurst, P. (2005). *"Stammerer" or "person who stammers"? A comparison of the impact of two labels on the general public.* Unpublished sociolinguistics project. De Montfort University, Leicester, UK.

Collier, R. (2012). Person-first language: Noble intent but to what effect? *CMAJ (Canadian Medical Association Journal), 184,* 1977–1978.

Dietrich, S., Jensen, K. H., & Williams, D. E. (2001). Effects of the label "stuttering" on student perceptions. *Journal of Fluency Disorders, 26,* 55–66.

St. Louis, K. O. (1999). Person-first labeling and stuttering. *Journal of Fluency Disorders, 24,* 1–24.

ON LEADING A SUPPORT GROUP

If you have volunteered or been appointed to lead a support or related group, you are to be congratulated. You are in the position to help others in ways you may not even imagine. Your group may well be the first place where a young man who stutters tells others, "I stutter." It might be the first really safe place that a woman who has spent her entire life successfully hiding a stuttering problem reveals that she has become so worried she will be found out that she has begun to avoid most speaking situations.

Whether you are a new or seasoned leader, you must realize that others have entrusted very important parts of their lives to you. And while you are in an enviable position to help them, a number of important responsibilities come with that. By all means, you should read carefully and abide by any and all aspects of the code of ethics of the organization you serve. Among many other important mandates, several are worth mentioning here.

Perhaps most important, your group must be, and remain, a safe haven for the participants. This means you cannot contribute to—or cannot condone—any violations of any participant's privacy, dignity, or trust. "What happens in Vegas stays in Vegas" is a good principle to follow here. And when a person shares something that is especially difficult or private, it is worth reminding the group members that they have become trustees, in a sense, and cannot talk about what happened outside the group.

Also important is that you must accept what anyone says as their own truth. Participants must not attack or criticize others, regardless of what someone may believe. No one should receive messages that what they believe is wrong or unacceptable. That does not mean that you or everyone else should agree. The group should be or be becoming a forum for participants to test out their beliefs with others. A good way to foster free exchange of ideas without belittling anyone's views is to suggest and help everyone learn to make "I statements." In other words, they should learn to say something like, "If *I* understand you, *I'm* not sure *I* would explain/interpret/do it that way, *I* would…" This issue has come up numerous times in our group regarding a particular approach to therapy. A participant comes to the group for the first time after experiencing a very successful approach to becoming more fluent. The new person then might easily begin offering advice to others to either attend Program "X" or to try Strategy "Y." The leader must step in immediately and remind the enthusiastic new member that this group is not about anyone advising others what to do. If that person wishes to share his or her own experiences, that is fine, but judging or coaching others is off limits.

You also must create a climate in the group where everyone has a chance to speak, share, and be accepted, even those who are typically very quiet. Sometimes that may involve saying something like, "Jerry, I wonder if you have something to offer about…" Or you might sometimes need to interrupt someone who has monopolized a conversation and say something like, "Joan, I really like what you've said, but in the limited time we have, I want to be sure everyone has a chance to speak."

In the Company of Friends is intended for support groups—not for group psychotherapy! Sometimes a thin line separates the two, but a support group leader must have a clear sense of what issues go beyond the purposes of the support group. In rare instances in our experience, people have shared something about themselves that is decidedly more personal or more potentially damaging than the typical issues faced in stuttering. If or when that happens, it is up to you, the group leader, to gracefully accept what was said, perhaps with a long inhalation and a few seconds of silence, and then intervene and say something like, "Yes, that is a very difficult and significant problem for you. I'd like to suggest that we talk after the meeting, and maybe I can help you find a better place to deal with that issue." In other words, if issues such as drug addictions, sexual assaults, criminal activity, or suicide come up, you must intercept the conversation and steer it back to the topic at hand. If you can, help the person find an appropriate referral to a mental health specialist who is equipped to manage the problem.

Occasionally, participants willfully or inadvertently advocate for a particular religious or political position. Here, again, you should interrupt immediately and inform the persons involved that the purpose of the group is to deal with stuttering—not X, Y, or Z. And then you should redirect the group immediately to the topic at hand.

Following are some other tips, that we have learned over the years, which promote positive interactions and effective groups.

- Stay aware of the time, and do your best to start and end on time.
- Provide large name tags that everyone prints themselves, using first names only. Pass materials to newcomers, and ask them to write their name so everyone can read it.
- Provide water or soft drinks and individually wrapped snacks in the middle of the table.
- Introduce new members to everyone in the group yourself, so they do not need to do so. If you stutter doing so, it will set the tone for acceptance of any and all stuttering.
- Remind everyone when a newcomer arrives that "Everything is optional in this group. We encourage everyone to participate, but if anyone does not want to, he or she can say or wave 'Pass.' Simply observing is just fine."
- Avoid saying, "Let's go around the room and tell us X" because many people who stutter have had spectacular failures with their speech doing so. Instead, always preface an instruction with "in no particular order, who would like to volunteer to X." If an activity is "going around the room," it is often helpful to break the pattern yourself and share something.
- Accept long silences while participants think of what they want to say and, if necessary, remind everyone that "silence is golden" sometimes, especially any guests who do not stutter. After a few sessions, people become more comfortable with silence.

- As a leader, try to position yourself so you have a clear view of everyone's face. Scan everyone when you ask for sharing to be sure that someone is not trying to overcome a silent block while trying to get started talking. If that happens and someone starts talking sooner, you might say, "Juan, you looked like you were going to say something. Is that right? Go ahead, we can wait."
- Inasmuch as possible, maintain good eye contact with every speaker, even during very long blocks.
- Engage early arrivers in small talk as they are comfortable doing so, and include others in the conversation as they arrive.
- If you are comfortable doing so, help everyone see that humor is sometimes a wonderful healer.
- Be yourself. Be the best yourself you can be.
- At the end, sincerely thank everyone for coming, especially any newcomers.
- Provide opportunities for stutterers or others to participate remotely with Zoom or another electronic meeting platform.

Clearly, this book is intended to be a guide for leaders of support groups for people who stutter. But it can also be adapted and used as a guide for leaders of any support or healing group. You can adapt any of the plans to suit your own needs. For example, all of the plans call for reading the National Stuttering Association's "Welcoming Words" and "Closing Words." Those are not necessary if your group is not an NSA group or if they might not apply to the participants.

CONDUCTING A SUPPORT GROUP

THE SETTING

Effective support groups can be carried out almost anywhere. Just as social gatherings or parties "happen" in a variety of settings, support groups can too. Still, as any experienced "social chair" will tell you, some settings make for better gatherings or parties than others. Virtually all support groups meet in spaces designed for other activities, whether that be a church basement room, a room in a restaurant, a family living room, a university or high school classroom, or the conference room of a local business. And these are typically determined by who a regular participant might know, who might volunteer a meeting room or space at no cost, the time of the meeting, and so on.

Whatever space is available, it should be rendered as compatible to a support group as possible. Following are some considerations that can make the difference between a marginal setting and an excellent setting:

- The room should be heated / air conditioned / vented such that it will be physically comfortable for participants accustomed to the local climate.

- Most adults interact most easily while sitting around a large table or a few tables pulled together in as close to a square or circle as possible. Tables are also amenable to writing, manipulating materials, etc.

- Library-style chairs often encourage more movement and flexibility than large easy-chairs or couches. They also put everyone on roughly the same eye level. Folding chairs may or may not be comfortable for middle-aged to older participants.

- Since some people, especially older people, have difficulty hearing in a noisy environment, the room should be essentially quiet—not in or next to loud talking or loud music. It should also be free of excessive external noises such as sirens, loudspeaker announcements, etc. Everyone should be able to hear a soft speaker with little difficulty.

- The room should have a door that can be closed, to encourage personal sharing and the feel of a private, safe place.

- Ideally, the room should have a large screen that can be used for playing videos from a computer or for participants who wish to join the group remotely, through Skype or another electronic meeting format.

- Ideally, as well, the room should have access to a white board (or traditional blackboard) or flip chart for writing by the leader or participants for everyone to see.

- The leader should ensure that the group will not be interrupted frequently by others who are unaware of the support group.

- Water, coffee, tea, soft drinks, juice and/or snacks can help make a support group setting inviting and friendly as well as permit some participants to come who otherwise would have to seriously delay a meal.

SCHEDULING AND TIME

Support groups can be carried out at any time, depending on the participants' schedules, average age, work commitments, home responsibilities, and so on. This book presents lesson plans that were developed for stuttering individuals, many of whom were college students and/or current or former clients in a university speech clinic. Nevertheless, over the years we have had participants with a variety of circumstances including some who were working in local businesses or for themselves, retirees, and even individuals who drove up to four hours to attend sessions.

The duration of the meetings should partly be determined by the frequency of the meetings. Our meetings typically met on a weekly basis, so most meetings were designed for one hour, although we often exceeded that time by 10–15 minutes. Other support groups that meet monthly often meet for 1½ to 2 hours.

Our group opted for a late afternoon / early evening time from 6:00 to 7:00 p.m. in order to accommodate most people who work until 5:00 or 5:30 and to accommodate those who attend regular meetings or activities later in the evening. Partly for this reason, we always provided drinks and light snacks for participants who may not have been able to eat dinner before the meeting.

PUBLICIZING AND NOTIFYING

Clearly, if a support group is to be successful, those individuals who might wish to attend must first learn of the group. Most stuttering organizations, such as the NSA, have excellent suggestions on their websites of how to announce and advertise an individual chapter or group. Word-of-mouth, newspaper, radio, television, internet sites, and social media should all be considered in promoting a new support group. For stuttering groups, it is worthwhile to make contact with local speech-language pathologists (SLPs) and/or university training programs for SLPs to notify them of a new support group. And new leaders must be patient in the early stages when either no one or only one or two participants come to groups. This is a very common experience of most leaders.

Once a group has been established, consistency is a big reason that it continues. Changing the monthly/bimonthly/weekly meeting date, the meeting time, or the meeting venue should be done only when absolutely necessary and infrequently. Participants, if they are to be regular, must be able to fit the meeting into their life routine, which has numerous other demands on their time and loyalty. Since most participants do not come to every meeting, there must be a go-to person, email address, website, or social media site to regularly and easily confirm meeting dates and times, special events, cancellations, and so on. The leader or administrator of these announcements must respond to queries immediately and tactfully. Sometimes it takes months before a stuttering person will have the courage to try a support group meeting. If that person comes to a place where the meeting is no longer held or has been cancelled, he or she may never try again.

In our NSA group, we have had an email list for years with everyone on it who has expressed an interest in the group and has given permission for his or her name to be added. The day before every support group meeting a group reminder email is sent to everyone on the list announcing the date, the time, the location, and, often, a teaser related to the topic of the upcoming meeting. In recent years, our NSA group has had a Facebook page where a similar announcement is posted before every meeting, usually along with a humorous meme that is relevant to the meeting's topic. Anyone who wishes their name to be removed from the email list is immediately accommodated. Interestingly, however, the email list contains addresses of persons who have not come to the group in years. And several times a year, someone writes back to offer a comment, to wish us well, or to catch us up on their life. Apparently, our weekly email is not a burden to most of these individuals.

WELCOMING GUESTS

The dynamics of any group are changed by the addition of one new person. That is one reason successful support groups for stuttering encourage nonstuttering persons to attend the meetings. If a group is near a university SLP training program, it is often the case that arrangements are made for students to come to the NSA support group to observe and participate. Students have brought a great deal of vitality to our group over the years, and virtually all of them benefitted greatly from the experience. Local SLPs also are frequent guests, sometimes bringing a high school student who stutters or the parent of a youngster who stutters. These SLPs must be forewarned that NSA support groups are not places to send stuttering clients to simply practice their fluency shaping target or practice voluntary control techniques. Of course, it is fine if their clients practice on their own, but if not, no feedback or coaching is to be given. The support group is not intended to be a speech therapy group that is simply an extension of individual speech therapy.

Any other guests can bring renewal and additional liveliness to well-led support groups. This gives regular participants the opportunity to share their stories of stuttering with those who typically know little about the speech disorder. This is often a highly therapeutic accomplishment. At the same time, guests are educated about stuttering and the special difficulties faced by individuals who stutter.

Occasionally, a guest will speak more than perhaps is desired. When that happens, just as with any participant, the leader should intervene fairly quickly. An easy way to do this is to express appreciation for the guest's contribution but point out that the group seeks to allow everyone to contribute, especially if they have not yet done so.

Regular support group participants may not need or wish to hear the confidentiality words each meeting, but when guests are present, it may be wise to read them at the beginning of the session, or at any other time that is more appropriate. Most of the activities in this book are designed to include nonstuttering individuals; thus, the confidentiality statement will easily be seen as applying to everyone.

SPECIAL STRUCTURE OF THE SUPPORT GROUP MEETING PLANS

INDIVIDUAL LESSON PLANS

The plans in this book are designed to deal with a plethora of topics related to living with stuttering. The table of contents identifies titles, themes, and sub-themes for each plan. Additionally, it gives a code for each plan in terms of three levels of difficulty typically faced by people who stutter. Recognizing that individual stutterers might view these differently, plans designated as "1" involve only discussion with the group, plans identified as "2" involve carrying out verbal interchanges that are role plays or other atypical interactions, and those marked "3" involve talking with others outside the group. Ordinarily, the "1" plans are best when new stuttering participants are present, while "2" and "3" plans would be more appropriate for more experienced participants. Finally, each plan lists a few goals that relate to the themes being targeted.

COMMON OBJECTIVES

Overarching objectives also characterize the plans. Most of them are designed to foster greater insight regarding one's own and others' stuttering and/or desensitization to one's stuttering. Stuttering is often regarded as mysterious. Therefore, greater insight will reduce its mystery. Stuttering is also greatly dreaded, avoided, or hidden because it is associated with anxiety or fear, embarrassment, shame, guilt, frustration, and anger. Reducing mystery will assist in reducing some of these feelings or emotions about stuttering, which is desensitization. However, numerous other strategies are specifically helpful in desensitizing a person to his or her stuttering. The purpose of desensitization is for a person to be able to speak, and eventually feel comfortable speaking, in spite of stuttering. Of course, not all stuttering persons achieve that entirely, but any progress in "taking the edge off" the stuttering will be immediately felt as a positive step in enjoying a happier and better quality of life.

MAXIMIZING PARTICIPATION OF NONSTUTTERING PARTICIPANTS

Most of the 111 different plans were designed to accommodate nonstuttering participants in the support groups. And many of them encourage participants, sometimes even the stutterers, to identify an issue that will be targeted in the activity and discussion. Often, understanding the problems of stuttering within the context of other life difficulties helps stutterers to understand that their struggles are not unique and helps nonstutterers to appreciate that, except for stuttering, stutterers are really struggling in the same way they do.

Although not consistently specified in the plans, nonstuttering issues should be something that a person has experienced considerable-to-great difficulty dealing/living with in the past. It should not be something trivial, which might have only occasionally caused distress such as a bad hair day or an unpleasant experience on one date. Instead, it should be something in the person's physical body, family or culture, emotional adjustment, life circumstances, etc. that presented (and ideally still presents) a challenge. The issue to be chosen should not, however, be so troubling or traumatic that it should be brought up only with a mental health professional, nor should it be something that the person would not want anyone in the group to know about under any circumstances. Examples that have been shared by nonstuttering participants include continuing problems with weight gain, getting through and getting past an unfortunate romantic breakup, long-term skin problems, diagnosis and subsequent management of a chronic disease, lack of acceptance by family members for some reason, and having a learning or reading disorder.

OFF-LIMIT COMMENTS

As noted, insight and desensitization are common objectives of support groups. Nevertheless, it is absolutely critical for the group leader to communicate by statement and by interactions that the goal of the support group is to help one another on their own journeys toward better insight and greater desensitization toward stuttering—not to suggest to or tell them that they "should" feel or do anything. A well-known speech-language pathologist who stuttered and went on to help hundreds of others who stutter, David Daly, often told his clients to "Stop 'shoulding' on yourselves!" Everyone feels what he or she feels; one cannot really will oneself to feel relief or not to feel shame. Those changes come from experiences, and they come to everyone differently on unique, individual schedules.

Also as noted, the goal of support group meetings is not to make the participants speak more fluently, that is, with less or no stuttering. In fact, such activities in organizations such as the NSA are forbidden in their chapter meetings. That is not to say that some stutterers will have as a personal goal to speak with less stuttering, which is perfectly acceptable. But it is not acceptable for another person—a stutterer, an SLP, or a nonstuttering guest—to coach anyone on how to speak more easily, with less stuttering, etc. Of course, a stuttering person is encouraged to share their own experiences of what works for them, but to stop there.

HAVING FUN

Our support groups over the years have always sought to include something fun in every meeting. We did not achieve that every time, but it was always part of our plan. Often the warms-ups or icebreaker activities included just enough quirkiness, silliness, or built-in humor to bring out grins or belly laughs at the outset. When any group can start out with safe humor, participants are simply more willing to engage, to encourage, to share, and to risk. Though not a goal of the support group, because not everyone can do it, when someone is able to begin to find some humor in their own stuttering—or stuttering in general—that person no longer views himself or herself as a victim.

SEEKING REAL, PERSONAL EXPERIENCE—NOT JUST AN INTELLECTUAL EXPERIENCE

One might hear an interesting lecture on the genetics of stuttering, and that might be an excellent session in a class on stuttering or at a conference on stuttering. But unless it were to trigger or connect with a significant personal memory or past experience with your or a friend's stuttering, it would remain just an intellectual experience. The plans in this book are designed as much as possible to tap into, trigger, or bring up memories of stuttering (or other issues) that have or had special significance to the individual. Their purpose is to get at the gut level aspects of stuttering. Sometimes the plans rely on memory; sometimes they generate the experiences in the meeting, e.g., from everyone calling a hotel and asking for prices while stuttering.

PROCESSING AND LESSONS

Most plans, therefore, have a primary activity designed to elicit a real, personal experience with stuttering. Next, the plans seek to process or digest the information brought forth. The processing component takes many forms, from reviewing lists of "defining moments" on a white board to participants reading anonymous compliments given to them by others in the group. Whenever possible, the leader follows this processing stage by inviting participants and guests to share what they learned or what the lesson(s) of the activities might be. Each plan is followed by some lessons that past group members have pointed out or that might tie the group experience to what is known about stuttering. These can be shared by the leader or not, as judged appropriate.

CARRYING OUT THE MEETING

Every group will develop its own unique personality. Ours certainly did, and this book is based on our traditions. Over two decades we found that the sequence was an effective way to encourage stuttering and nonstuttering participants with highly varied backgrounds and ages to interact effectively. The general structure followed in most of our meetings is presented below, although we always were willing to change or even abandon the structure when the group dynamics moved us in a different direction.

In recent years, more and more groups include people who participate from remote locations with a computer via Zoom or another electronic meeting platform. Our support group has utilized this technology effectively by arranging for some individuals to be a part of the group by appearing on a large screen through Skype for several years. A camera and microphone is used to let the remote person(s) see and hear the group activities, and the screen and a speaker permits the group to see and hear the remote participant. We have also hosted a speaker from Europe to speak to our group via a telephone hookup and speaker, without the video. And a few times, we used FaceTime on a smartphone to include a person with a small group. During the 2020–2021 COVID-19 pandemic, we met entirely on the Zoom platform, modifying plans as necessary. To the extent that participants can join in remotely, it is possible to extend the benefits of the support group to far more people and to alleviate numerous problems that interfere with attendance, such as bad weather. Admittedly, it requires foresight and advance notification to the group leader or a designee to arrange and test the electronic connections. Also, if a person plans to join with video conferencing, e.g., Skype or Zoom, the group plan must be tailored so that the person can at least share in most of the activities and not simply observe. Occasionally, some materials can be emailed to the person prior to the meeting such as if participants are asked to play a role from a pre-determined set of instructions.

For support group meetings that are scheduled for more than one hour, leaders may wish to add a regular component of simple sharing at some point, perhaps after the icebreaker. We have done this in the past, and it is simply a time where the participants who stutter are free to talk about anything they want.

NSA'S WELCOMING WORDS

The facilitator asks if anyone would like to read the Welcoming Words (*also shown in Appendix E*). Typically, one person would read them, but in some NSA chapters, several copies are available so that the stutterers could read them chorally together (where stuttering almost always disappears).

Welcome to the _____ Chapter of the National Stuttering Association. The National Stuttering Association is a nonprofit organization dedicated to bringing hope, dignity, support, education, and empowerment to children and adults who stutter, their families, and professionals through support, education, advocacy, and research.

If you are a person who stutters, or have a special interest in stuttering, you are welcome here. For the time we meet here, this room is a very special place.

It is a place where we are accepted and supported;

It is a place where we can relax and speak freely;

It is a place where we can stutter openly without fear and embarrassment;

It is a place where we can practice whatever speaking and communicating techniques with which we may feel comfortable.

Together, we will help each other, and we will help ourselves to accept and cope with our stuttering, to build our self-confidence, and to improve our verbal communication skills to the best of our abilities.

We who stutter, and those who support and help us, are not alone. Together we are strong.*

CONFIDENTIALITY WORDS

This is optional, but if used, the leader, or the person who read the Welcoming Words, should read:

Because this meeting is a safe place where participants can discuss personal matters in a supporting environment, everything said here must remain strictly confidential. Let us share the hope and encouragement we receive here with others, but keep all the details to ourselves.

---

* Included with permission of the National Stuttering Association.

SETTING GOALS

In no particular order everyone is asked to set and share aloud a goal for themselves for the meeting, which they will individually evaluate at the end of the meeting on a scale from 1 (did not meet it at all) to 10 (met it very well). The goals can be anything a person might want to practice, think about, learn, or even enjoy at the meeting. Some stutterers might wish to work on their eye contact, a slower rate of speech, pull-outs, not substituting words, or just talking without worrying about stuttering. Guests might wish to reduce their "um's" or fillers, to learn something new, to learn everyone's name, or to reveal something about themselves. Goal setting should take no more than a few minutes.

ICEBREAKER

Each session begins with a warm-up or icebreaker, which is designed to ordinarily take no more than about five minutes. Most icebreakers that one might find on the internet are designed to help fairly large groups of individuals who don't know each other to get acquainted and, thus, are typically quite time consuming. The icebreakers in each plan, as well as 100 extras in Appendix A, were designed primarily to inject humor immediately into the meeting. Those with the plans were included because they are at least peripherally related to the themes of the sessions. The leader is encouraged to consider the one included in a plan but is free to choose any icebreaker that he or she feels would set the best stage for the meeting plan.

ACTIVITY AND PROCESSING

Coming up with ideas for interesting and effective support group meetings is often the most difficult challenge faced by group leaders. *In the Company of Friends* was written to make available the best examples of two decades of one-hour, weekly planned sessions for subsequent support groups in Morgantown, West Virginia. Accordingly, leaders are invited to review the various titles, themes, sub-themes, difficulty levels, and meeting goals included and select a meeting that most meets the needs, desires, and support-group experience level of the likely participants of the next meeting. Our group met during the university semester schedule on a weekly basis and then infrequently or not at all during the holiday breaks or summer semester. By contrast, most NSA chapters meet on a monthly basis. If one were to meet 12 times a year, enough fresh plans would be provided in this book for nine years. Even with meeting twice a month, sufficient new material would be available for rotating leaders for several years.

It bears repeating that the plans should be considered *guides* for groups—not prescriptions for exactly what will take place. It is important always to remember that if a support group meeting moves in a new direction—so long as that direction is in keeping with the purpose of the group—the leader should encourage that and keep the plan only as a backup. More likely, leaders will read a plan and think of ways that it could be adapted or changed to better fit the needs and purposes of their individual group.

TAKE AWAYS

At this point, the leader asks what everyone learned or can take away from the meeting. As appropriate, he or she might read some of the provided "lessons learned" to help crystallize the purpose of the meeting.

EVALUATING GOALS

At the end, and in no particular order, participants are asked to rate their performance relative to their goal on a scale from 1 to 10. This can contribute to the fun of the meeting when a participant admits, "I forgot all about my goal the whole time, so I'll give myself a 2." Or it can be a significant achievement when someone says, "I only avoided one word tonight. I give myself a 9." Or when a guest says, "I can't believe how warm and accepting everyone was. I learned everyone's name plus I learned a lot about myself. I'll give myself a 10!"

CLOSING WORDS

Finally, as with the Welcoming Words, the leader asks if someone would like to read the Closing Words.

May the spirit we have shared tonight help our speech in the coming weeks, until we meet again. May we go forth gladly into speaking situations, without force or struggle, accepting ourselves regardless of our fluency, and listening always to the music of our voices. We are not alone. Together we are strong.**

And optionally, the following confidentiality reminder:

Please remember the confidential nature of this meeting. Take the help and encouragement with you, and leave the details behind.

SAMPLE MEETINGS

Appendix J provides written summaries of two of our meetings, presented as samples. Their purpose is to show some of the flesh on the skeleton plans provided. These were both actual sessions, with real comments and reactions, but with names and dates changed for anonymity.

** Included with permission of the National Stuttering Association.

LESSON PLANS

1. PERSONALIZING THE SUPPORT GROUP

PREPARATION

- Have access to a whiteboard or other display device.
- Have one or more blindfolds available.
- At the beginning and end of the meeting, ask someone to read the Welcoming Words and Closing Words (*Appendix E*).

GOALS

1. To consider what this support group is really all about.
2. To create an internet presence for the group.

THE MEETING

WELCOMING WORDS

ICEBREAKER

Ask the participants to pair up and move to a hallway if possible. One by one, or all at once with a large group, have one of each pair put on a blindfold and then be guided to the other end of the hall by verbal directions of the partner. They should switch roles and return. Caution the guiding partner to stop the person if he/she is about to hit something. (*Or see Appendix A.*)

INDIVIDUAL GOALS

Ask each one in attendance (stutterers, facilitators, visitors) to identify a personal goal for the meeting, and share it with the group. Inform them that, at the end of the meeting, they will be reminded of their goals and have an opportunity to evaluate themselves. (If necessary, prompt ones who are having difficulty choosing a goal with some examples, like those in Appendix G.)

ACTIVITY

(Announce that participation in any activity is strictly voluntary. Everyone should join only those exercises with which they feel comfortable.)

1. Invite participants to share their own ideal concept of a support group for stuttering. Ask a volunteer to write the various ideas on a whiteboard.

2. Discuss and possibly adopt various ways to stay connected and how to publicize the support group.

3. Create a Facebook (or other social media) page and write a short description of the group's mission, or what it hopes to do. This will be a place where group members—and friends and supporters—can keep posted about upcoming meetings and events, share ideas and information, and generally maintain communication and support. As a group, decide on a photo or graphic for the page, a public description of the page's purpose, who will be the administrators, etc.

TAKEAWAY LESSONS

Encourage participants to share what stands out for them, or what they may have learned about themselves, their issues, and each other.

CONSIDER:

1. Every support group has its own personality and structure. Regular attendees should be free to offer suggestions for an initial presence or for changes.

2. Being able to communicate easily with potential group members, or for attendees to stay connected with one another, enhances the support individuals can receive from a support group.

3. With a social media presence, each meeting can be posted in advance (perhaps with a humorous meme or quote to give a "teaser" about the topic of the meeting). The leader can see who has seen the post and have an idea of who is following (possibly interested) and who replies (likely coming).

INDIVIDUAL GOAL EVALUATIONS

Ask participants to go back to the goals that they stated at the beginning of the meeting, and grade themselves on a scale from 1 to 10. They may share their grades with the group if they choose.

CLOSING WORDS

2. IDENTIFYING SUPPORT FOR STUTTERING

PREPARATION

- Make copies of the *Personal Appraisal of Support for Stuttering–Adult (PASS–Ad)* (*Appendix F*) to hand out to participants.
- At the beginning and end of the meeting, ask someone to read the Welcoming Words and Closing Words (*Appendix E*).

GOALS

1. To consider some of the ways nonstutterers support stutterers, and which are helpful or not helpful.
2. To search for ways stutterers might be able to guide nonstutterers into more effective ways of helping.

THE MEETING

WELCOMING WORDS

ICEBREAKER

Ask the participants to respond to this question, "When someone was trying to help you, what's the worst advice you have ever been given." (*Or see Appendix A.*)

INDIVIDUAL GOALS

Ask each one in attendance (stutterers, facilitators, visitors) to identify a personal goal for the meeting, and share it with the group. Inform them that, at the end of the meeting, they will be reminded of their goals and have an opportunity to evaluate themselves. (If necessary, prompt ones who are having difficulty choosing a goal with some examples, like those in Appendix G.)

ACTIVITY

(Announce that participation in any activity is strictly voluntary. Everyone should join only those exercises with which they feel comfortable.)

1. Ask nonstutterers to identify a long-term difficult issue they have faced (and ideally still face) and report it to the group. The stutterers will be addressing stuttering.

2. Hand out the *Personal Appraisal of Support for Stuttering—Adult (PASS–Ad)* and allow 10–15 minutes for participants to complete it. Inform the nonstutterers to substitute their own issues for stuttering and rate as many items as they can that make sense.

3. Ask everyone to review their responses and share five of the items rated the highest (5 or closest to 5) and five rated the lowest (1 or closest to 1).

4. Ask the stutterers to pick one or two of their highest- and lowest-rated items and explain what their actual experiences were in terms of support or lack of support.

5. Ask stutterers how they would react if they unexpectedly met another stutterer. What, if anything, would they do to help the stutterer feel supported?

6. If time permits, ask for discussion of what stutterers could do to help nonstuttering people better help them.

TAKEAWAY LESSONS

Encourage participants to share what stands out for them, or what they may have learned about themselves, their issues, and each other.

CONSIDER:

1. There are numerous ways for nonstutterers to demonstrate support or lack of support for stutterers.

2. Although there are common patterns, there is no clear list of "Dos" and "Don'ts" for nonstutterers in their interactions with stuttering. A study of 150 adults who stuttered resulted in the following: *When first interacting with a person who stutters …, be engaging, patient, accepting, friendly, and as comfortable as possible, all the while being a good listener. After getting to know the person, learn more about stuttering and be flexible about modifying your interactions according the person's personal preferences for being supported, realizing that sometimes a particular action, such as trying to guess and fill in a word being stuttered, though generally not advised, is sometimes desired. After considerable interaction, you may gently inquire if you should ask questions about the stuttering, offer advice or referrals, or otherwise comment on the stuttering, but be ready to respect the stuttering person's wishes.* (p. 10). St. Louis, K. O., Irani, F., Gabel, R. M., Hughes, S., Langevin, M., Rodriguez, M., Scott, K. S., & Weidner, M. E. (2017). Evidence-based guidelines for being supportive of people who stutter in North America. *Journal of Fluency Disorders, 53,* 1–13.

3. As stutterers, we can help the nonstuttering majority adopt better ways of supporting us.

INDIVIDUAL GOAL EVALUATIONS

Ask participants to go back to the goals they stated at the beginning of the meeting, and grade themselves on a scale from 1 to 10. They may share their grades with the group if they choose.

CLOSING WORDS

"After learning and sharing the challenges of everyone in the group, it made me more courageous. I feel I owe my professional success to that experience."

3. SEEKING THE SUPPORT WE NEED

PREPARATION

- Have access to a whiteboard or other display device.
- Supply paper and pens or pencils.
- At the beginning and end of the meeting, ask someone to read the Welcoming Words and Closing Words (*Appendix E*).

GOALS

1. To consider the support we need from others.
2. To learn ways to achieve more support from others, especially from those who do not stutter.

THE MEETING

WELCOMING WORDS

ICEBREAKER

Have participants stand in a circle facing one another. Ask them to count off and remember their number. Have participants extend their hands into the center and grasp someone else's hands with their own. Call out a number and have that person give instructions to the others on how to unravel the "knot," without letting go. (*Or see Appendix A.*)

INDIVIDUAL GOALS

Ask each one in attendance (stutterers, facilitators, visitors) to identify a personal goal for the meeting, and share it with the group. Inform them that, at the end of the meeting, they will be reminded of their goals and have an opportunity to evaluate themselves. (If necessary, prompt ones who are having difficulty choosing a goal with some examples, like those in Appendix G.)

ACTIVITY

(Announce that participation in any activity is strictly voluntary. Everyone should join only those exercises with which they feel comfortable.)

1. Ask participants to each draw a large circle on a piece of paper. Across the top of the whiteboard, write "How I get the support I need." Draw a circle on the whiteboard, and outside the circle, begin a list with these three points: (a) others reaching out, (b) putting yourself in the right place or environment, and (c) what you say and do.

2. Tell the group that these three points are important ways we receive support from others, whether in relation to stuttering or any other need or concern. Ask if there are other applicable categories, and add them to the list if necessary.

3. Ask everyone to make a pie chart from the circle they have drawn: make a point in the center, and divide the circle into different-sized wedges expressing the relative importance of the types of support they need.

4. Invite discussion of the charts, and of getting the support we need in general. Ask participants to identify something they can do right now to help move them closer to receiving the support they need.

TAKEAWAY LESSONS

Encourage participants to share what stands out for them, or what they may have learned about themselves, their issues, and each other.

CONSIDER:

1. We all need and thrive on support from others, in varying degrees.

2. A support group is unique in that it provides an atypical place where we can talk about our need for support.

3. Support is a two-way street; it is a process of both giving and receiving. An analogy might be of a person being held up or supported by a large number of people holding a net and then, over time, transitioning to hold up part of the net as a support for others.

INDIVIDUAL GOAL EVALUATIONS

Ask participants to go back to the goals they stated at the beginning of the meeting, and grade themselves on a scale from 1 to 10. They may share their grades with the group if they choose.

CLOSING WORDS

4. THE STUTTERING AND THE STUTTERER

PREPARATION

- Before people arrive for the meeting, place a variety of small objects on a table and cover them with a large towel or cloth.
- This session requires an internet-connected computer and a monitor large enough to display the videos to the group. Before the meeting, find online videos of three to five stutterers, with varying severity, and bookmark them.
- At the beginning and end of the meeting, ask someone to read the Welcoming Words and Closing Words (*Appendix E*).

GOALS

1. To understand the discrepancy between overt symptoms of stuttering and the stutterer's reaction to stuttering.
2. To begin to match internalized feelings about stuttering to overt symptoms of stuttering.
3. To become desensitized to one's stuttering by comparing it to a variety of stutters.

THE MEETING

WELCOMING WORDS

ICEBREAKER

Play "Kim's Game," from the book by Rudyard Kipling. Casually lift the cover off the objects, let people look at them for a minute, and replace the cover. Then, tell the group to cooperate to name as many of the items as they can, while one person writes them down. Remove the cover again and see how successful the group was. (*Or see Appendix A.*)

INDIVIDUAL GOALS

Ask each one in attendance (stutterers, facilitators, visitors) to identify a personal goal for the meeting, and share it with the group. Inform them that, at the end of the meeting, they will be reminded of their goals and have an opportunity to evaluate themselves. (If necessary, prompt ones who are having difficulty choosing a goal with some examples, like those in Appendix G.)

ACTIVITY

(Announce that participation in any activity is strictly voluntary. Everyone should join only those exercises with which they feel comfortable.)

1. Tell participants that they will be watching videos of stutterers, will be asked to rate the severity of the stutterer on a scale of 1 (no stuttering) to 10 (very severe stuttering), and will be invited to comment on their ratings.

2. First they will watch the stutterers with the audio muted, and respond only to the stutterer's face or gestures. Show the videos, with the audio off. After each one, pause and ask participants to share their ratings.

3. Repeat the above, with the audio on.

4. Ask the participants to look at their ratings and think about the extent to which their ratings were on how the person likely perceived their stuttering ("the stutterER") versus how much the ratings were on the actual observable and/or audible symptoms ("the stutterING"). Invite them to share their insights.

5. Ask the stutterers to rate, on the same scale, both their own overt stuttering symptoms and their feelings, thoughts, and adjustments to them.

TAKEAWAY LESSONS

Encourage participants to share what stands out for them, or what they may have learned about themselves, their issues, and each other.

CONSIDER:

1. There is no necessary connection between the severity of our stuttering symptoms and our reaction to it.

2. What we and others perceive as "bad" stuttering may not be as bad as we or they think. And perhaps the word "bad" should be replaced by the words, "more frequent" or "more severe," because stuttering is not a "bad" thing.

3. We tend to see other people as we do because we compare them to our own experiences.

INDIVIDUAL GOAL EVALUATIONS

Ask participants to go back to the goals they stated at the beginning of the meeting, and grade themselves on a scale from 1 to 10. They may share their grades with the group if they choose.

CLOSING WORDS

5. INDIVIDUAL AND SITUATIONAL FACTORS AFFECTING THE SEVERITY OF STUTTERING

PREPARATION

- Have access to a whiteboard or other display device.
- At the beginning and end of the meeting, ask someone to read the Welcoming Words and Closing Words (*Appendix E*).

GOALS

1. To explore what factors affect the severity of stuttering for each individual.
2. To compare common person-based and situation-based influences on stuttering severity.

THE MEETING

WELCOMING WORDS

ICEBREAKER

Ask people about different cures for hiccups. (*Or see Appendix A.*)

INDIVIDUAL GOALS

Ask each one in attendance (stutterers, facilitators, visitors) to identify a personal goal for the meeting, and share it with the group. Inform them that, at the end of the meeting, they will be reminded of their goals and have an opportunity to evaluate themselves. (If necessary, prompt ones who are having difficulty choosing a goal with some examples, like those in Appendix G.)

ACTIVITY

(Announce that participation in any activity is strictly voluntary. Everyone should join only those exercises with which they feel comfortable.)

1. Ask those in attendance to talk about specific situations or occasions—not related to stuttering—which cause them embarrassment or frustration, or situations they avoid because they know it will be uncomfortable.

2. Ask for discussion of how situations might be more or less bothersome at different times, and what factors might be responsible for the difference. Which of these factors are inherent in the situation itself, and which are really about the individual experiencing it? Have someone divide the whiteboard into two columns, and write these factors under the heading "Situation" or "Individual."

3. Repeat this exercise for factors relating to the severity of our stuttering. Ask participants to consider which of the factors listed on the board are applicable to variations in stuttering severity, which are not, and what factors were not listed because they relate specifically to stuttering.

TAKEAWAY LESSONS

Encourage participants to share what stands out for them, or what they may have learned about themselves, their issues, and each other.

CONSIDER:

1. *Stuttering severity* is a generic term that includes how frequently we stutter, how long each stuttering lasts, the types of stuttering we have, the amount and visibility of our accessory behaviors, the amount we are disfluent even when not stuttering, etc.

2. Our stuttering severity may be affected by situational factors like the purpose of the communication, the words we must use (e.g., "hello" on the phone), and time pressure in some situations. It is also affected by individual factors related to past failures we may or may not remember, such as by certain letters or sounds or by characteristics of conversation partners.

3. Understanding what affects the severity of our stuttering removes much of the mystery surrounding it.

INDIVIDUAL GOAL EVALUATIONS

Ask participants to go back to the goals they stated at the beginning of the meeting, and grade themselves on a scale from 1 to 10. They may share their grades with the group if they choose.

CLOSING WORDS

6. UNDERSTANDING ACCESSORY BEHAVIORS

PREPARATION

- Have a large mirror on hand, at least 12 by 18 inches.
- Have access to a whiteboard or other display device.
- At the beginning and end of the meeting, ask someone to read the Welcoming Words and Closing Words (*Appendix E*).

GOALS

1. To better understand the idea of accessory or secondary behaviors in stuttering.
2. To consider the impact our own accessory behaviors have on others.

THE MEETING

WELCOMING WORDS

ICEBREAKER

Ask participants whether they would rather be able to turn invisible, or able to read minds. (*Or see Appendix A.*)

INDIVIDUAL GOALS

Ask each one in attendance (stutterers, facilitators, visitors) to identify a personal goal for the meeting, and share it with the group. Inform them that, at the end of the meeting, they will be reminded of their goals and have an opportunity to evaluate themselves. (If necessary, prompt ones who are having difficulty choosing a goal with some examples, like those in Appendix G.)

ACTIVITY

(Announce that participation in any activity is strictly voluntary. Everyone should join only those exercises with which they feel comfortable.)

1. Explain that "accessory behaviors" are tricks or habits that stutterers use to help them avoid or minimize stuttering (*Appendix H*). Ask each stutterer to name one of these behaviors, and think about the first time they became aware of it. Ask

nonstutterers to name one habit they have picked up dealing with communication, such as exaggerated gesturing, pausing, using filler words (*like, so, basically, et cetera*), fidgeting, and the like. Have someone list these on a whiteboard, or other device if available, along with the name of the person.

2. Pair the participants—with stutterers partnered with nonstutterers as much as possible. Assign each pair a potentially controversial debate topic prepared beforehand (e.g., meat should be promoted versus vegetarian diets should be promoted), and assign one of the pair to debate each side. One pair at a time, have participants conduct a brief, informal debate on the topic, while each person uses the other's accessory behavior in an exaggerated way.

3. After the exercise, ask the group to discuss how each person did modeling his partner's behavior, and how distracting or annoying your own behavior is when you see it in someone else.

4. Stand the mirror up where each person in turn can sit or stand and watch himself or herself talk. Have a facilitator stand off to the side with a list of scenarios (see *Appendix A*). One at a time, each person will face the mirror and respond to a scenario posed by the facilitator.

5. Invite the group to discuss the exercise, and to consider why we adopt these accessory or secondary behaviors, how they affect our communication, and how we can change them.

TAKEAWAY LESSONS

Encourage participants to share what stands out for them, or what they may have learned about themselves, their issues, and each other.

CONSIDER:

1. We often use our accessory behaviors as a crutch when we feel uncomfortable, out of control, or panicked.

2. Although secondary behaviors might seem helpful, they more often limit us by making our overt stuttering more distracting to listeners or even more severe.

INDIVIDUAL GOAL EVALUATIONS

Ask participants to go back to the goals they stated at the beginning of the meeting, and grade themselves on a scale from 1 to 10. They may share their grades with the group if they choose.

CLOSING WORDS

7. DEFINING MOMENTS OF STUTTERING

PREPARATION

- At the beginning and end of the meeting, ask someone to read the Welcoming Words and Closing Words (*Appendix E*).

GOALS

1. To promote insight into stuttering by recalling defining moments throughout participants' lives.

2. To consider ways to reduce negative impacts of stuttering throughout participants' lives.

THE MEETING

WELCOMING WORDS

ICEBREAKER

Ask those in attendance to think of a favorite food, and imagine that they were hungry and saw the only available portion of that food fall on the floor or ground. What would the condition of the floor or ground need to be in for them to be willing or unwilling to pick up the food and eat it? (*Or see Appendix A.*)

INDIVIDUAL GOALS

Ask each one in attendance (stutterers, facilitators, visitors) to identify a personal goal for the meeting, and share it with the group. Inform them that, at the end of the meeting, they will be reminded of their goals and have an opportunity to evaluate themselves. (If necessary, prompt ones who are having difficulty choosing a goal with some examples, like those in Appendix G.)

ACTIVITY

(Announce that participation in any activity is strictly voluntary. Everyone should join only those exercises with which they feel comfortable.)

1. Ask participants to briefly relate something someone said to them which has affected their lives in a positive way.

2. Ask them to next relate something said to them which has had a negative effect on their lives.

3. Ask each one to share the first real memory he or she has involving stuttering.

4. Mention the theme of the meeting again, "Defining moments in stuttering," and comment on what a life-defining moment is. It's a moment that alters your life and moves you in a new direction. It could be sudden, powerful, or even subtle at the time of onset. Ask each participant to share one or two life-defining moments related to stuttering.

5. Ask the group to discuss how we could reduce the negative effects or reactions of stuttering.

TAKEAWAY LESSONS

Encourage participants to share what stands out for them, or what they may have learned about themselves, their issues, and each other.

CONSIDER:

1. We all have memories of specific comments or events that we never forget and that have permanently changed our lives in both positive and negative ways.

2. Recalling defining moments often helps us understand why we react to various situations as we do.

3. As important as they are, negative defining moments of stuttering can, with insight and effort, be weakened and replaced by more positive memories.

INDIVIDUAL GOAL EVALUATIONS

Ask participants to go back to the goals they stated at the beginning of the meeting, and grade themselves on a scale from 1 to 10. They may share their grades with the group if they choose.

CLOSING WORDS

8. NAGGING PROBLEMS ASSOCIATED WITH STUTTERING

PREPARATION

- At the beginning and end of the meeting, ask someone to read the Welcoming Words and Closing Words (*Appendix E*).

GOALS

1. To learn about others' insight into our problems.
2. To realize we often have the answers to our own nagging questions.

THE MEETING

WELCOMING WORDS

ICEBREAKER

Ask everyone to share their individual quirks about using soap in the shower or sink. For example, when a bar of soap gets so small it breaks, what do you do? When a bottle of liquid soap is almost empty, what do you do? (*Or see Appendix A.*)

INDIVIDUAL GOALS

Ask each one in attendance (stutterers, facilitators, visitors) to identify a personal goal for the meeting, and share it with the group. Inform them that, at the end of the meeting, they will be reminded of their goals and have an opportunity to evaluate themselves. (If necessary, prompt ones who are having difficulty choosing a goal with some examples, like those in Appendix G.)

ACTIVITY

(Announce that participation in any activity is strictly voluntary. Everyone should join only those exercises with which they feel comfortable.)

1. Ask everyone to think about a problem that they have nagging questions about. For stutterers, the problem could be something about their stuttering. For non-stutterers, ask that the problem not be something trivial, but something that is a real problem right now. Have everyone write down a persistent nagging question—

something really troubling—they have had about the problem. Allow a few minutes for everyone to write down a question.

2. Explain that each participant is now going to assume the role of someone with all the answers to life's questions. Have everyone write their name on their papers and then collect all the questions. Ask each participant in turn to come forward and sit in a chair facing the group. Read the person's own question to them, and ask them to give their best answer as an all-knowing sage, even if they are unsure.

3. Thank everyone for their courage in participating. Next, ask everyone to think about something that impressed them about someone else's part in the exercise, and compliment that person on some specific element of what they said. There are three rules in this part of the activity: say nothing negative, give no advice, and the person receiving the complimentary feedback may not refute it.

TAKEAWAY LESSONS

Encourage participants to share what stands out for them, or what they may have learned about themselves, their issues, and each other.

CONSIDER:

1. We may have more insight about our nagging problems of stuttering than we thought. For example, we often know the reason why we face difficult problems even if the problem cannot be solved.

2. It is hard to truly appreciate another person's problem. We cannot understand a person unless we "walk a mile in their shoes." One reason is that every stutter and stutterer is different.

3. However, a little empathy from others gives us courage to tackle those difficult problems.

INDIVIDUAL GOAL EVALUATIONS

Ask participants to go back to the goals they stated at the beginning of the meeting, and grade themselves on a scale from 1 to 10. They may share their grades with the group if they choose.

CLOSING WORDS

9. KEEPING UP MORALE IN DIFFICULT CIRCUMSTANCES

PREPARATION

- Have a supply of envelopes, index cards, and pens or pencils on hand.
- At the beginning and end of the meeting, ask someone to read the Welcoming Words and Closing Words (*Appendix E*).

GOAL

1. To share stories of challenging situations, and to consider the perspectives of others in dealing with situations.

THE MEETING

WELCOMING WORDS

ICEBREAKER

Ask participants what they would do if they found 100 dollars on the ground. (*Or see Appendix A.*)

INDIVIDUAL GOALS

Ask each one in attendance (stutterers, facilitators, visitors) to identify a personal goal for the meeting, and share it with the group. Inform them that, at the end of the meeting, they will be reminded of their goals and have an opportunity to evaluate themselves. (If necessary, prompt ones who are having difficulty choosing a goal with some examples, like those in Appendix G.)

ACTIVITY

(Announce that participation in any activity is strictly voluntary. Everyone should join only those exercises with which they feel comfortable.)

1. Give everyone an envelope, and ask them to write their names on them. Place index cards where everyone can reach them.

2. Ask people to think of a time when stuttering or some other issue caused a problem that spiraled out of control and affected them for some time. After a minute to

think, have people, one at a time, tell a little about the experience.

3. After the end of each speaker's story, ask the listeners to take an index card and write a brief comment completing the thought, "I am not you and I don't know if this would work for your situation, but I would…" Pass the speaker's envelope around, and let people put in their cards. Keep the envelopes in a stack until everyone who chooses to participate has done so.

4. Distribute the envelopes, and allow a couple of minutes for everyone to silently read his or her comments.

5. Ask each speaker to briefly tell what they actually did in the situation, and whether any of the comments from the group seem like they may have been a good idea.

6. Invite general discussion.

TAKEAWAY LESSONS

Encourage participants to share what stands out for them, or what they may have learned about themselves, their issues, and each other.

CONSIDER:

1. We cannot avoid the occasional situation that spirals out of control.

2. When stuttering becomes out of control, it is easy to lose perspective and our morale plummets into hopelessness.

3. Support from others is often the best medicine when our morale is low.

INDIVIDUAL GOAL EVALUATIONS

Ask participants to go back to the goals they stated at the beginning of the meeting, and grade themselves on a scale from 1 to 10. They may share their grades with the group if they choose.

CLOSING WORDS

10. UNDERSTANDING THOUGHTS AND EMOTIONS ASSOCIATED WITH STUTTERING

PREPARATION

- Prepare index cards with general topics for a brief extemporaneous speech, such as:
  - » the longest trip I ever took
  - » one of my earliest music favorites
  - » the ideal pizza
  - » my hometown
  - » the last movie I saw
  - » the best car I or my family ever had
  - » one job which is underpaid
  - » the worst habit of local drivers
- Bookmark an image of the "iceberg of stuttering" to show the group.
- At the beginning and end of the meeting, ask someone to read the Welcoming Words and Closing Words (*Appendix E*).

GOALS

1. To discuss the thoughts and feelings surrounding stuttering.
2. To share different strategies for managing or accepting them.

THE MEETING

WELCOMING WORDS

ICEBREAKER

Ask participants to think about the first time they jumped off a high diving board, rappelled over a cliff, or some other scary activity. Ask them to briefly share their thoughts and feelings before, during, and after the activity. (*Or see Appendix A.*)

INDIVIDUAL GOALS

Ask each one in attendance (stutterers, facilitators, visitors) to identify a personal goal for the meeting, and share it with the group. Inform them that, at the end of the meeting, they will be reminded of their goals and have an opportunity to evaluate themselves. (If necessary, prompt ones who are having difficulty choosing a goal with some examples, like those in Appendix G.)

ACTIVITY

(Announce that participation in any activity is strictly voluntary. Everyone should join only those exercises with which they feel comfortable.)

1. Announce that participants will each be standing in front of the group and giving an impromptu speech for one to two minutes, without any time for preparation. Topics will be randomly handed out just before the speech begins.

2. Invite participants to come to the front, hand them a random card with a topic, and let them make the short speech.

3. After everyone willing to participate has done so, invite the group to discuss their feelings and thoughts:

    » when the speech exercise was announced

    » while waiting their turn

    » during the speech

    » after the speech

4. Show the "iceberg of stuttering" image and point out that most of stuttering is not observable, and what's not observable involves the thoughts and feelings about it. Discuss how the feelings and thoughts about this exercise compare with real-life situations and strategies people used both in the meeting and in real life.

TAKEAWAY LESSONS

Encourage participants to share what stands out for them, or what they may have learned about themselves, their issues, and each other.

CONSIDER:

1. Thoughts and feelings about our stuttering are as important—if not more important—than the actual disfluencies in our speech.

2. We can overcome negative thoughts and feelings about stuttering even if we cannot or choose not to reduce our actual stuttering.

3. Public speaking is ranked as one of the most feared activities by nonstutterers. It is likely ranked higher overall by stutterers.

INDIVIDUAL GOAL EVALUATIONS

Ask participants to go back to the goals they stated at the beginning of the meeting, and grade themselves on a scale from 1 to 10. They may share their grades with the group if they choose.

CLOSING WORDS

"Even though it's hard to face yourself sometimes, I think it's beneficial because you get to learn about yourself."

11. YOUR LIFE JOURNEY

PREPARATION

- Make copies of the "Life Journey" template for each participant (*Appendix F*).
- Supply graph paper and pencils.
- If no copier is available, draw the graph on a whiteboard or other display device, and have participants copy it.
- At the beginning and end of the meeting, ask someone to read the Welcoming Words and Closing Words (*Appendix E*).

GOALS

1. To think about how our personal issues change over time, and what factors might make problems more or less troublesome at different times.
2. To review an issue (like stuttering) that has negatively affected one's life, and consider how the issue has progressed.

THE MEETING

WELCOMING WORDS

ICEBREAKER

Ask the participants to imagine the following scenario. You are embarking on a vacation in Southeast Asia and have just landed in a large city. When you arrive in the airport, you are stopped by an Immigration official. You and a family member accidentally switched passports through the course of the trip. Your family member managed to get through customs with your passport but he or she is nowhere to be seen. You must satisfy the official's questions before being able to enter the country. The official does not speak English at all, and you do not speak any of the language there. There is a line behind you, so, in a short period of time, show us how you will, without the support of a common language, explain yourself to the official through pantomiming. (*Or see Appendix A.*)

INDIVIDUAL GOALS

Ask each one in attendance (stutterers, facilitators, visitors) to identify a personal goal for the meeting, and share it with the group. Inform them that, at the end of the meeting, they will be reminded of their goals and have an opportunity to evaluate themselves. (If necessary, prompt ones who are having difficulty choosing a goal with some examples, like those in Appendix G.)

ACTIVITY

(Announce that participation in any activity is strictly voluntary. Everyone should join only those exercises with which they feel comfortable.)

1. Ask the participants to choose something that has been a troubling or difficult issue in their personal lives that has lasted at least a year. For the participants who stutter, encourage them to choose stuttering as their issue. Nonstutterers will choose another issue, and everyone present will participate. Provide the graph paper, or provide blank paper and instruct participants to draw two intersecting axes. Label the horizontal axis "Time" and write "Born" at the left end and "Now" at the right end. Label the vertical axis "Seriousness."

2. Ask each participant to determine when their issue began in their lives and how serious it was at that time, and mark an "X" on their graphs. Ask them to place another "X" at the end of the horizontal axis, above the "Now" label, to indicate how serious the same issue is for them currently. Ask them to place another "X," or two or more of them, at points in life when they feel the issue was especially serious, or significantly less serious.

3. After time to complete the graphs, ask participants to summarize their journeys with their issues for the group. Have each one explain why he or she believes the issue was more or less serious at different times throughout their life. If participants have difficulty starting the discussion, prompt them by saying that past participants have responded with some of the following:

   » The problem became more serious in stressful times, like moving to a new area or beginning college.

   » Some problems can limit someone's ability to participate in sports, which leads to feeling left out.

   » Parents can sometimes be slow to recognize or respond to their child's difficulties.

4. If you have access to a whiteboard or other display, list the factors that made the issues better or worse as the participants discuss their journeys. Otherwise, list them on paper to refer to later. Allow the group to discuss the similarities and differences in their experiences.

TAKEAWAY LESSONS

Encourage participants to share what stands out for them, or what they may have learned about themselves, their issues, and each other.

CONSIDER:

1. We all face ups and downs in our lives.

2. Sometimes we can't control the events that make our problems worse; sometimes we can.

3. Managing stuttering is a journey, and everyone's journey is different.

INDIVIDUAL GOAL EVALUATIONS

Ask participants to go back to the goals they stated at the beginning of the meeting, and grade themselves on a scale from 1 to 10. They may share their grades with the group if they choose.

CLOSING WORDS

> "Individual and group therapy are my safe havens. I feel very comfortable in the group. It relaxes me, and I find comfort in the people who come."

12. TELLING OUR "STORY OF STUTTERING"

PREPARATION

- At the beginning and end of the meeting, ask someone to read the Welcoming Words and Closing Words (*Appendix E*).

GOALS

1. To explore how our "stories of stuttering" can be helpful in understanding our experiences.
2. To consider how our stories can be changed.

THE MEETING

WELCOMING WORDS

ICEBREAKER

Ask participants to imagine that they will be stranded on an island with only the group participants. Ask everyone to identify only one thing they will have with them on the island, but it must be something that they have with them right now. (*Or see Appendix A.*)

INDIVIDUAL GOALS

Ask each one in attendance (stutterers, facilitators, visitors) to identify a personal goal for the meeting, and share it with the group. Inform them that, at the end of the meeting, they will be reminded of their goals and have an opportunity to evaluate themselves. (If necessary, prompt ones who are having difficulty choosing a goal with some examples, like those in Appendix G.)

ACTIVITY

(Announce that participation in any activity is strictly voluntary. Everyone should join only those exercises with which they feel comfortable.)

1. Ask everyone to think about their "story of stuttering," or "story" of some other serious issue for the nonstutterers, for several minutes. After some time for thought, ask each stutterer to share his story in a few minutes.

2. Ask everyone to rate on a scale of 1 to 10 how they view their stuttering overall, with 1 being extremely negatively and 10 being extremely positively. Then, ask everyone to reflect on their stories and share whether or not the examples they gave accurately reflected their 1–10 ratings.

3. Invite everyone to share one way that they believe they could change their story.

TAKEAWAY LESSONS

Encourage participants to share what stands out for them, or what they may have learned about themselves, their issues, and each other.

CONSIDER:

1. We all have a "story of stuttering" that summarizes our experience. Most likely, our stories will quite precisely reflect the degree to which we feel both negative and positive about our stuttering.

2. We can change our stories, especially in a safe place.

INDIVIDUAL GOAL EVALUATIONS

Ask participants to go back to the goals they stated at the beginning of the meeting, and grade themselves on a scale from 1 to 10. They may share their grades with the group if they choose.

CLOSING WORDS

13. OUR STUTTERING AND OUR TRAITS

PREPARATION

- Have access to a whiteboard or other display device.
- Have on hand the deck of green (adjective) cards from the *Apples to Apples* game (e.g., awkward, cowardly, delightful, boring, absurd, busy, chunky, crazed).
- If possible, seat participants around a table.
- At the beginning and end of the meeting, ask someone to read the Welcoming Words and Closing Words (*Appendix E*).

GOALS

1. To take stock of positive and negative traits.
2. To appreciate that stuttering does not define who we are.

THE MEETING

WELCOMING WORDS

ICEBREAKER

Draw three vertical lines on the whiteboard, to divide it into four sections. At the top, label the sections "Unusual Job Experience," "Rare Skills," "Surprising Education," and "Obscure Honors" (or make up different categories). Compile a group "resumé," inviting those in attendance to share items from their own lives to add to each category. (*Or see Appendix A.*)

INDIVIDUAL GOALS

Ask each one in attendance (stutterers, facilitators, visitors) to identify a personal goal for the meeting, and share it with the group. Inform them that, at the end of the meeting, they will be reminded of their goals and have an opportunity to evaluate themselves. (If necessary, prompt ones who are having difficulty choosing a goal with some examples, like those in Appendix G.)

ACTIVITY

(Announce that participation in any activity is strictly voluntary. Everyone should join only those exercises with which they feel comfortable.)

1. Spread the green *Apples to Apples* cards (or self-generated adjectives), face up, on the table. Ask participants to each take three cards that they feel describe themselves. Set the remaining cards aside. Have participants pass in their cards, face down, and stack them. Do this without shuffling, so each group of three cards stays together.

2. Reveal the cards three at a time, and ask the group to guess which member chose those three as their self-description. Have the person who chose those three identify themselves, and briefly explain why. Let the group react to this, and comment on it.

3. Spread the cards face up again, and ask everyone to choose one card that has something to do with their stuttering (or another continuing life challenge, for nonstutterers), either positive or negative.

4. Have everyone tell which card they chose, and why. Allow the group to react.

TAKEAWAY LESSONS

Encourage participants to share what stands out for them, or what they may have learned about themselves, their issues, and each other.

CONSIDER:

1. Despite our stuttering, we have and can recognize many positive assets.

2. We have some degree of control over our positive and negative traits.

INDIVIDUAL GOAL EVALUATIONS

Ask participants to go back to the goals they stated at the beginning of the meeting, and grade themselves on a scale from 1 to 10. They may share their grades with the group if they choose.

CLOSING WORDS

14. OUR ASSETS: LETTING IN THE GOOD STUFF

PREPARATION

- Have index cards and pens or pencils on hand. Access to a whiteboard or other display device is helpful.
- At the beginning and end of the meeting, ask someone to read the Welcoming Words and Closing Words (*Appendix E*).

GOAL

1. To review our assets and consider how they could help us work through an issue, such as stuttering, that we have carried through life.

THE MEETING

WELCOMING WORDS

ICEBREAKER

Ask each person in turn to pay a compliment—genuine or humorous—to the person on his or her right. (*Or see Appendix A.*)

INDIVIDUAL GOALS

Ask each one in attendance (stutterers, facilitators, visitors) to identify a personal goal for the meeting, and share it with the group. Inform them that, at the end of the meeting, they will be reminded of their goals and have an opportunity to evaluate themselves. (If necessary, prompt ones who are having difficulty choosing a goal with some examples, like those in Appendix G.)

ACTIVITY

(Announce that participation in any activity is strictly voluntary. Everyone should join only those exercises with which they feel comfortable.)

1. Ask each one in attendance to write down what they consider to be their greatest asset. If someone has trouble deciding, they can write two. Instruct them to not share this information with their neighbors.

2. Collect the cards, shuffle them, and one by one read them to the group. If a whiteboard or other display device is available, write a list of the responses, or have someone do it. As you read each card, invite the group to guess who wrote it.

3. Ask each one to let the group know why they chose to write what they did, and what makes that asset a strong positive characteristic.

4. Call attention to the list of assets, and ask the group to discuss how their assets have or could be used to assist them with their stuttering, or another troublesome issue for nonstutterers.

TAKEAWAY LESSONS

Encourage participants to share what stands out for them, or what they may have learned about themselves, their issues, and each other.

CONSIDER:

1. It is easy to focus on our faults or liabilities rather than our assets, especially in terms of what we "should" do. Perhaps we need to stop "should-ing" on ourselves.

2. Talking about our positive attributes with people can be beneficial and become a morale booster.

3. Our assets can and do assist us in managing the problems associated with our stuttering.

INDIVIDUAL GOAL EVALUATIONS

Ask participants to go back to the goals they stated at the beginning of the meeting, and grade themselves on a scale from 1 to 10. They may share their grades with the group if they choose.

CLOSING WORDS

15. OUR LIABILITIES: OPENING UP AND TRUSTING

PREPARATION

- At the beginning and end of the meeting, ask someone to read the Welcoming Words and Closing Words (*Appendix E*).

GOALS

1. To identify our personal liabilities.

2. To explore the challenges and benefits of becoming vulnerable to share our liabilities with others.

THE MEETING

WELCOMING WORDS

ICEBREAKER

Ask everyone to think of one true and one false statement about themselves. Let people take turns sharing the statements, and let the others guess which is which. (*Or see Appendix A.*)

INDIVIDUAL GOALS

Ask each one in attendance (stutterers, facilitators, visitors) to identify a personal goal for the meeting, and share it with the group. Inform them that, at the end of the meeting, they will be reminded of their goals and have an opportunity to evaluate themselves. (If necessary, prompt ones who are having difficulty choosing a goal with some examples, like those in Appendix G.)

ACTIVITY

(Announce that participation in any activity is strictly voluntary. Everyone should join only those exercises with which they feel comfortable.)

1. Ask each one in the group to identify a troubling liability—an issue that has affected them quite negatively. Encourage stutterers to choose something related to stuttering, and encourage nonstutterers not to choose a relatively trivial issue, such as a bad hair day. Ask each one to state that liability to the group, without explaining it or elaborating.

2. Separate the group into pairs. As best as possible, pair stutterers and nonstutterers. Send each pair to a place as private as possible, with the instruction to discuss their liabilities for five minutes

3. Once the group reconvenes, ask each pair to say a little about how the activity went—not the subject matter, just the exercise of talking about a personal liability.

4. Ask people to talk a little about how it feels to become vulnerable.

5. Ask each person to say something positive about how their partner communicated during their discussion—not the problem being discussed, but just the way they did it.

6. Ask any nonstutterers to say a little about the experience of hearing about issues in stuttering.

7. Ask any stutterers who were paired with nonstutterers to say something about the experience.

TAKEAWAY LESSONS

Encourage participants to share what stands out for them, or what they may have learned about themselves, their issues, and each other.

CONSIDER:

1. Although we may know it intellectually, talking about our liabilities in a safe place helps us to unburden, makes our issues feel less heavy to bear, and reduces the power they have over us.

2. Becoming a little more vulnerable to others in an appropriate place (such as a support group) is typically viewed positively by others.

INDIVIDUAL GOAL EVALUATIONS

Ask participants to go back to the goals they stated at the beginning of the meeting, and grade themselves on a scale from 1 to 10. They may share their grades with the group if they choose.

CLOSING WORDS

16. OUR SELF-IMAGE AND OUR STUTTERING

PREPARATION

- Have access to a whiteboard or other display device.
- At the beginning and end of the meeting, ask someone to read the Welcoming Words and Closing Words (*Appendix E*).

GOAL

1. To gain insight into how self concepts regarding stuttering (and other issues such as our body image) affect us and may be limiting us.

THE MEETING

WELCOMING WORDS

ICEBREAKER

Ask the participants to imagine that they just won $20 million from the lottery. What will they do with the money? (*Or see Appendix A.*)

INDIVIDUAL GOALS

Ask each one in attendance (stutterers, facilitators, visitors) to identify a personal goal for the meeting, and share it with the group. Inform them that, at the end of the meeting, they will be reminded of their goals and have an opportunity to evaluate themselves. (If necessary, prompt ones who are having difficulty choosing a goal with some examples, like those in Appendix G.)

ACTIVITY

(Announce that participation in any activity is strictly voluntary. Everyone should join only those exercises with which they feel comfortable.)

1. Introduce the concept of body image, and allow the group to briefly discuss what it means and how it can affect our life choices.

2. Ask attendees to identify one thing they don't like about their bodies, something that has limited them in some way. Mention that it could be a strictly physical attribute like height, weight, skin, teeth, etc., or something to do with ability,

like not being good at athletics or dancing, or being dissatisfied with their voice. Have someone list the responses on a whiteboard, if available. Invite discussion of why they have let these things limit them, and whether the limitations have been unavoidable, or something they have allowed to happen.

3. Ask stutterers for examples of how stuttering has limited them. Invite discussion of to what extent the limitations were unavoidable, or to what extent they have been allowed to happen.

4. Ask participants to think back to the physical attributes they identified earlier, and imagine that the condition is suddenly and completely gone. Ask the group to discuss how their lives would be different, or how they would think or behave differently.

5. Ask which participants would choose: a magic wand to remove or correct their issue or a $20 million lottery winning. For anyone who chose $20 million, start with $1 and go up until they would have a difficult time deciding which to choose, the money or correcting their issue.

TAKEAWAY LESSONS

Encourage participants to share what stands out for them, or what they may have learned about themselves, their issues, and each other.

CONSIDER:

1. Most of us are concerned about how other people see us in a negative way, but other people are very likely concerned about how we see them.

2. To the extent we can, our quality of life is enhanced if we do not focus excessively on other people's presumed judgments of us.

3. Our insecurities make us who we are.

INDIVIDUAL GOAL EVALUATIONS

Ask participants to go back to the goals they stated at the beginning of the meeting, and grade themselves on a scale from 1 to 10. They may share their grades with the group if they choose.

CLOSING WORDS

17. DETERMINATION AND ACHIEVEMENT

PREPARATION

- Have access to a whiteboard or other display device.
- At the beginning and end of the meeting, ask someone to read the Welcoming Words and Closing Words (*Appendix E*).

GOALS

1. To discuss long-term goals and the efforts required to accomplish them.
2. To share stories of accomplishments achieved and not achieved.

THE MEETING

WELCOMING WORDS

ICEBREAKER

Ask participants to talk about something they find very difficult, but other people do easily. (*Or see Appendix A.*)

INDIVIDUAL GOALS

Ask each one in attendance (stutterers, facilitators, visitors) to identify a personal goal for the meeting, and share it with the group. Inform them that, at the end of the meeting, they will be reminded of their goals and have an opportunity to evaluate themselves. (If necessary, prompt ones who are having difficulty choosing a goal with some examples, like those in Appendix G.)

ACTIVITY

(Announce that participation in any activity is strictly voluntary. Everyone should join only those exercises with which they feel comfortable.)

1. Ask participants to think about and share something reasonably challenging, not related to stuttering, that they wanted to do and then followed through to complete or were mostly successful with.

2. Ask them to think about something not related to stuttering, that was at least as challenging as their successful accomplishment that they wanted to do but was not successful. Point out that they may have started it but did not put in sufficient time and/or effort to make it happen.

3. Ask the stutterers to think of a stuttering-related challenge in which they succeeded and another one in which they did not.

4. Invite a discussion of the differences between when they followed through and succeeded and when they did not follow through and did not succeed. Ask participants to explain what kept them from following through on their goal and ask a volunteer to summarize the reasons on one side of the whiteboard.

5. Ask participants to call out words that are associated with "determination" while the volunteer writes them on the other side of the whiteboard.

TAKEAWAY LESSONS

Encourage participants to share what stands out for them, or what they may have learned about themselves, their issues, and each other.

CONSIDER:

1. The difference between following through to success or abandoning a goal can depend on our abilities, the difficulty of the goal, and the level of our determination.

2. Determination is a complex concept that involves opportunity, perceived difficulty, past history of success, individual personalities, etc. It is not as simple as what we often hear—"If I can do it, anyone can do it."

3. Determination is important in overcoming problems associated with our stuttering, but it must be balanced with a healthy amount of acceptance of what we cannot change.

INDIVIDUAL GOAL EVALUATIONS

Ask participants to go back to the goals they stated at the beginning of the meeting, and grade themselves on a scale from 1 to 10. They may share their grades with the group if they choose.

CLOSING WORDS

18. CONTEMPLATING THE FUTURE

PREPARATION

- At the beginning and end of the meeting, ask someone to read the Welcoming Words and Closing Words (*Appendix E*).

GOALS

1. To explore how stuttering or another personal issue affects our lives.

2. To discuss the future in five years' time and contemplate how stuttering or a personal issue may affect our future goals.

3. To contemplate the benefits and drawbacks of thinking about the future with regards to stuttering or another personal issue.

THE MEETING

WELCOMING WORDS

ICEBREAKER

Have everyone take turns "reading the palm" of the person on their right. Get creative! Come up with three future events. (*Or see Appendix A.*)

INDIVIDUAL GOALS

Ask each one in attendance (stutterers, facilitators, visitors) to identify a personal goal for the meeting, and share it with the group. Inform them that, at the end of the meeting, they will be reminded of their goals and have an opportunity to evaluate themselves. (If necessary, prompt ones who are having difficulty choosing a goal with some examples, like those in Appendix G.)

ACTIVITY

(Announce that participation in any activity is strictly voluntary. Everyone should join only those exercises with which they feel comfortable.)

1. Ask participants, "Where do you see yourself in five years? Add any relevant details, such as where you will be, who you will be with, if you will be married with children,

what you will be doing, and so on. Also, share how you are preparing for this 'five-year plan' in any way, big or small."

2. Ask participants to identify an issue they are currently facing in life. Encourage the stutterers to choose stuttering, but everyone should choose one issue they find to be seriously hindering in some way. Ask each person to name the issue they have chosen.

3. Ask the group, "How is your chosen issue potentially affecting any part of your five-year plan?"

4. Ask, "To what extent do you think your chosen issue will impact your future, on a scale of 1–10?"

5. Ask each person to contemplate the benefits and drawbacks of being concerned with their future regarding their chosen issue.

TAKEAWAY LESSONS

Encourage participants to share what stands out for them, or what they may have learned about themselves, their issues, and each other.

CONSIDER:

1. Setting future goals for ourselves increases the likelihood we will achieve them.

2. Identifying potential obstacles in advance may help us reduce their impact.

3. Stuttering may or may not be a serious obstacle to our future plans, depending on how we view it and/or what we do about it.

INDIVIDUAL GOAL EVALUATIONS

Ask participants to go back to the goals they stated at the beginning of the meeting, and grade themselves on a scale from 1 to 10. They may share their grades with the group if they choose.

CLOSING WORDS

19. PREPARING FOR JOB INTERVIEWS

PREPARATION

- Video recording and viewing equipment is needed. Choose a spot for two speakers to sit facing each other across a table, and set up the equipment to record that area.

- Someone needs to be prepared to conduct mock interviews for a generic job, with questions focusing on the applicant's oral communication skills. A guest who has done job interviews would be ideal, if such a person can be recruited. If not, the leader can assume this role.

- At the beginning and end of the meeting, ask someone to read the Welcoming Words and Closing Words (*Appendix E*).

GOALS

1. To practice a high-stress speaking situation—a job interview.

2. To watch recordings of the interviews as a group, and discuss the emotions involved in the activity and aspects of effective or less effective communication.

THE MEETING

WELCOMING WORDS

ICEBREAKER

Ask what people do when they want to impress someone. (*Or see Appendix A.*)

INDIVIDUAL GOALS

Ask each one in attendance (stutterers, facilitators, visitors) to identify a personal goal for the meeting, and share it with the group. Inform them that, at the end of the meeting, they will be reminded of their goals and have an opportunity to evaluate themselves. (If necessary, prompt ones who are having difficulty choosing a goal with some examples, like those in Appendix G.)

ACTIVITY

(Announce that participation in any activity is strictly voluntary. Everyone should join only those exercises with which they feel comfortable.)

1. Ask participants to participate, one at a time, in a brief, two-minute portion of a job interview. The interviewer should ask questions and discuss the applicant's communication skills in a friendly, supportive way.

2. After all the interviews, play the recordings such that the group can watch. After each interview, pause the recording and let the individual applicant tell about how he or she feels they did, what they did well and what could be improved.

3. Repeat the first two steps, but with the interviewer being very skeptical of the applicant's ability to do the job, and impatient with the applicant's answers. In the response portion of the activity, ask participants to discuss differences in their emotions or stress levels involved in the two interviews.

4. Ask stutterers to comment on what, if anything, they did to disclose their stuttering. Ask for group discussion of opinions regarding the question, to disclose or not to disclose.

TAKEAWAY LESSONS

Encourage participants to share what stands out for them, or what they may have learned about themselves, their issues, and each other.

CONSIDER:

1. Formal speaking situations such as job interviews are stressful for most people, and especially so for stutterers. Still we must learn to face and do our best in them.

2. Carrying out mock interviews, like any practice sessions, can assist us in managing our stuttering in later, real interviews.

INDIVIDUAL GOAL EVALUATIONS

Ask participants to go back to the goals they stated at the beginning of the meeting, and grade themselves on a scale from 1 to 10. They may share their grades with the group if they choose.

CLOSING WORDS

20. THOUGHTS AND FEELINGS BEFORE, DURING, AND AFTER STUTTERING

PREPARATION
- Have access to a whiteboard or other display device.
- At the beginning and end of the meeting, ask someone to read the Welcoming Words and Closing Words (*Appendix E*).

GOAL
1. To cultivate insight toward stuttering by exploring the moment of stuttering in terms of its anticipation, its present reality, and its aftereffects.

THE MEETING

WELCOMING WORDS

ICEBREAKER
Ask members what they do when they need to order from a menu without time to read it thoroughly. (*Or see Appendix A.*)

INDIVIDUAL GOALS
Ask each one in attendance (stutterers, facilitators, visitors) to identify a personal goal for the meeting, and share it with the group. Inform them that, at the end of the meeting, they will be reminded of their goals and have an opportunity to evaluate themselves. (If necessary, prompt ones who are having difficulty choosing a goal with some examples, like those in Appendix G.)

ACTIVITY
(Announce that participation in any activity is strictly voluntary. Everyone should join only those exercises with which they feel comfortable.)

1. Ask the participants to think back to a time when they had to get a vaccination or get blood drawn, and think about all the thoughts and feelings that went through their head before, during, and after. Give the participants a few minutes to think back. Ask participants to share their feelings before the procedure, and list them

on a whiteboard or other display under the heading "Before." Repeat for feelings "During" and "After" the procedure.

2. Ask what thoughts and feelings participants experience before, during, and after a particularly memorable stuttering situation, and add the responses to the lists on the board. Invite discussion of the similarities and differences.

TAKEAWAY LESSONS

Encourage participants to share what stands out for them, or what they may have learned about themselves, their issues, and each other.

CONSIDER:

1. Most of us can anticipate a stutter before it happens, and this often triggers past fears.

2. We all experience the occurrence of stuttering differently.

3. After stuttering, some stutterers experience temporary relief. Well-known stuttering expert Joseph Sheehan said, "Fluency is followed by stuttering, and stuttering is followed by fluency."

4. After stuttering, some stutterers experience embarrassment, shame, or guilt.

INDIVIDUAL GOAL EVALUATIONS

Ask participants to go back to the goals they stated at the beginning of the meeting, and grade themselves on a scale from 1 to 10. They may share their grades with the group if they choose.

CLOSING WORDS

21. THE RELATIONSHIP BETWEEN THOUGHTS AND FEELINGS

PREPARATION

- Before the meeting, either draw the "Thoughts, Feelings, and Actions" graphic on a whiteboard or other display, or make copies of the version in Appendix F to hand out to the group. Become familiar with the ideas represented in the graphic, and be prepared to explain and discuss them.
- At the beginning and end of the meeting, ask someone to read the Welcoming Words and Closing Words (*Appendix E*).

GOALS

1. To examine the "Thoughts, Feelings, and Actions" relationship chart.
2. To discuss the two-way relationship of thoughts and feelings in relation to stuttering.

THE MEETING

WELCOMING WORDS

ICEBREAKER

Ask people in attendance what was their dream job when they were young. (*Or see Appendix A.*)

INDIVIDUAL GOALS

Ask each one in attendance (stutterers, facilitators, visitors) to identify a personal goal for the meeting, and share it with the group. Inform them that, at the end of the meeting, they will be reminded of their goals and have an opportunity to evaluate themselves. (If necessary, prompt ones who are having difficulty choosing a goal with some examples, like those in Appendix G.)

ACTIVITY

(Announce that participation in any activity is strictly voluntary. Everyone should join only those exercises with which they feel comfortable.)

1. Briefly explain the "Thoughts, Feelings, and Actions" chart, and announce that the focus of the meeting will be on the two-way relationship between thoughts and feelings. Ask participants—stutterers and nonstutterers—to try to separate thoughts and feelings during the discussion.

2. As an example, offer the following scenario. (If your participants are not students, try to create a more generic example.)

    » Situation: You fail an exam.
    » Thoughts: I am stupid. I'm going to flunk this class. I might need to drop out.
    » Feelings: Anger, anxiety, depression.

3. Ask the group to discuss other thoughts, which might lead to different feelings.

4. Explain that many people believe that their feelings are generated by events and situations and that there's very little anyone can do to change their feelings. But, in the model represented in this graphic, that's not the case. Feelings can come from thoughts about what is happening, not directly from what's happening, and there is often an opportunity to change our feelings by consciously changing our thoughts.

5. Ask participants to think of an unresolved issue in their lives that causes strong feelings. Invite participants to share what the situation is, and what the feelings are. Ask what thoughts are creating these feelings.

6. For each situation, ask participants to imagine they are able to consciously alter their feelings, even if they really feel that this is not possible. What new thoughts would be desirable? How would these altered thoughts lead to altered feelings?

7. Invite stutterers to apply this exercise to some stuttering-related condition or situation that causes strong feelings, and to share it with the group.

TAKEAWAY LESSONS

Encourage participants to share what stands out for them, or what they may have learned about themselves, their issues, and each other.

CONSIDER:

1. Our thoughts and feelings about stuttering are very much related.

2. Talking about our stuttering with others typically results in greater acceptance (thoughts), which in turn results in less fear and avoidance (feelings).

INDIVIDUAL GOAL EVALUATIONS

Ask participants to go back to the goals they stated at the beginning of the meeting, and grade themselves on a scale from 1 to 10. They may share their grades with the group if they choose.

CLOSING WORDS

"No matter what happens it will be okay, because it is always okay."

22. IDENTIFYING EMOTIONS ASSOCIATED WITH STUTTERING

PREPARATION

- At the beginning and end of the meeting, ask someone to read the Welcoming Words and Closing Words (*Appendix E*).

GOALS

1. To identify the different emotions associated with being a stutterer.

2. To provide insight into and desensitization to the emotions that are often associated with stuttering.

THE MEETING

WELCOMING WORDS

ICEBREAKER

Ask the group members to imagine that they are at an upscale dinner party and being served something that looks very unappetizing. Ask what they would be thinking and how they would react. (*Or see Appendix A.*)

INDIVIDUAL GOALS

Ask each one in attendance (stutterers, facilitators, visitors) to identify a personal goal for the meeting, and share it with the group. Inform them that, at the end of the meeting, they will be reminded of their goals and have an opportunity to evaluate themselves. (If necessary, prompt ones who are having difficulty choosing a goal with some examples, like those in Appendix G.)

ACTIVITY

(Announce that participation in any activity is strictly voluntary. Everyone should join only those exercises with which they feel comfortable.)

1. Ask each participant to try to think of a time when their stuttering, or another difficult issue for nonstutterers, made them angry, and share it with the group. Allow brief discussion.

2. Repeat Step 1, but asking for a time when people were embarrassed, then a time when they were afraid, then frustrated, then ashamed.

3. Ask each person to rank the severity of each of these emotions—anger, embarrassment, fear, frustration, and shame—on a scale from 1 to 5, with 1 being the least personally troubling, and 5 being the worst. Ask each person to explain his/her ranking.

TAKEAWAY LESSONS

Encourage participants to share what stands out for them, or what they may have learned about themselves, their issues, and each other.

CONSIDER:

1. Our emotions are innate, unlearned responses. We cannot will them not to occur; they just are.

2. Our emotions may cause us to jump to unnecessary—and often false—conclusions about our stuttering.

3. If we have progressed to feeling shame or guilt because of our stuttering, changing the stutter itself may have little effect on these emotions.

INDIVIDUAL GOAL EVALUATIONS

Ask participants to go back to the goals they stated at the beginning of the meeting, and grade themselves on a scale from 1 to 10. They may share their grades with the group if they choose.

CLOSING WORDS

23. CLARIFYING THE EMOTIONS OF STUTTERING

PREPARATION

- Have access to a whiteboard or other display device.
- Have pencil and paper available.
- At the beginning and end of the meeting, ask someone to read the Welcoming Words and Closing Words (*Appendix E*).

GOALS

1. To discuss negative emotions surrounding stuttering or any other issue.
2. To share strategies for managing or understanding negative emotions.

THE MEETING

WELCOMING WORDS

ICEBREAKER

Ask participants what job they believe would be the worst, and why it would be so bad for them. (*Or see Appendix A.*)

INDIVIDUAL GOALS

Ask each one in attendance (stutterers, facilitators, visitors) to identify a personal goal for the meeting, and share it with the group. Inform them that, at the end of the meeting, they will be reminded of their goals and have an opportunity to evaluate themselves. (If necessary, prompt ones who are having difficulty choosing a goal with some examples, like those in Appendix G.)

ACTIVITY

(Announce that participation in any activity is strictly voluntary. Everyone should join only those exercises with which they feel comfortable.)

1. Ask stutterers to think about how various emotions are related to their stuttering. Ask nonstutterers to do the same regarding another especially troubling personal issue that causes negative emotions in their lives. After a brief time to think, ask nonstutterers to share what issue they will be discussing.

2. Have the following negative emotions written on the whiteboard: a) embarrassment, b) frustration, c) fear, d) anger, and e) shame or guilt. Explain that the group will be encouraged to discuss them.

3. For each of them, ask participants to think about and write a reminder note for themselves for each of the following questions:

    » What emotions do you feel with your stuttering (or other issue)? Rate it on a scale of 1–10 in terms of not applicable to very extreme.

    » What situations typically cause you to feel this/these emotions?

    » Why do you think you feel this way?

    » Is there anything you have learned that helps (or doesn't help) endure or manage the emotions?

TAKEAWAY LESSONS

Encourage participants to share what stands out for them, or what they may have learned about themselves, their issues, and each other.

CONSIDER:

1. Our past speaking failures and negative reactions of others when we stuttered are the seeds of later emotions that become linked to stuttering, or even the thought of stuttering.

2. Everyone is different, but most commonly, stuttering-related emotions often proceed from surprise to embarrassment, then to frustration, then to anxiety or fear, and then to shame or guilt. Anger may or may not occur.

3. Emotions cannot be willed to stop. They simply are.

4. With greater acceptance of negative emotions, they need not dictate our lives. It is what we do with them that matters.

INDIVIDUAL GOAL EVALUATIONS

Ask participants to go back to the goals they stated at the beginning of the meeting, and grade themselves on a scale from 1 to 10. They may share their grades with the group if they choose.

CLOSING WORDS

24. EMBARRASSMENT AND SHAME IN STUTTERING

PREPARATION

- At the beginning and end of the meeting, ask someone to read the Welcoming Words and Closing Words (*Appendix E*).

GOALS

1. To share experiences of feeling shame or embarrassment.
2. To discuss different ways of dealing with embarrassment or shame, and the lingering effects of these emotions.

THE MEETING

WELCOMING WORDS

ICEBREAKER

Ask those in attendance to think of examples of thoughtless comments that end up embarrassing the speaker. (If people are having trouble thinking of anything, supply an example, such as, "What's different about you today? You look really good. ... Not that you don't always look good.") (*Or see Appendix A.*)

INDIVIDUAL GOALS

Ask each one in attendance (stutterers, facilitators, visitors) to identify a personal goal for the meeting, and share it with the group. Inform them that, at the end of the meeting, they will be reminded of their goals and have an opportunity to evaluate themselves. (If necessary, prompt ones who are having difficulty choosing a goal with some examples, like those in Appendix G.)

ACTIVITY

(Announce that participation in any activity is strictly voluntary. Everyone should join only those exercises with which they feel comfortable.)

1. Ask everyone present to think of a time when they remember feeling embarrassment that they are willing to share with the group. For stutterers this will probably be in relation to speech, but others should choose a personal story to share.

2. After time for thought, ask people to share their stories. Ask them to include any memories of how they felt just before the embarrassment, during it, and afterward. How long did the situation last? How long after the incident did the person keep coming back to the memory and experiencing the embarrassment again?

3. Repeat Step 2 but for feeling shame.

4. Discuss the similarities and differences of the feeling and experience of embarrassment versus shame.

TAKEAWAY LESSONS

Encourage participants to share what stands out for them, or what they may have learned about themselves, their issues, and each other.

CONSIDER:

1. We all feel embarrassment when we make a gaffe, when we slip up, when we have a social "accident," etc. Our feelings may be intense at the time, but they typically diminish relatively quickly. Later, memories of embarrassment are often funny.

2. Much less commonly, we feel shame. It may result from some of the same circumstances that caused embarrassment, but it also is typically associated with a value judgment of being or doing something "bad." Shame may occur immediately but ordinarily develops over time. Children who are "black and white" versus "shades of gray" thinkers are more prone to feeling shame immediately than adults. However, childhood shame persists into adulthood.

3. If we stutter and feel ashamed by it, we have a longer journey to being okay with our stuttering than if we felt only embarrassed by it.

INDIVIDUAL GOAL EVALUATIONS

Ask participants to go back to the goals they stated at the beginning of the meeting, and grade themselves on a scale from 1 to 10. They may share their grades with the group if they choose.

CLOSING WORDS

25. FEELING TRAPPED BY STUTTERING

PREPARATION
- Have access to a whiteboard or other display device.
- Ask someone to write on the board during the group activity.
- At the beginning and end of the meeting, ask someone to read the Welcoming Words and Closing Words (*Appendix E*).

GOALS
1. To consider what it means to be "trapped."
2. To discover strategies for moving out of the feeling of being trapped.

THE MEETING

WELCOMING WORDS

ICEBREAKER

Ask participants to answer one of the following questions: In a job interview you are asked, "Have you ever stolen anything from your employer?" or Your significant other asks, "What do you think is the worst thing about me?" (*Or see Appendix A.*)

INDIVIDUAL GOALS

Ask each one in attendance (stutterers, facilitators, visitors) to identify a personal goal for the meeting, and share it with the group. Inform them that, at the end of the meeting, they will be reminded of their goals and have an opportunity to evaluate themselves. (If necessary, prompt ones who are having difficulty choosing a goal with some examples, like those in Appendix G.)

ACTIVITY

(Announce that participation in any activity is strictly voluntary. Everyone should join only those exercises with which they feel comfortable.)

1. Announce that this meeting is about feeling trapped. Ask participants what they think of when they hear the word "trap." Allow a few minutes for responses.

2. Ask everyone to tell about a time when they felt trapped by a situation not involving stuttering. This should be a situation that is no longer happening, one in which they eventually got out of the trap or just moved on from it. Allow each one to briefly describe their experience. As this discussion is going on, have someone divide the whiteboard in half, and label one half "trap" and the other half "freedom." Have this person write some key words in the "trap" area about some of the feelings (*feelings*, not the details of the situation) expressed as the group discusses their experiences.

3. Ask the stutterers to talk about a time when they felt trapped by their stuttering, and have key words from this discussion listed on the board along with the other "trap" words.

4. Ask the participants to talk about their feelings when they got out of their trap, and have some key words listed under "freedom." Ask the group what other words should be added to the two lists.

TAKEAWAY LESSONS

Encourage participants to share what stands out for them, or what they may have learned about themselves, their issues, and each other.

CONSIDER:

1. Almost all of us have felt trapped by something, and most of us have learned either to get out of the trap or to manage it.

2. Traps tend to be more in our minds than in reality.

3. Because every person's journey is unique, we may consider something a trap that others may not be bothered by.

INDIVIDUAL GOAL EVALUATIONS

Ask participants to go back to the goals they stated at the beginning of the meeting, and grade themselves on a scale from 1 to 10. They may share their grades with the group if they choose.

CLOSING WORDS

26. IDENTIFYING AUTOMATIC NEGATIVE THOUGHTS

PREPARATION

- Have access to a whiteboard or other display device.
- At the beginning and end of the meeting, ask someone to read the Welcoming Words and Closing Words (*Appendix E*).

GOALS

1. To achieve greater insight into stuttering through examining different types of automatic negative thoughts, where they come from, and why we have them.

2. To promote desensitization toward stuttering by assisting participants to place their automatic negative thoughts into a realistic perspective.

THE MEETING

WELCOMING WORDS

ICEBREAKER

Ask what participants would do if they were in a car being driven by their boss, and the boss started texting while driving. (*Or see Appendix A.*)

INDIVIDUAL GOALS

Ask each one in attendance (stutterers, facilitators, visitors) to identify a personal goal for the meeting, and share it with the group. Inform them that, at the end of the meeting, they will be reminded of their goals and have an opportunity to evaluate themselves. (If necessary, prompt ones who are having difficulty choosing a goal with some examples, like those in Appendix G.)

ACTIVITY

(Announce that participation in any activity is strictly voluntary. Everyone should join only those exercises with which they feel comfortable.)

1. Write five situations on the board: 1) interviewing for a job, 2) speaking in front of a large group, 3) meeting your significant other's family for the first time, 4) testifying in court about an accident you witnessed, and 5) giving complex directions to a

stranger who is lost. Ask everyone to think about which situation would make them the most apprehensive.

2. Have each participant identify the scenario they chose, and list their names next to the situation they chose.

3. Tell the group that the goal in this session is to demonstrate that it is not the situation itself that causes the stress but the negative thoughts about the results. Ask each person to repeat the situation that would make them negative and briefly say why.

4. One at a time, remind the group of each participant's response, and ask the group to discuss what might be the worst possible outcome of the situation, and what might be the best possible outcome. Then ask that individual what would probably be the most likely outcome.

5. Invite discussion of how we have unrealistic, negative thoughts and fears, and where these thoughts come from.

TAKEAWAY LESSONS

Encourage participants to share what stands out for them, or what they may have learned about themselves, their issues, and each other.

CONSIDER:

1. We all tend to have automatic negative thoughts, and we rarely think about where they come from.

2. Identifying automatic negative thoughts is a first step in helping to get past them, but actually achieving that takes courage, hard work, and experiencing fearful situations over and over.

3. Some stuttering therapy involves going into real situations over and over in order to weaken the anxious, negative thoughts associated with speaking to various people.

INDIVIDUAL GOAL EVALUATIONS

Ask participants to go back to the goals they stated at the beginning of the meeting, and grade themselves on a scale from 1 to 10. They may share their grades with the group if they choose.

CLOSING WORDS

27. ANALYZING AUTOMATIC NEGATIVE THOUGHTS

PREPARATION

- Download a list of unusual phobias from the internet and print them.
- Have access to a whiteboard or other display device.
- At the beginning and end of the meeting, ask someone to read the Welcoming Words and Closing Words (*Appendix E*).

GOALS

1. To discuss automatic negative thoughts and their effect on our lives.
2. To share experiences with negative thinking and possible ways to limit it.

THE MEETING

WELCOMING WORDS

ICEBREAKER

Write various phobias on the board, and ask the participants to guess what specific fears the words represent. Next, ask the participants to share a unique phobia that they have. (*Or see Appendix A.*)

INDIVIDUAL GOALS

Ask each one in attendance (stutterers, facilitators, visitors) to identify a personal goal for the meeting, and share it with the group. Inform them that, at the end of the meeting, they will be reminded of their goals and have an opportunity to evaluate themselves. (If necessary, prompt ones who are having difficulty choosing a goal with some examples, like those in Appendix G.)

ACTIVITY

(Announce that participation in any activity is strictly voluntary. Everyone should join only those exercises with which they feel comfortable.)

1. Invite a few minutes of discussion about automatic negative thoughts: what they are, where they come from, etc.

2. Ask each one in attendance—stutterers and nonstutterers—to think of one type of anxious negative thought that they are prone to. Allow a minute for people to think, then ask everyone to share their thought.

3. For the stutterers, and for the nonstutterers as time permits, ask the following questions about the person's anxious, negative thought:

    » Is it true?

    » Are you 100% sure, guaranteed, it is true?

    » How does it feel when you think the thought?

    » How would you feel if you didn't have the thought?

    » Who would you be if you didn't have the thought?

    » Turn the original thought around. What if the opposite were true? Is it true more often than the anxious negative thought? (from Amen, 2019) https://www.amenclinics.com/blog/number-one-habit-develop-order-feel-positive/

TAKEAWAY LESSONS

Encourage participants to share what stands out for them, or what they may have learned about themselves, their issues, and each other.

CONSIDER:

1. When evaluated, many of our negative thoughts and fears about stuttering are not accurate.

2. It is possible to change our "scripts" (or what we tell ourselves) by evaluating the way we view our thoughts and attitudes.

3. Although self-evaluation is important, it is not always a solution. Some thoughts/fears are deeply ingrained. The purpose of analyzing our anxious, negative thoughts is not to put a guilt trip on us but rather to help us evaluate our negative thoughts based on what is actually likely to happen.

INDIVIDUAL GOAL EVALUATIONS

Ask participants to go back to the goals they stated at the beginning of the meeting, and grade themselves on a scale from 1 to 10. They may share their grades with the group if they choose.

CLOSING WORDS

28. DEALING WITH NEGATIVE THOUGHTS AND EMOTIONS

PREPARATION

- At the beginning and end of the meeting, ask someone to read the Welcoming Words and Closing Words (*Appendix E*).

GOALS

1. To acknowledge negative emotions/thoughts that are experienced in certain speaking situations.

2. To evaluate what fuels these emotions/thoughts.

3. To discuss what can be done to reduce the power of negative thoughts/feelings.

THE MEETING

WELCOMING WORDS

ICEBREAKER

When you get up in the morning and look into the mirror, what is the first thing you notice? (*Or see Appendix A.*)

INDIVIDUAL GOALS

Ask each one in attendance (stutterers, facilitators, visitors) to identify a personal goal for the meeting, and share it with the group. Inform them that, at the end of the meeting, they will be reminded of their goals and have an opportunity to evaluate themselves. (If necessary, prompt ones who are having difficulty choosing a goal with some examples, like those in Appendix G.)

ACTIVITY

(Announce that participation in any activity is strictly voluntary. Everyone should join only those exercises with which they feel comfortable.)

1. Announce that everyone will be giving a one- to two-minute speech on a major tragedy in their lives. The speeches will be video recorded for the others to view and

comment on. The group will be given two minutes to think about the speeches, and prepare to speak. Wait two minutes.

2. Reveal that the speeches will not actually be made. Ask the group to discuss the thoughts or emotions they experienced while they were thinking about making the speech. Of people's negative thoughts, which ones were rational or realistic, and which were emotional? Where do these thoughts come from, and what keeps them going? Are any of the thoughts useful?

TAKEAWAY LESSONS

Encourage participants to share what stands out for them, or what they may have learned about themselves, their issues, and each other.

CONSIDER:

1. Anticipation of events often produces strong emotions.
2. Emotions cannot be willed; they simply occur.
3. Emotions, in turn, can produce both rational and irrational thoughts.
4. Sometimes, we can react to negative emotions with intentional, positive thinking.

INDIVIDUAL GOAL EVALUATIONS

Ask participants to go back to the goals they stated at the beginning of the meeting, and grade themselves on a scale from 1 to 10. They may share their grades with the group if they choose.

CLOSING WORDS

29. PROCESSING NEGATIVE EARLY MEMORIES OF STUTTERING

PREPARATION

- At the beginning and end of the meeting, ask someone to read the Welcoming Words and Closing Words (*Appendix E*).

GOALS

1. To gain insight into stuttering by discussing memories and what participants wish they would have been told as a young stutterer.

2. To talk about emotional wounds and how we can move past them.

THE MEETING

WELCOMING WORDS

ICEBREAKER

Ask each participant to share the first dream in their memory. (*Or see Appendix A.*)

INDIVIDUAL GOALS

Ask each one in attendance (stutterers, facilitators, visitors) to identify a personal goal for the meeting, and share it with the group. Inform them that, at the end of the meeting, they will be reminded of their goals and have an opportunity to evaluate themselves. (If necessary, prompt ones who are having difficulty choosing a goal with some examples, like those in Appendix G.)

ACTIVITY

(Announce that participation in any activity is strictly voluntary. Everyone should join only those exercises with which they feel comfortable.)

1. Ask the group to share their first memory of a troubling communicative experience. For the people who stutter, ask them to share the first time they can remember their stuttering being a problem for them. For the guests in the group, ask them to share an early memory of a time where they have struggled communicatively in other ways.

2. Next, ask the people who stutter to share what they wish someone would have told them about stuttering when they were children.

3. As time permits, ask the same of the nonstutterers regarding their communication experience.

4. Next, ask participants to speak about the "wounds," or those misunderstandings that stuttering or other communication difficulties may have caused. Invite discussion of steps anyone has taken to move past those wounds.

5. Next, ask for discussion about the value of talking about stuttering when one is young.

TAKEAWAY LESSONS

Encourage participants to share what stands out for them, or what they may have learned about themselves, their issues, and each other.

CONSIDER:

1. Children typically remember things as "black or white" and "good or bad." They don't remember things in "shades of gray" or as both "good and bad."

2. Therefore, we all have wounds from what was said or not said to us as children.

3. These wounds often were not intentionally inflicted. Our parents often did the best they could.

4. It is possible to move past our wounds in a productive manner. We can even become "wounded healers."

INDIVIDUAL GOAL EVALUATIONS

Ask participants to go back to the goals they stated at the beginning of the meeting, and grade themselves on a scale from 1 to 10. They may share their grades with the group if they choose.

CLOSING WORDS

30. UNBURDENING NEGATIVE MEMORIES

PREPARATION

- Have paper and pens or pencils for everyone. Have a clipboard ready. Set up two chairs facing each other, where the group can see.
- Print a picture of the "iceberg of stuttering" from the internet.
- Gather together several items of various weights, each small enough to fit in one's hand.
- At the beginning and end of the meeting, ask someone to read the Welcoming Words and Closing Words (*Appendix E*).

GOALS

1. To evaluate the effects of leaving things unsaid, which often burdens us.
2. To realize that more often than not, some specific experience shapes our views, reactions, and behaviors.
3. To consider addressing a burden sooner rather than later, so less of the weight of that burden will be felt.

THE MEETING

WELCOMING WORDS

ICEBREAKER

Invite participants to line up against a wall. The leader will show them a horizontal line marked on a sheet of paper on the wall about 4 feet from the floor. Participants will close their eyes while the leader puts an item in their hand. When the item is placed in their hand, each person will raise it to try to meet the exact height of the line marked on the wall without opening their eyes. (*Or see Appendix A.*)

INDIVIDUAL GOALS

Ask each one in attendance (stutterers, facilitators, visitors) to identify a personal goal for the meeting, and share it with the group. Inform them that, at the end of the meeting, they will be reminded of their goals and have an opportunity to evaluate themselves. (If necessary, prompt ones who are having difficulty choosing a goal with some examples, like those in Appendix G.)

ACTIVITY

(Announce that participation in any activity is strictly voluntary. Everyone should join only those exercises with which they feel comfortable.)

1. Ask everyone to think for a minute or two and then choose one specific instance when they did not say something and wish they had. It could be really life-changing or relatively trivial, but it should be something that has stayed on their mind. Encourage stutterers to select an incident involving their stuttering.

2. Ask each participant to place a "weight value" on how heavy the burden of remembering the incident is—not *at the time*, but how heavy remembering it *now* is. Call the weight 10 pounds if it is very light, 50 pounds if it is a serious mental burden, and 100 pounds if it is too much to bear. Have people share their weight estimates with the group.

3. Ask everyone to write on a sheet of paper the name of the person or people they wish they had said something to. (Instead of a name, it could be a descriptor, like sister, neighbor, boss, etc.)

4. Tell participants that they will now have an opportunity to say what they should have said. Invite anyone to do the following: briefly identify the situation to the group, place the paper with the person's name or descriptor on a clipboard, prop the clipboard up on one of the chairs, and sit facing the chair and say what needs to be said as if the person were there. Assure the group that this exercise is voluntary.

5. Ask participants how it felt to do the exercise. Ask if it lessened the weight they previously said they felt, and by how much. Invite general discussion of saying things, leaving things unsaid, and the consequences.

TAKEAWAY LESSONS

Encourage participants to share what stands out for them, or what they may have learned about themselves, their issues, and each other.

CONSIDER:

1. There is often a burden or "weight on our chest" felt when things go unsaid.

2. It's not healthy to carry a burden if it can be lessened.

3. We must be judicious about where we unburden. It must be in a safe place with people who are invested in us and our feelings.

4. In terms of the "iceberg of stuttering," by unburdening, we can melt away what is below the surface of the iceberg.

INDIVIDUAL GOAL EVALUATIONS

Ask participants to go back to the goals they stated at the beginning of the meeting, and grade themselves on a scale from 1 to 10. They may share their grades with the group if they choose.

CLOSING WORDS

"I am gaining confidence and losing a lot of those negative emotions."

31. UNDERSTANDING WHY WE AVOID

PREPARATION

- Provide paper and pens or pencils.
- At the beginning and end of the meeting, ask someone to read the Welcoming Words and Closing Words (*Appendix E*).

GOAL

1. To consider aspects of avoidance behavior, including various motivations for it and when it may or may not be helpful.

THE MEETING

WELCOMING WORDS

ICEBREAKER

Ask group members to pair up and then pose this question, "How do you make and eat your favorite sandwich?" One in each pair will explain the sandwich procedure to their partner, but they are not allowed to make eye contact at all. After the first speaker, they will switch roles. (*Or see Appendix A.*)

INDIVIDUAL GOALS

Ask each one in attendance (stutterers, facilitators, visitors) to identify a personal goal for the meeting, and share it with the group. Inform them that, at the end of the meeting, they will be reminded of their goals and have an opportunity to evaluate themselves. (If necessary, prompt ones who are having difficulty choosing a goal with some examples, like those in Appendix G.)

ACTIVITY

(Announce that participation in any activity is strictly voluntary. Everyone should join only those exercises with which they feel comfortable.)

1. Announce that the topic for this meeting is avoidance. People will be asked to think of certain avoidance situations and to write down a phrase or a sentence concerning it, so they can remember to bring it up in the discussion.

2. For this first part, ask participants to think of two non-speech-related avoidances they have done or typically do, one motivated by fear and one not. For example, avoiding dogs because you were once bitten, avoiding phone calls because you are behind on some bills, or avoiding social situations because you are shy, are fear motivated. Avoiding the phone because you have to get work done, avoiding cats because you are allergic, or avoiding politics at a family gathering because it will cause an argument, are not based on fear, and are probably smart decisions. After a brief time for thinking, invite discussion.

3. Next, ask participants to think of one non-speech-related avoidance that worked out well for them, and one that did not. Ask participants to share and discuss their experiences, and whether they were based on fear or not.

4. Ask stutterers to think of avoidance behaviors they have done, or routinely do, because of stuttering. After a brief time for reflection, invite participants to share their examples, and discuss them in relation to the ideas discussed earlier.

5. Ask for discussion of the pros and cons of avoidance in various situations.

TAKEAWAY LESSONS

Encourage participants to share what stands out for them, or what they may have learned about themselves, their issues, and each other.

CONSIDER:

1. Avoidance serves a useful purpose for all animals, including humans, to reduce or eliminate danger. In such cases, avoidance is appropriate.

2. Most social avoidance is motivated by not wanting others to judge us negatively.

3. Fear-motivated social avoidance often creates more problems than it solves, such as low self-esteem and missing out on desired experiences.

4. Typically avoidance is not necessarily based on facts or real experiences but rather on conceptions that we have in our heads, such as avoiding certain sports because we believe that everyone is judging us.

INDIVIDUAL GOAL EVALUATIONS

Ask participants to go back to the goals they stated at the beginning of the meeting, and grade themselves on a scale from 1 to 10. They may share their grades with the group if they choose.

CLOSING WORDS

32. AVOIDING AND MISSING OPPORTUNITIES

PREPARATION

- At the beginning and end of the meeting, ask someone to read the Welcoming Words and Closing Words (*Appendix E*).

GOALS

1. To consider the cost of avoidance.

2. To explore the role of risk in not avoiding stuttering in potentially good opportunities.

THE MEETING

WELCOMING WORDS

ICEBREAKER

Ask participants to imagine the following scenario: You are romantically unattached and are riding the bus home one night and begin talking to an amazing person sitting beside you. You realize as you are talking that this person could be your soulmate…you have never felt this way about someone before. Instant connection! Then the bus stops, the person says goodbye, and begins to walk off the bus. You immediately start thinking to yourself, get their number! Or ask if you can see each other again…something! Then the bus door shuts and the bus begins to drive away. Five years later you run into this person at a party, and he or she instantly recognizes you. What are you going to say to the person? (*Or see Appendix A.*)

INDIVIDUAL GOALS

Ask each one in attendance (stutterers, facilitators, visitors) to identify a personal goal for the meeting, and share it with the group. Inform them that, at the end of the meeting, they will be reminded of their goals and have an opportunity to evaluate themselves. (If necessary, prompt ones who are having difficulty choosing a goal with some examples, like those in Appendix G.)

ACTIVITY

(Announce that participation in any activity is strictly voluntary. Everyone should join only those exercises with which they feel comfortable.)

1. Ask those in attendance to think of a time they missed an opportunity through inaction, something they realistically could have done at the time. After a minute for reflection, invite people to share their experience. After everyone has shared, invite discussion of the experiences, and what feelings people have about the incident now. Ask for discussion of why they failed to act when they saw an opportunity.

2. Ask stutterers to share a time they missed a potentially wonderful opportunity because they avoided saying something because of their stuttering. Ask how they feel about it now.

3. Brainstorm strategies that will reduce the likelihood that people will miss potentially wonderful opportunities that are only temporarily available.

TAKEAWAY LESSONS

Encourage participants to share what stands out for them, or what they may have learned about themselves, their issues, and each other.

CONSIDER:

1. Taking advantage of fleeting opportunities requires risk, and we all tolerate different amounts of risk.

2. We all can push ourselves to risk at least a little bit more than usual to take advantage of a unique opportunity.

3. Reflecting on our "risk quotient" in a group such as this might help us be better prepared not to let avoidance result in lost opportunities.

INDIVIDUAL GOAL EVALUATIONS

Ask participants to go back to the goals they stated at the beginning of the meeting, and grade themselves on a scale from 1 to 10. They may share their grades with the group if they choose.

CLOSING WORDS

33. AVOIDING AVOIDANCE

PREPARATION
- At the beginning and end of the meeting, ask someone to read the Welcoming Words and Closing Words (*Appendix E*).

GOALS
1. To explore the forms and ramifications of avoidance.
2. To encourage acceptance of stuttering rather than avoidance or substitutions.

THE MEETING

WELCOMING WORDS

ICEBREAKER
If you were going to a costume party, what costume would you wear and what would you do if you could do anything without any negative ramifications? (*Or see Appendix A.*)

INDIVIDUAL GOALS
Ask each one in attendance (stutterers, facilitators, visitors) to identify a personal goal for the meeting, and share it with the group. Inform them that, at the end of the meeting, they will be reminded of their goals and have an opportunity to evaluate themselves. (If necessary, prompt ones who are having difficulty choosing a goal with some examples, like those in Appendix G.)

ACTIVITY
(Announce that participation in any activity is strictly voluntary. Everyone should join only those exercises with which they feel comfortable.)

1. Inform the group that the topic of the meeting will be avoidance behavior. Ask the group to briefly discuss how someone might avoid each of the situations below. Create more if you like.

    » At a meeting, you are handed an announcement and asked to read it to the group.

- » You and another person are mutually attracted, but you are in a relationship and your partner is suspicious.
- » You cover your baldness with a comb-over, and you are asked to participate in an activity that will probably expose it.
- » You are embarrassed about scarring on your arms.
- » You have a tattoo on your lower neck that you discovered is the same as the logo of a recently popularized crime syndicate.

2. Ask the group to discuss the short-term and long-term ramifications of their avoidance behaviors.

3. Next ask the group to apply similar ideas to stuttering, by discussing the following situations, plus others from their own experience. How did they avoid stuttering or minimize people's awareness of the stuttering?

    - » Being introduced to your fiancé's/fiancée's parents for the first time
    - » Meeting someone in person from online dating
    - » Getting pulled over by a police officer
    - » Selling something to strangers
    - » Being interviewed for a position over the phone

4. Again, invite discussion of the short- and long-term results of avoidance.

5. Ask members of the group to tell about situations in which they use avoidance behaviors relating to stuttering, and the results of the avoidance. What would be the ramifications of avoiding the avoidance instead?

TAKEAWAY LESSONS

Encourage participants to share what stands out for them, or what they may have learned about themselves, their issues, and each other.

CONSIDER:

1. Sometimes, it may be best or easiest to avoid, when the consequences of disclosure might be extremely negative or we will never see the person again.

2. However, for most secrets, sooner or later our friends and family will find out. In those cases, disclosing (avoiding avoidance) is probably a better option.

3. The more we avoid a situation and the more successful we become at avoidance, the higher the stakes become for failure to avoid in the future. This is common for covert stutterers.

INDIVIDUAL GOAL EVALUATIONS

Ask participants to go back to the goals they stated at the beginning of the meeting, and grade themselves on a scale from 1 to 10. They may share their grades with the group if they choose.

CLOSING WORDS

"Not that I fixed my stutter, but it's more of a confidence issue. My stutter isn't gone, but I definitely don't care nearly as much as when I started attending the group."

34. CONFRONTING AVOIDANCE

PREPARATION

- Write examples of rude or thoughtless behavior on index cards, such as spilling coffee on someone, spontaneously letting a serious curse word slip out, jumping ahead of someone in line, belching, shaking a wet umbrella on someone, being drunk and crass at the family picnic, causing a fender bender, eating very sloppily or rapidly, stepping on someone's heel.

- At the beginning and end of the meeting, ask someone to read the Welcoming Words and Closing Words (*Appendix E*).

GOALS

1. To recognize situations we are avoiding and feelings associated with avoidance, and to understand the benefits of confronting our avoidances.

2. To identify strategies to promote desensitization and decrease instances of avoidance.

THE MEETING

WELCOMING WORDS

ICEBREAKER

One at a time, hand participants a card and have them "apologize" to someone in the group for that behavior. (*Or see Appendix A.*)

INDIVIDUAL GOALS

Ask each one in attendance (stutterers, facilitators, visitors) to identify a personal goal for the meeting, and share it with the group. Inform them that, at the end of the meeting, they will be reminded of their goals and have an opportunity to evaluate themselves. (If necessary, prompt ones who are having difficulty choosing a goal with some examples, like those in Appendix G.)

ACTIVITY

(Announce that participation in any activity is strictly voluntary. Everyone should join only those exercises with which they feel comfortable.)

98 | *In the Company of Friends*

1. Ask participants to identify a current situation, involving another person or persons, in which they are avoiding doing something they ought to do. Ask for discussion. How important is this? How long has the avoidance been going on? Why?

2. Ask participants to identify another situation that they were avoiding but in which they finally did act. Allow discussion.

3. Ask for ideas on the difference in the two situations. Is there some consistent factor that makes any of the participants more likely to continue avoidance or to finally act?

4. Ask if stuttering is a factor in any situation anyone has avoided in the past or is currently avoiding.

5. Ask for any realistic suggestions for what we can do to avoid avoidance.

TAKEAWAY LESSONS

Encourage participants to share what stands out for them, or what they may have learned about themselves, their issues, and each other.

CONSIDER:

1. Avoidance of stuttering can be insidious; it often sneaks up on us in the form of old or new accessory (secondary) behaviors.

2. Confrontation of avoidance should be done as soon as possible; we should not wait too long to confront avoidances because delay strengthens the tendency to avoid.

3. Avoiding stuttering is often harder on us than the people we talk to.

4. For those of us in speech therapy, strategies are more effective and more permanent when we *don't try not to stutter but, rather, try to talk in a new way.*

INDIVIDUAL GOAL EVALUATIONS

Ask participants to go back to the goals they stated at the beginning of the meeting, and grade themselves on a scale from 1 to 10. They may share their grades with the group if they choose.

CLOSING WORDS

35. ACCEPTING WHAT WE CANNOT CHANGE

PREPARATION

- At the beginning and end of the meeting, ask someone to read the Welcoming Words and Closing Words (*Appendix E*).

GOALS

1. To explore the concept of acceptance.
2. To consider the difference between changing what we can and accepting things we cannot change.

THE MEETING

WELCOMING WORDS

ICEBREAKER

Ask each participant to say "yes" when you announce a body part that he or she would give up if they never stuttered again. For nonstutterers, have them pretend that they stuttered. Pausing between parts, progress as follows: both legs, one leg, both arms, one arm, both hands, one hand, one thumb, one index finger, one little finger, one big toe, one middle toe, one external ear, one ear lobe, one middle toenail. (*Or see Appendix A.*)

INDIVIDUAL GOALS

Ask each one in attendance (stutterers, facilitators, visitors) to identify a personal goal for the meeting, and share it with the group. Inform them that, at the end of the meeting, they will be reminded of their goals and have an opportunity to evaluate themselves. (If necessary, prompt ones who are having difficulty choosing a goal with some examples, like those in Appendix G.)

ACTIVITY

(Announce that participation in any activity is strictly voluntary. Everyone should join only those exercises with which they feel comfortable.)

1. Ask participants to think of a situation they have been forced to accept. This could be about family or partner relations, health, personal traits, irrevocable life choices, etc.

2. Ask participants to discuss why the situation was hard to accept and what it took to finally accept it.

3. Ask for discussion of where people are with accepting the fact that they stutter and what has helped them learn acceptance.

4. Ask for discussion of how to know if something can be changed or must be accepted.

TAKEAWAY LESSONS

Encourage participants to share what stands out for them, or what they may have learned about themselves, their issues, and each other.

CONSIDER:

1. Accepting our stuttering can be a difficult thing to do.

2. Accepting is not the same as giving up.

3. The "Serenity Prayer" is relevant here: *Grant me the serenity to accept the things I cannot change, courage to change the things I can, and wisdom to know the difference.*

INDIVIDUAL GOAL EVALUATIONS

Ask participants to go back to the goals they stated at the beginning of the meeting, and grade themselves on a scale from 1 to 10. They may share their grades with the group if they choose.

CLOSING WORDS

36. VOLUNTARY STUTTERING: WHAT IS IT AND WHY DO IT?

PREPARATION

- At the beginning and end of the meeting, ask someone to read the Welcoming Words and Closing Words (*Appendix E*).

GOALS

1. To understand the common desensitization strategy of voluntary stuttering.

2. To experiment with voluntary stuttering as a strategy for reducing fear and avoidance.

THE MEETING

WELCOMING WORDS

ICEBREAKER

Ask participants to compliment the person next to them on something about their ears. (*Or see Appendix A.*)

INDIVIDUAL GOALS

Ask each one in attendance (stutterers, facilitators, visitors) to identify a personal goal for the meeting, and share it with the group. Inform them that, at the end of the meeting, they will be reminded of their goals and have an opportunity to evaluate themselves. (If necessary, prompt ones who are having difficulty choosing a goal with some examples, like those in Appendix G.)

ACTIVITY

(Announce that participation in any activity is strictly voluntary. Everyone should join only those exercises with which they feel comfortable.)

1. If a professional speech-language pathologist is present, ask him or her to briefly explain the idea of voluntary stuttering as a therapeutic strategy. Otherwise, read the definition in the glossary (*Appendix H*).

2. Remind participants that the exercise is entirely voluntary. Those who feel comfortable participating are invited to do so, and others are free to decline. Participants will leave the meeting room, and voluntarily stutter as they ask a stranger a common question, such as, Where is the elevator or restroom, What time is it, Is it still raining (snowing, hot, cold) outside, etc. Everyone should plan what they will ask, and on what words they will stutter. Choose a time for the group to reassemble, allowing about 15 minutes for the activity, and have everyone participating leave.

3. Ask participants to discuss the experience. How did the stranger react? How was it different from their expectations? Has anyone used voluntary stuttering as a part of therapy?

TAKEAWAY LESSONS

Encourage participants to share what stands out for them, or what they may have learned about themselves, their issues, and each other.

CONSIDER:

1. Voluntary stuttering is a unique way of desensitization. It is impossible for us to avoid stuttering and seek to do it at the same time.

2. Voluntary stuttering works differently for all of us. One stutterer who found it extremely helpful described it as her "reset" button.

3. Voluntarily stuttering to strangers many times in quick succession often results in a dramatic reduction in fear of stuttering and also in the frequency of stuttering, at least temporarily. Over time, these fear and stuttering reductions can last for longer and longer periods of time.

INDIVIDUAL GOAL EVALUATIONS

Ask participants to go back to the goals they stated at the beginning of the meeting, and grade themselves on a scale from 1 to 10. They may share their grades with the group if they choose.

CLOSING WORDS

37. VOLUNTARY STUTTERING TO WEAKEN FEAR OF PHONE CALLS

PREPARATION

- Compile a list of local businesses or offices where the public might call for information—restaurants, movie theaters, bus or train companies, churches, etc. Write the business or office names and phone numbers on index cards, plus a question people might typically ask when making this call. On each card, also write a one-syllable word (not typically stuttered) that stutterers will be asked to stutter voluntarily on (e.g., *from*, *the*, *is*, *will*, *I*, *your*, and *the*).
- At the beginning and end of the meeting, ask someone to read the Welcoming Words and Closing Words (*Appendix E*).

GOALS

1. To understand the common desensitization strategy of voluntary stuttering.
2. To reduce the fear or anxiety of making telephone calls.

THE MEETING

WELCOMING WORDS

ICEBREAKER

Play the game "telephone." Whisper "Making phone calls to five strangers while using voluntary stuttering might desensitize you." to one of the participants. Have them pass it on around the room, and see what the phrase becomes after it has passed from person to person. (*Or see Appendix A.*)

INDIVIDUAL GOALS

Ask each one in attendance (stutterers, facilitators, visitors) to identify a personal goal for the meeting, and share it with the group. Inform them that, at the end of the meeting, they will be reminded of their goals and have an opportunity to evaluate themselves. (If necessary, prompt ones who are having difficulty choosing a goal with some examples, like those in Appendix G.)

ACTIVITY

(Announce that participation in any activity is strictly voluntary. Everyone should join only those exercises with which they feel comfortable.)

1. Read aloud the Icebreaker sentence again, and point out that making phone calls is the purpose of this session. Remind them again that participation is entirely voluntary; observing can be helpful as well. Explain that participants will be making phone calls to local businesses and offices and asking for typical information these businesses give over the phone. Participants—stutterers and nonstutterers—will be voluntarily stuttering during these conversations, with either repetition or prolongation on selected words or sounds. Repetitions should be five times or more, and prolongations should be at least three seconds.

2. One at a time, hand a card to a participant, both stutterers and nonstutterers, and allow them to plan one sentence in which they will say one of the words on the card. Have them choose whether they will be stuttering voluntarily using a repetition or prolongation on the word, in such a way that the listener will have no doubt that they stuttered on it. All three of the following possibilities will be considered a success: 1) they only stutter voluntarily on the word, 2) their stuttering turns real on the word, or 3) they start out stuttering voluntarily and find it turns real. Participants can be fluent, stutter voluntarily, or stutter for real on any other words in the calls. But, the focus is on that one planned word. Make the calls, either one by one with a small group or in clusters of three or four with a large group.

3. After all the calls are made, discuss the anxiety level participants felt, how much doing this with others listening increased anxiety, and how the listeners responded.

4. If time remains, ask participants to think of a phone call that would make them especially anxious. (If necessary, prompt the group with examples like asking for a date, checking on the status of a loan application, telling someone you have been fired or failed a class, etc.) Ask for discussion of the value of choosing a word on which to stutter voluntarily at the outset of such a call.

5. Invite any stutterer who is interested to try to do the calling activity ten times in one day before the next meeting and report the result.

TAKEAWAY LESSONS

Encourage participants to share what stands out for them, or what they may have learned about themselves, their issues, and each other.

CONSIDER:

1. Voluntary stuttering can be a very powerful technique to reduce our tendencies to fear and avoid. This turns the usual dynamic of speaking upside down. We typically hope we will not stutter; with voluntary stuttering, we know we will stutter. With repeated practice, voluntary stuttering sometimes even reduces the occurrence of our stuttering.

2. Our voluntary stuttering can, but need not, duplicate our ordinary stuttering.

3. Many of us who stutter find telephone calls to be especially challenging, so repeatedly doing them also reduces fear and avoidance.

INDIVIDUAL GOAL EVALUATIONS

Ask participants to go back to the goals they stated at the beginning of the meeting, and grade themselves on a scale from 1 to 10. They may share their grades with the group if they choose.

CLOSING WORDS

"The scared feeling is gone."

38. ANTICIPATING AND RECEIVING PHONE CALLS

PREPARATION

- Well before the meeting, get someone (or more than one person) from outside the group to agree to participate by making a series of phone calls during the meeting. During the meeting, after you call and say to begin, this person will call your phone, and ask for general information, such as:
    » a good restaurant, and how to get there
    » the best (or worst) thing about living in this area
    » a good movie to watch on a first date
    » what the stuttering group is all about
    » how bad the winters (or summers) are in the area where the group is
- Make up more topics if a larger number of participants is expected.
- Have pencil and paper available.
- At the beginning and end of the meeting, ask someone to read the Welcoming Words and Closing Words (*Appendix E*).

GOALS

1. To discuss the anxiety caused by anticipating having to answer a stranger's questions on the phone.
2. To practice talking on the phone with a stranger.
3. To compare anxiety levels and strategies for managing phone calls.

THE MEETING

WELCOMING WORDS

ICEBREAKER

Ask participants what they do or think while having blood drawn or getting a shot. (*Or see Appendix A.*)

INDIVIDUAL GOALS

Ask each one in attendance (stutterers, facilitators, visitors) to identify a personal goal for the meeting, and share it with the group. Inform them that, at the end of the meeting, they will be reminded of their goals and have an opportunity to evaluate themselves. (If necessary, prompt ones who are having difficulty choosing a goal with some examples, like those in Appendix G.)

ACTIVITY

(Announce that participation in any activity is strictly voluntary. Everyone should join only those exercises with which they feel comfortable.)

1. Announce to the group that you have arranged for a stranger to make a series of phone calls to your phone, asking for general information that anyone should be able to provide. Different participants answer the caller's questions.

2. Invite participants to discuss how much anxiety this causes them, how much difficulty they anticipate in managing the calls, and whether they believe having an "audience" will affect their anxiety level or their ability to handle the call.

3. Determine a random order for the participants to answer the phone. Tear a sheet of paper into strips, put numbers on them, and let participants draw numbers, or use any other randomization method. Call your off-site collaborator(s) and say you are ready to begin.

4. Let participants answer the phone and complete the exercise. After everyone has taken a turn, discuss topics such as how much the audience affected anyone's performance or emotions, strategies anyone used to minimize either the stuttering or the emotions surrounding it, how the stress of the actual call compared with the stress people anticipated when they first heard about the activity, and anything positive anyone noticed about someone else's performance.

TAKEAWAY LESSONS

Encourage participants to share what stands out for them, or what they may have learned about themselves, their issues, and each other.

CONSIDER:

1. Most stutterers experience initiating phone calls differently than receiving phone calls. For some of us, initiating calls is easier; for others, receiving calls is easier.

2. Dreaded anticipation of stuttering typically makes stuttering more likely and more severe. Also, the dread and fear make the call more emotionally draining.

3. Sometimes, the only way to reduce the feared anticipation of stuttering is to jump in and get it over with.

INDIVIDUAL GOAL EVALUATIONS

Ask participants to go back to the goals they stated at the beginning of the meeting, and grade themselves on a scale from 1 to 10. They may share their grades with the group if they choose.

CLOSING WORDS

"No matter what is going on with my stuttering,
I am my Number One critic."

39. MANAGING STRESSORS THAT INCREASE STUTTERING

PREPARATION

- Have access to a whiteboard or other display device.
- At the beginning and end of the meeting, ask someone to read the Welcoming Words and Closing Words (*Appendix E*).

GOALS

1. To examine the stress that can come from stuttering.
2. To explore ways to better understand or reduce stuttering-induced stress.

THE MEETING

WELCOMING WORDS

ICEBREAKER

Distribute to everyone a piece of paper with one of the following emotions printed on it: angry, nervous, sad, happy, or anxious. Ask participants, while stating a goal for the meeting, to do so as if they are experiencing the emotion stated on their paper. After the goals have been shared, ask the group to guess who illustrated what emotion. (*Or see Appendix A.*)

INDIVIDUAL GOALS

Ask each one in attendance (stutterers, facilitators, visitors) to identify a personal goal for the meeting, and share it with the group. Inform them that, at the end of the meeting, they will be reminded of their goals and have an opportunity to evaluate themselves. (If necessary, prompt ones who are having difficulty choosing a goal with some examples, like those in Appendix G.)

ACTIVITY

(Announce that participation in any activity is strictly voluntary. Everyone should join only those exercises with which they feel comfortable.)

1. Ask stuttering participants to discuss the stressors that accompany stuttering or that make stuttering worse. For nonstutterers, ask them to think of a troubling issue,

possibly related to communicating, that is worse in some situations. Prompt the group by saying that stressors are often associated with the person or group involved in the speech situation, the words or sounds involved in the situation, the subject matter, the setting, the importance of the communication itself, the speaker's mood, etc.

2. Ask everyone to identify the most important stressors that affect their stuttering or other issue. After everyone has reported, ask each participant to provide the best specific example in their recent or distant memory to illustrate the impact of that stressor.

3. With a volunteer writing new ideas, as they emerge, on the whiteboard, ask participants to offer a strategy they might have used—or would now use in a similar situation—to mitigate or reduce the impact of each of their stressors.

4. Ask everyone to look at all of the strategies and suggest ways to combine them into a short list of general strategies that will help some or most stutterers manage stuttering stressors.

TAKEAWAY LESSONS

Encourage participants to share what stands out for them, or what they may have learned about themselves, their issues, and each other.

CONSIDER:

1. Many of the stressors that increase the likelihood or severity of stuttering cannot be changed. Therefore, if we can develop effective strategies to handle them, our quality of life will be enhanced.

2. Avoiding stressors can sometimes be successful, but avoiding typically creates more fear and avoidance.

3. One of the most effective strategies to handle stressors is to disclose our stuttering, matter-of-factly or humorously.

4. A healthy acceptance of our own stuttering typically becomes obvious to our listeners, and that often makes difficult communications easier.

INDIVIDUAL GOAL EVALUATIONS

Ask participants to go back to the goals they stated at the beginning of the meeting, and grade themselves on a scale from 1 to 10. They may share their grades with the group if they choose.

CLOSING WORDS

40. HUMOR AND STUTTERING

PREPARATION

- Video viewing equipment is needed.
- Bring the board game Anomia to the meeting.
- At the beginning and end of the meeting, ask someone to read the Welcoming Words and Closing Words (*Appendix E*).

GOALS

1. To cultivate insight toward stuttering by identifying ways that humor is related to stuttering.
2. To explore how humor can help those who stutter.

THE MEETING

WELCOMING WORDS

ICEBREAKER

Show an internet video where two or three people take a spectacular fall (and probably hurt themselves). After everyone laughs, ask the participants, "Why did everyone laugh?" (*Or see Appendix A.*)

INDIVIDUAL GOALS

Ask each one in attendance (stutterers, facilitators, visitors) to identify a personal goal for the meeting, and share it with the group. Inform them that, at the end of the meeting, they will be reminded of their goals and have an opportunity to evaluate themselves. (If necessary, prompt ones who are having difficulty choosing a goal with some examples, like those in Appendix G.)

ACTIVITY

(Announce that participation in any activity is strictly voluntary. Everyone should join only those exercises with which they feel comfortable.)

1. Announce that the group is now going to play the game Anomia. Point out that the game will likely result in increased stuttering or tripping over one's words.

Anomia plays off the fact that our minds are positively brimming with all sorts of random information: things to eat, pop songs, websites, etc. Sure, under normal circumstances, it's easy to give an example of a frozen food or a dog breed, but you'll find that your brain works a little differently under pressure!

To play, draw and reveal a card from the center pile. Does the symbol on your card match one on another player's card? If so, you must quickly face-off with the other player by giving an example of the person, place, or thing on his card before he can do the same for yours. If you blurt out a correct answer first, you win his card and the drawing continues.

Sounds simple, right? Wrong! Wild cards allow unlike symbols to match, increasing the number of things to which you must pay attention. Cascading face-offs can occur when you hand over a lost card, thereby revealing a new top card on your play pile.

2. Pose this question: "Why was everyone laughing during the game, when everyone was stuttering and tripping over their words?"

3. Invite a few minutes of discussion on each of the following questions:

    » Can stuttering be funny? Why, or why not?

    » Who is allowed to laugh or find humor in stuttering?

    » Why do people laugh at stuttering?

    » When is it appropriate to find humor in stuttering?

4. Ask if any of the stutterers in the group believe that humor could sometimes be a tool to help them deal with their stuttering. Ask if anyone has had an experience in which stuttering was funny.

TAKEAWAY LESSONS

Encourage participants to share what stands out for them, or what they may have learned about themselves, their issues, and each other.

CONSIDER:

1. Humor can be cruel when people laugh at our stuttering. Still, it is a reality that we who stutter must learn to deal with.

2. Humor is a way of disclosing information and can be a light way of letting people know we are okay with our stuttering.

3. There is a thin line between when it is or is not appropriate to laugh at stuttering. In the end, it is us—the stutterers—who get to decide when humor is okay or not.

INDIVIDUAL GOAL EVALUATIONS

Ask participants to go back to the goals they stated at the beginning of the meeting, and grade themselves on a scale from 1 to 10. They may share their grades with the group if they choose.

CLOSING WORDS

"Before I started coming to the support group, stuttering was my ever-opened umbrella. It seemed to cover everything in my life. It was always in the way. It absorbed every phone call, every interaction, and every self-thought. The group helped me to fold the umbrella and walk in the rain.
I am forever grateful!"

41. HOW STUTTERERS ARE SEEN BY NONSTUTTERERS

PREPARATION

- This meeting would be especially appropriate when there are at least two nonstutterers present.
- Find videos of three stutterers of varying severity (www.stutteringhelp.org is one source), and have a way to show them to the participants.
- At the beginning and end of the meeting, ask someone to read the Welcoming Words and Closing Words (*Appendix E*).

GOALS

1. To encourage a better understanding of how stutterers are perceived by nonstutterers.
2. To understand how stutterers' reactions to listener reactions are important in later perceptions of stutterers by the nonstutterers.

THE MEETING

WELCOMING WORDS

ICEBREAKER

Ask participants, "If a movie were being made of your life, what actor or actress would play you? Why?" (*Or see Appendix A.*)

INDIVIDUAL GOALS

Ask each one in attendance (stutterers, facilitators, visitors) to identify a personal goal for the meeting, and share it with the group. Inform them that, at the end of the meeting, they will be reminded of their goals and have an opportunity to evaluate themselves. (If necessary, prompt ones who are having difficulty choosing a goal with some examples, like those in Appendix G.)

ACTIVITY

(Announce that participation in any activity is strictly voluntary. Everyone should join only those exercises with which they feel comfortable.)

1. Show the three videos of stutterers with varying degrees of severity. After seeing them all, remind the participants of the three stutterers with a word or two and ask for their overall impressions of each of the speakers. Invite nonstutterers to comment first.

2. Invite discussion of what each person's impression of the stuttering speakers suggests about the majority public opinion? What has influenced each person's impression?

3. Knowing what stuttering is, that is, an involuntary inability to say a sound, syllable, or word the speaker knows full well how to say, ask the nonstutterers present if they have ever, even once, "stuttered." Ask them to explain. Did their experience of "stuttering" color their views of confirmed stutterers?

4. Ask the stutterers to share an experience in which a listener reacted to their stuttering in a very noticeable or negative way. Invite discussion of why that happened.

TAKEAWAY LESSONS

Encourage participants to share what stands out for them, or what they may have learned about themselves, their issues, and each other.

CONSIDER:

1. Nonstutterers often have a surprised reaction to our stuttering when it first occurs. That is ordinarily not a negative reaction. Our verbal or nonverbal responses, after their surprised reactions, typically determine the nonstutterers' impressions.

2. Most nonstutterers can recall a time that they "stuttered," and it typically was when they were nervous, scared, or very excited. This may be part of the reason why many view stutterers as nervous, shy, introverted, weak, or psychologically involved.

3. The severity of our stuttering can affect listeners' perceptions of us.

INDIVIDUAL GOAL EVALUATIONS

Ask participants to go back to the goals they stated at the beginning of the meeting, and grade themselves on a scale from 1 to 10. They may share their grades with the group if they choose.

CLOSING WORDS

42. HANDLING UNHELPFUL ADVICE

PREPARATION

- Have access to a whiteboard or other display device.
- At the beginning and end of the meeting, ask someone to read the Welcoming Words and Closing Words (*Appendix E*).

GOALS

1. To share experiences with well-meaning but unhelpful advice.
2. To discuss options in how to respond to unhelpful advice.

THE MEETING

WELCOMING WORDS

ICEBREAKER

Ask participants what was the worst or most bizarre gift they ever received, and how they reacted. (*Or see Appendix A.*)

INDIVIDUAL GOALS

Ask each one in attendance (stutterers, facilitators, visitors) to identify a personal goal for the meeting, and share it with the group. Inform them that, at the end of the meeting, they will be reminded of their goals and have an opportunity to evaluate themselves. (If necessary, prompt ones who are having difficulty choosing a goal with some examples, like those in Appendix G.)

ACTIVITY

(Announce that participation in any activity is strictly voluntary. Everyone should join only those exercises with which they feel comfortable.)

1. Read some of the following scenarios to the group one at a time, and ask them to discuss some particularly unhelpful advice someone might expect to receive in these situations.

    » your car is stuck in snow

- » you have won ten million dollars
- » you've spilled a lot of coffee on yourself
- » you have just found out you have a new "hidden" relative from Ancestry.com
- » your pet has died

2. Ask stuttering participants to share and discuss any unhelpful advice they have received regarding stuttering. Arrange for a volunteer to write these on the whiteboard.

3. Discuss some reasons why people might be so quick to give advice even if it is not helpful.

4. Take the "unhelpful stuttering advice" listed on the whiteboard, and one at a time, offer ways individual stutterers would handle such advice. If necessary, to get participants started, mention ignoring it, educating the person giving the advice, reproaching them, etc. If possible, seek to get a limited consensus of how different responses might be appropriate in different situations.

TAKEAWAY LESSONS

Encourage participants to share what stands out for them, or what they may have learned about themselves, their issues, and each other.

CONSIDER:

1. If unhelpful advice comes from a person who is not important to us, or someone we're unlikely to see again, it might be easiest to simply ignore the advice.

2. If an important person in our life gives us advice out of ignorance that is hurtful to us, we typically feel better about ourselves if we respond.

3. Sometimes we get unhelpful, or incorrect, advice from people who care about us. It is important to correct the incorrect advice, and redirect the unhelpful advice, in a way that doesn't insult the other person. Winston Churchill is quoted as saying "Tact is the ability to tell someone to go to hell in such a way that they look forward to the trip."

4. Al Franken wrote: "There are as many forms of advice as there are colors of the rainbow. Remember that good advice can come from bad people and bad advice from good people. The important thing about advice is that it is simply that. Advice."

INDIVIDUAL GOAL EVALUATIONS

Ask participants to go back to the goals they stated at the beginning of the meeting, and grade themselves on a scale from 1 to 10. They may share their grades with the group if they choose.

CLOSING WORDS

"I think that we can all build off of one another."

43. UNDERSTANDING AND DEALING WITH NEGATIVE REACTIONS TO STUTTERING

PREPARATION

- Prepare at least as many impromptu speaking topics as participants and guests (*See Appendix B*).
- At the beginning and end of the meeting, ask someone to read the Welcoming Words and Closing Words (*Appendix E*).

GOALS

1. To gain insight into negative reactions to stuttering by the public.
2. To experience confronting negative reactions productively in communicative situations.

THE MEETING

WELCOMING WORDS

ICEBREAKER

Ask participants how they would accommodate or react to having to "use the bathroom" in the woods. (*Or see Appendix A.*)

INDIVIDUAL GOALS

Ask each one in attendance (stutterers, facilitators, visitors) to identify a personal goal for the meeting, and share it with the group. Inform them that, at the end of the meeting, they will be reminded of their goals and have an opportunity to evaluate themselves. (If necessary, prompt ones who are having difficulty choosing a goal with some examples, like those in Appendix G.)

ACTIVITY

(Announce that participation in any activity is strictly voluntary. Everyone should join only those exercises with which they feel comfortable.)

1. Pair up the participants with a partner for role plays. One participant will play the "stuttering" partner while the other "nonstuttering" partner acts negatively toward

the stutterer according to one of the following assigned roles: filling in words, interrupting, laughing at stutters, talking loudly as if the stutterer can't understand, mimicking, or looking away while the person stutters. (*Ideas from Appendix D.*)

2. Next, read a list of different strategies to combat rude and unhelpful behaviors, and allow the group to discuss them one by one. The strategies are joking lightly about the stutter, confronting the conversation partner for being unhelpful, disclosing the stutter at the beginning of the conversation to allow the person to be at ease, telling the person to stop, making eye contact and being friendly to engage the person, using humor, continuing to stutter through an interruption, and saying "I'm not finished yet" or "That's not really helpful."

3. Conduct the same role play, reversing roles with the "stutterer" using one of the strategies discussed.

4. Discuss whether utilization of those strategies aided in the flow of the conversations during the role plays.

5. Invite discussion of personal experiences with negative listener reactions and how helpful some of the strategies discussed in this meeting might be in promoting communication.

TAKEAWAY LESSONS

Encourage participants to share what stands out for them, or what they may have learned about themselves, their issues, and each other.

CONSIDER:

1. Most adult listeners try to be patient and helpful, whether or not we perceive them to be.

2. A few listeners are rude and insensitive.

3. It takes courage to wear our stuttering insecurities on our sleeve; yet, this speaks to our character to be able to talk about it.

4. It may be helpful to acknowledge our stuttering in conversational situations involving negative listener reactions.

INDIVIDUAL GOAL EVALUATIONS

Ask participants to go back to the goals they stated at the beginning of the meeting, and grade themselves on a scale from 1 to 10. They may share their grades with the group if they choose.

CLOSING WORDS

44. CONFRONTING NEGATIVE PERSONAL MESSAGES

PREPARATION

- At the beginning and end of the meeting, ask someone to read the Welcoming Words and Closing Words (*Appendix E*).

GOALS

1. To share experiences of hurtful remarks that had a long-lasting effect.

2. To consider what reply to the hurtful remark might have been appropriate and to role play making the reply.

3. To discuss whether this exercise, or any other technique, might help lessen the lasting negative feelings from a hurtful remark.

THE MEETING

WELCOMING WORDS

ICEBREAKER

Ask participants to share an embarrassing story with everyone. It could be an awkward moment, a situation, or an event that they feel was embarrassing but can laugh about now. Ask if any nicknames resulted from this story or if there was any lasting impression. (*Or see Appendix A.*)

INDIVIDUAL GOALS

Ask each one in attendance (stutterers, facilitators, visitors) to identify a personal goal for the meeting, and share it with the group. Inform them that, at the end of the meeting, they will be reminded of their goals and have an opportunity to evaluate themselves. (If necessary, prompt ones who are having difficulty choosing a goal with some examples, like those in Appendix G.)

ACTIVITY

(Announce that participation in any activity is strictly voluntary. Everyone should join only those exercises with which they feel comfortable.)

1. Ask participants to remember a time when someone made a negative remark to them that caused lasting negative feelings. Encourage stutterers to choose an inci-

dent related to stuttering or fluency. Nonstutterers may choose another memory of a negative remark that caused negative feelings.

2. After time for thought, ask for volunteers to share their stories, including the situation, the person who made the remark, and why the feelings from the incident were so long-lasting.

3. Ask those who shared their experiences to think of what they wish they had said at the time. After a few minutes for thought, announce that they will now have the opportunity to say it. Place two chairs facing each other, and invite participants to come one at a time and speak to the empty chair as if the person were there.

4. After everyone has done this, ask for discussion of how it felt to participate, and the extent to which they believe an activity like this could provide any lasting benefit.

TAKEAWAY LESSONS

Encourage participants to share what stands out for them, or what they may have learned about themselves, their issues, and each other.

CONSIDER:

1. Isolated, negative remarks of others typically do not (but can) have a profound effect on us.

2. In a supportive environment, responding—even vicariously—to past negative remarks can reduce their negative power by bringing them to light and then putting them behind us.

INDIVIDUAL GOAL EVALUATIONS

Ask participants to go back to the goals they stated at the beginning of the meeting, and grade themselves on a scale from 1 to 10. They may share their grades with the group if they choose.

CLOSING WORDS

45. MESSAGES ABOUT STUTTERING FROM OUR CHILDHOOD

PREPARATION

- At the beginning and end of the meeting, ask someone to read the Welcoming Words and Closing Words (*Appendix E*).

GOALS

1. To share experiences of how stuttering was treated when group members were children.
2. To explore ways of re-processing memories of negative messages received as children.

THE MEETING

WELCOMING WORDS

ICEBREAKER

Ask those in attendance what is the craziest thing on their "bucket list." (*Or see Appendix A.*)

INDIVIDUAL GOALS

Ask each one in attendance (stutterers, facilitators, visitors) to identify a personal goal for the meeting, and share it with the group. Inform them that, at the end of the meeting, they will be reminded of their goals and have an opportunity to evaluate themselves. (If necessary, prompt ones who are having difficulty choosing a goal with some examples, like those in Appendix G.)

ACTIVITY

(Announce that participation in any activity is strictly voluntary. Everyone should join only those exercises with which they feel comfortable.)

1. Ask the stutterers in the group to discuss their earliest memory of what they were told or led to believe about stuttering when they were young, and who (parents, other relatives, teachers, etc.) gave them these ideas. Ask nonstutterers to recall a similar memory about why they or another child they knew about had a serious health issue or accident.

2. Ask how participants feel now about the way stuttering or the other issue was explained to them as children.

3. Ask what was helpful about what they were led to believe about stuttering as children. What was not helpful?

4. Ask for discussion about what the most important things for grownups to impart to a stuttering child are and about ways they might get the message across.

TAKEAWAY LESSONS

Encourage participants to share what stands out for them, or what they may have learned about themselves, their issues, and each other.

CONSIDER:

1. Most children know they stutter, but for some reason, it is often one of those things that children pretend does not bother them. Therefore, stuttering is something that too often has been swept under the rug.

2. For some of us who stutter, our families or communities do not always act optimally because they simply do not understand stuttering. Many years ago, the speech-language pathologist Wendell Johnson recommended to parents to ignore stuttering and it will go away. While stuttering goes away more often than not, its remission or persistence has little to do with parents.

3. As children, we were very impressionable, and the messages we received about stuttering may well be those we still hold, correctly or incorrectly.

4. Ideally, parents of children who stutter would have access to accurate, up-to-date information about stuttering to share, as appropriate, with their children.

INDIVIDUAL GOAL EVALUATIONS

Ask participants to go back to the goals they stated at the beginning of the meeting, and grade themselves on a scale from 1 to 10. They may share their grades with the group if they choose.

CLOSING WORDS

46. COMPLIMENTS THAT AREN'T

PREPARATION

- At the beginning and end of the meeting, ask someone to read the Welcoming Words and Closing Words (*Appendix E*).
- Prepare slips of paper stating different social problems.

GOALS

1. To share experiences of receiving positive or negative compliments.
2. To explore the relationship between unflattering compliments and teasing.

THE MEETING

WELCOMING WORDS

ICEBREAKER

Ask participants to discuss what they would do if they were on a date, or out with a new acquaintance, and find they can't stand the person. (*Or see Appendix A.*)

INDIVIDUAL GOALS

Ask each one in attendance (stutterers, facilitators, visitors) to identify a personal goal for the meeting, and share it with the group. Inform them that, at the end of the meeting, they will be reminded of their goals and have an opportunity to evaluate themselves. (If necessary, prompt ones who are having difficulty choosing a goal with some examples, like those in Appendix G.)

ACTIVITY

(Announce that participation in any activity is strictly voluntary. Everyone should join only those exercises with which they feel comfortable.)

1. Ask those in attendance—stutterers and nonstutterers—to share something flattering and unflattering about themselves and why they feel that way.
2. Ask them to share an instance in which someone has said something to them that is flattering and that they took as a sincere compliment. Then ask about a time someone said something about them that they took as unflattering.

3. Discuss the differences between the flattering and unflattering comments. What difference can the setting, or who is speaking, make in whether something comes across as positive or negative? Has anyone seen their attitude change over time, as to what they find positive or negative? What differences, if any, are there between unflattering comments and teasing?

TAKEAWAY LESSONS

Encourage participants to share what stands out for them, or what they may have learned about themselves, their issues, and each other.

CONSIDER:

1. A thin line often differentiates a comment as flattering or unflattering. The difference can be the truth of the comment, our comfort with the issue commented on, the alignment of the comment with our own standards, the degree to which the person has made us feel special, and whether or not the person has some other agenda.

2. Sometimes, as stutterers, we prefer that people would simply accept our progress in accepting or changing our stutter and feel no urge to comment. But if they do, we can accept the compliments or correct the unflattering remarks.

INDIVIDUAL GOAL EVALUATIONS

Ask participants to go back to the goals they stated at the beginning of the meeting, and grade themselves on a scale from 1 to 10. They may share their grades with the group if they choose.

CLOSING WORDS

47. UNDERSTANDING OUR REACTIONS TO TEASING

PREPARATION

- At the beginning and end of the meeting, ask someone to read the Welcoming Words and Closing Words (*Appendix E*).
- Prepare slips of paper with different social problems, such as:
    - » body odor
    - » food stuck between teeth
    - » bad breath
    - » lipstick stains on teeth
    - » dripping wet from sweat
    - » large stain on clothing
    - » zipper undone
- Have a roll of tape available.

GOALS

1. To gain insight through examining our reactions in situations in which we were teased about stuttering or another insecurity.
2. To identify strategies for responding to teasing, which might decrease negative emotions.

THE MEETING

WELCOMING WORDS

ICEBREAKER

Every person is given a piece of paper to tape on their forehead as they walk in the door. The paper has a social problem and no one is allowed to look at their own paper, but can ask others yes or no questions about the issue taped on their forehead. (*Or see Appendix A.*)

INDIVIDUAL GOALS

Ask each one in attendance (stutterers, facilitators, visitors) to identify a personal goal for the meeting, and share it with the group. Inform them that, at the end of the meeting, they will be reminded of their goals and have an opportunity to evaluate themselves. (If necessary, prompt ones who are having difficulty choosing a goal with some examples, like those in Appendix G.)

ACTIVITY

(Announce that participation in any activity is strictly voluntary. Everyone should join only those exercises with which they feel comfortable.)

1. Ask each participant to think of some times when they were younger and were teased, belittled, or otherwise subjected to negativity about stuttering (or for non-stutterers, teasing or negative comments about another insecurity they had when younger). Wait a minute while participants think about this.

2. Ask each one to tell about a time when the teasing bothered them. Ask them to tell a little about what happened and how they reacted.

3. Ask each participant to tell about a time when they were teased and it did not bother them, or at least not as much.

4. Invite discussion of why teasing bothered us some times but not others. Consider the person who is teasing, the setting, being in a different mood, etc.

TAKEAWAY LESSONS

Encourage participants to share what stands out for them, or what they may have learned about themselves, their issues, and each other.

CONSIDER:

1. Teasers or bullies seek out people who are especially vulnerable. When teasing does not bother someone, they typically stop.

2. If we were teased and it bothered us, it is likely that we were not sure of ourselves or especially vulnerable with regard to stuttering or other issues.

3. Cruel and persistent teasing and bullying must be stopped because it can result in life-long self-esteem or health issues and even violence.

4. As we become more self-accepting or compensate in other ways, teasing increasingly does not bother us.

5. With close friends or family members, "friendly teasing" can be a positive thing, but that decision must always rest with the stutterer or person being teased.

INDIVIDUAL GOAL EVALUATIONS

Ask participants to go back to the goals they stated at the beginning of the meeting, and grade themselves on a scale from 1 to 10. They may share their grades with the group if they choose.

CLOSING WORDS

"It was 'a life-changing moment' for me to hear Scott's comment that he wished his stuttering was viewed as a personal quality rather than something that is wrong."

48. UNDERSTANDING AND MANAGING LISTENER REACTIONS

PREPARATION

- Cut out photos of faces of famous people from magazines, or, print some digital photos. Tape them, individually, to heavy paper or cardboard with a handle so participants can hold a photo up to their foreheads without looking at the photo.
- Prepare slips of paper with different speaker scenarios and listener attitudes. (*See Appendix D.*)
- At the beginning and end of the meeting, ask someone to read the Welcoming Words and Closing Words (*Appendix E*).

GOALS

1. To better understand normal listener reactions to stuttering.
2. To consider ways to reduce the impact of negative listener reactions.
3. To explore ways to positively change the reaction of a listener to help ensure that you are being heard in the way that you would like to be heard.

THE MEETING

WELCOMING WORDS

ICEBREAKER

Give everyone a face of a well-known person or character, face down, so they cannot see it. Next, one at a time, ask participants to display "their" face over their foreheads for other players to see. Everyone will take turns asking yes/no questions to guess their own characters. (*Or see Appendix A.*)

INDIVIDUAL GOALS

Ask each one in attendance (stutterers, facilitators, visitors) to identify a personal goal for the meeting, and share it with the group. Inform them that, at the end of the meeting, they will be reminded of their goals and have an opportunity to evaluate themselves. (If necessary, prompt ones who are having difficulty choosing a goal with some examples, like those in Appendix G.)

ACTIVITY

(Announce that participation in any activity is strictly voluntary. Everyone should join only those exercises with which they feel comfortable.)

1. Participants will work in pairs. One person will draw a "speaker scenario" paper, and the other will draw a "listener attitude" paper, then they will act out the scenario for a minute or two at the most. Speakers should try to act as "normal" as possible, and listeners should concentrate on their assigned attitude while still participating in the conversation.

2. Have participants switch partners, draw new scenarios, and act out the opposite role (speaker or listener) from the one they did the first time.

3. Ask everyone to identify types or characteristics of listeners they find most and least difficult to talk to.

4. Ask stutterers to consider strategies to manage difficult listeners.

5. Discuss strategies for dealing with difficult listeners or speakers.

TAKEAWAY LESSONS

Encourage participants to share what stands out for them, or what they may have learned about themselves, their issues, and each other.

CONSIDER:

1. We cannot change most initial listener reactions, but we can make future reactions more favorable by being authentic, honest, and open.

2. Disclosure of stuttering or humor often puts listeners at ease and makes their reactions more positive.

INDIVIDUAL GOAL EVALUATIONS

Ask participants to go back to the goals they stated at the beginning of the meeting, and grade themselves on a scale from 1 to 10. They may share their grades with the group if they choose.

CLOSING WORDS

49. MANAGING SPEAKING SITUATIONS IN WHICH WE ARE JUDGED

PREPARATION

- At the beginning and end of the meeting, ask someone to read the Welcoming Words and Closing Words (*Appendix E*).

GOALS

1. To become aware of speaking situations where judgment may occur based on the response.
2. To recognize and explore coping mechanisms that might be effective when confronting judgmental situations.

THE MEETING

WELCOMING WORDS

ICEBREAKER

Ask everyone to explain how they would approach getting a passport or driver's license photo where there would be only one try after being strictly told not to smile. Then ask participants to assume and hold their pose for three seconds. (*Or see Appendix A.*)

INDIVIDUAL GOALS

Ask each one in attendance (stutterers, facilitators, visitors) to identify a personal goal for the meeting, and share it with the group. Inform them that, at the end of the meeting, they will be reminded of their goals and have an opportunity to evaluate themselves. (If necessary, prompt ones who are having difficulty choosing a goal with some examples, like those in Appendix G.)

ACTIVITY

(Announce that participation in any activity is strictly voluntary. Everyone should join only those exercises with which they feel comfortable.)

1. Ask each stutterer to imagine the following situation. At the end of the probationary period at your job, you are scheduled to go out to dinner with your boss and his

or her spouse, but at the last minute the boss has to cancel and you are now dining alone with the spouse. Paired with a nonstutterer as the spouse, spend 5 minutes in dinner conversation. At the end of each conversation, ask participants to identify one thing the stutterer did well. Have the stutterer comment on one thing he or she could have done better.

2. Invite anyone to talk about a recent speaking situation in which he or she felt they may have been judged, and what they did well in the situation and not so well.

TAKEAWAY LESSONS

Encourage participants to share what stands out for them, or what they may have learned about themselves, their issues, and each other.

CONSIDER:

1. We would be well advised to accept the fact that we will be judged in some situations.

2. We can practice various strategies to help us foster the best impressions, such as following preliminary advice given to job interviewees (e.g., well-groomed, prompt, courteous, and good eye contact).

3. It is often advisable to disclose our stuttering when we are entering a situation where we will be judged overall.

INDIVIDUAL GOAL EVALUATIONS

Ask participants to go back to the goals they stated at the beginning of the meeting, and grade themselves on a scale from 1 to 10. They may share their grades with the group if they choose.

CLOSING WORDS

50. IDENTIFYING OUR PERSONAL STRENGTHS

PREPARATION

- Prepare copies of the test portion of a free personality test from the internet for each participant. A number of such scales are available. A test such as The Short Personality Test <https://www.personalityclub.com/short-personality-test/> or 16 Personalities <https://www.16personalities.com/free-personality-test/> is suggested because they feature the 16 widely known Myers-Briggs or Kiersey personality types. Make one copy of the characteristics of each personality type for each participant as well as one copy of a summary of each of the types to read to the group. If the test is to be taken online, each participant should be asked to bring a laptop to the meeting.
- Supply paper and pens or pencils.
- At the beginning and end of the meeting, ask someone to read the Welcoming Words and Closing Words (*Appendix E*).

GOALS

1. To explore the various personality types of the group and what that means to each individual.
2. To encourage use of personal strengths to succeed in difficult situations.

THE MEETING

WELCOMING WORDS

ICEBREAKER

Have those in attendance write down three little-known facts about themselves, and hand them in. Read these to the group, and have them guess which list is whose. (*Or see Appendix A.*)

INDIVIDUAL GOALS

Ask each one in attendance (stutterers, facilitators, visitors) to identify a personal goal for the meeting, and share it with the group. Inform them that, at the end of the meeting, they will be reminded of their goals and have an opportunity to evaluate themselves. (If necessary, prompt ones who are having difficulty choosing a goal with some examples, like those in Appendix G.)

ACTIVITY

(Announce that participation in any activity is strictly voluntary. Everyone should join only those exercises with which they feel comfortable.)

1. Have participants complete and score a personality test that requires at least 15 minutes.

2. Ask everyone to share their personality type results with the group.

3. Hand out or read descriptions of each personality type represented, and ask the group to discuss how accurate they feel the test is.

4. Ask participants to comment on their own personal strengths and abilities associated with their personality type. How can each person's strengths and abilities be used to better manage or cope with their stuttering?

TAKEAWAY LESSONS

Encourage participants to share what stands out for them, or what they may have learned about themselves, their issues, and each other.

CONSIDER:

1. We all have a unique personality type, which guides our preferences in choices we make throughout life.

2. Once we reach adulthood, our personality types do not change much; however, as we mature, we often gain experience in our non-preferred types.

3. Understanding our personality types and preferences can assist us in several ways: a) knowing that all of us are different in basic ways, we can inform significant others that we may not share all of their values; b) whereas our stuttering probably did not come from our personalities, our reactions to it and preferences for managing it likely are influenced by our unique personalities; and c) we can learn ways to compensate for less-developed aspects of our personalities to make better adjustments in our lives.

INDIVIDUAL GOAL EVALUATIONS

Ask participants to go back to the goals they stated at the beginning of the meeting, and grade themselves on a scale from 1 to 10. They may share their grades with the group if they choose.

CLOSING WORDS

51. STARTING OVER SUCCESSFULLY

PREPARATION

- Have access to a whiteboard or other display device.
- At the beginning and end of the meeting, ask someone to read the Welcoming Words and Closing Words (*Appendix E*).

GOALS

1. To examine the details of what makes one fresh-start attempt different from another and to focus on factors present in successful fresh starts.
2. To consider desirable fresh starts regarding stuttering and how modeling it on previous successes might increase the likelihood of future success.

THE MEETING

WELCOMING WORDS

ICEBREAKER

Ask people to talk about their pet peeves, or things they like to have done a certain way. (*Or see Appendix A.*)

INDIVIDUAL GOALS

Ask each one in attendance (stutterers, facilitators, visitors) to identify a personal goal for the meeting, and share it with the group. Inform them that, at the end of the meeting, they will be reminded of their goals and have an opportunity to evaluate themselves. (If necessary, prompt ones who are having difficulty choosing a goal with some examples, like those in Appendix G.)

ACTIVITY

(Announce that participation in any activity is strictly voluntary. Everyone should join only those exercises with which they feel comfortable.)

1. Ask those in attendance to think of a time when they made a fresh start—not necessarily related to stuttering—that turned out to be successful, and share it with the group. If they cannot think of anything, offer an example of learning a

new sport or outdoor activity and sticking with it or deciding to replace marathon television sessions with reading good books.

2. Ask participants to think of a time when a fresh start was not successful and to share that experience. Examples, if necessary, might include failed diets or attempts to quit smoking.

3. Prompt a discussion of how successful fresh starts were different from unsuccessful ones, whether it was the techniques used, the attitude, the timing, the amount of planning, etc. Arrange for a volunteer to summarize the reasons for success and lack of success on either side of a divided whiteboard.

4. Ask stuttering participants if they can think of a way some of these successful strategies might be used in making a fresh start regarding some aspect of stuttering, and to discuss them.

TAKEAWAY LESSONS

Encourage participants to share what stands out for them, or what they may have learned about themselves, their issues, and each other.

CONSIDER:

1. Success in new beginnings is more likely when a fresh start has immediate and continuous rewards. Success requires greater commitment when a fresh start requires replacing immediate rewards with greatly deferred satisfaction.

2. Habits related to stuttering or other behaviors are often difficult for us to replace with new habits.

3. For every fresh start, we must give up the often disguised "benefits" of not starting over.

INDIVIDUAL GOAL EVALUATIONS

Ask participants to go back to the goals they stated at the beginning of the meeting, and grade themselves on a scale from 1 to 10. They may share their grades with the group if they choose.

CLOSING WORDS

52. MAKING FRESH STARTS AFTER LIFE CHANGES

PREPARATION

- At the beginning and end of the meeting, ask someone to read the Welcoming Words and Closing Words (*Appendix E*).

GOALS

1. To discuss necessary life changes and how they affect other areas of daily living.
2. To share experiences of coping and adapting to change.
3. To explore strategies for increasing success with fresh starts.

THE MEETING

WELCOMING WORDS

ICEBREAKER

Ask participants to share a "foot-in-the-mouth" experience they have had or one they remember that someone else had. (*Or see Appendix A.*)

INDIVIDUAL GOALS

Ask each one in attendance (stutterers, facilitators, visitors) to identify a personal goal for the meeting, and share it with the group. Inform them that, at the end of the meeting, they will be reminded of their goals and have an opportunity to evaluate themselves. (If necessary, prompt ones who are having difficulty choosing a goal with some examples, like those in Appendix G.)

ACTIVITY

(Announce that participation in any activity is strictly voluntary. Everyone should join only those exercises with which they feel comfortable.)

1. Ask each person in attendance, stutterers and nonstutterers, to identify one major life change they have had to deal with.
2. Invite each person to talk about how their daily routine became different since making the change, including positive and negative changes.

3. Ask stutterers how their stuttering was affected by the new changes.

4. Invite discussion of what can be done when a fresh start appears to be necessary.

TAKEAWAY LESSONS

Encourage participants to share what stands out for them, or what they may have learned about themselves, their issues, and each other.

CONSIDER:

1. Major life changes occur for all of us and will continue for the rest of our lives. Therefore, we could be well advised to accept that fact.

2. Making a new start typically has some effect on our stuttering. For some, new surroundings or circumstances increase the stuttering; for others, they decrease (and sometimes temporarily eliminate) the stuttering.

3. Often, after going through a difficult life change, we experience renewed strength, confidence, and self-acceptance.

INDIVIDUAL GOAL EVALUATIONS

Ask participants to go back to the goals they stated at the beginning of the meeting, and grade themselves on a scale from 1 to 10. They may share their grades with the group if they choose.

CLOSING WORDS

53. KEEPING AND DISCLOSING SECRETS

PREPARATION

- Have available several small but diverse items in a bag or a covered bucket (e.g., a key, a "gorilla clip," a bottle cork, a small measuring cup, an AA battery, a Post-It note, a poker chip, a dollar bill, etc.)
- Have paper and pens or pencils on hand.
- At the beginning and end of the meeting, ask someone to read the Welcoming Words and Closing Words (*Appendix E*).

GOALS

1. To explore secrets and the effect they have on us.
2. To consider the pros and cons of disclosing secrets.

THE MEETING

WELCOMING WORDS

ICEBREAKER

Pass the bag or bucket around, and have participants feel the objects with one hand for 10 seconds, then write down a list of all the things they could identify. After everyone has had a turn, put the objects on the table, and see who made the most accurate list. Optional: award a prize. (*Or see Appendix A.*)

INDIVIDUAL GOALS

Ask each one in attendance (stutterers, facilitators, visitors) to identify a personal goal for the meeting, and share it with the group. Inform them that, at the end of the meeting, they will be reminded of their goals and have an opportunity to evaluate themselves. (If necessary, prompt ones who are having difficulty choosing a goal with some examples, like those in Appendix G.)

ACTIVITY

(Announce that participation in any activity is strictly voluntary. Everyone should join only those exercises with which they feel comfortable.)

146 | *In the Company of Friends*

1. Ask those in attendance to think of a small secret they would be willing to share with the group. It should be something that they consciously refrain from telling most people, not just something they don't tell because it isn't relevant. After a time for reflection, have volunteers share their secrets and explain a little.

2. Ask the group to think of something they used to keep secret, but now do not mind telling people, and to share their secret with the group. Why did they let the secret go?

3. Ask participants to think of a major secret that they will *not* be sharing with the group. After time for thought, invite people to share why they do not tell it to anybody.

4. Invite discussion of secrets, in general, and of the factors that cause people to decide whether to share information with others or not.

5. Ask for discussion of how we are affected by keeping secrets, or letting them go.

TAKEAWAY LESSONS

Encourage participants to share what stands out for them, or what they may have learned about themselves, their issues, and each other.

CONSIDER:
1. Trying to keep our stuttering a secret is typically unsuccessful, and it makes others uncomfortable because they do not want to upset us by mentioning it.

2. Some secrets probably should be kept if, after being shared, they might harm us or someone else.

3. Many secrets are based on our perception that others will think less of us if we shared the secrets.

INDIVIDUAL GOAL EVALUATIONS

Ask participants to go back to the goals they stated at the beginning of the meeting, and grade themselves on a scale from 1 to 10. They may share their grades with the group if they choose.

CLOSING WORDS

54. BEING THE BEST YOU

PREPARATION

- This meeting requires a table for participants to sit around.
- Gather a large number of small everyday objects—such as a rock, a spoon, sunglasses, earphones, ribbons, paper clips, pens and pencils, a paper wad, keys, a pocket knife, kitchen tools, a hat, a glove, a cup, a phone, coins, a watch, hand sanitizer, a belt, small tools, a business card, a flower, and other diverse items. Place all of them in the center of the table.
- Obtain Styrofoam cups or other small containers that can be written on.
- Provide pens or pencils and slips of paper for the group.
- At the beginning and end of the meeting, ask someone to read the Welcoming Words and Closing Words (*Appendix E*).

GOALS

1. To consider what aspects of ourselves we want others to see and how we present ourselves to others.
2. To appreciate different ways people define and represent themselves.

THE MEETING

WELCOMING WORDS

ICEBREAKER

Ask participants to share what they would change about themselves if they decided to adopt a "new look." (*Or see Appendix A.*)

INDIVIDUAL GOALS

Ask each one in attendance (stutterers, facilitators, visitors) to identify a personal goal for the meeting, and share it with the group. Inform them that, at the end of the meeting, they will be reminded of their goals and have an opportunity to evaluate themselves. (If necessary, prompt ones who are having difficulty choosing a goal with some examples, like those in Appendix G.)

ACTIVITY

(Announce that participation in any activity is strictly voluntary. Everyone should join only those exercises with which they feel comfortable.)

1. Instruct participants to use the objects on the table to make models of themselves. They are free to trade objects if they want. Allow five to ten minutes.

2. Let each participant explain their creation and why it represents them.

3. Instruct each participant to write one positive comment about each of the other participants on a slip of paper. Next, have each one write his or her name on a cup. Pass the cups around the group, and have everyone place their comments in the appropriate person's cup.

4. Invite discussion about what comments the participants found surprising. Then ask what comments were especially meaningful.

TAKEAWAY LESSONS

Encourage participants to share what stands out for them, or what they may have learned about themselves, their issues, and each other.

CONSIDER:

1. Stuttering is a very small part of us.
2. Although we know about our strengths, affirmation of those by others gives us joy and confidence.

INDIVIDUAL GOAL EVALUATIONS

Ask participants to go back to the goals they stated at the beginning of the meeting, and grade themselves on a scale from 1 to 10. They may share their grades with the group if they choose.

CLOSING WORDS

55. REDUCING THE BAGGAGE OF STUTTERING

PREPARATION

- Have cloth bags, with handles long enough to fit over the neck, available for each participant.
- Have Play-Doh available for each participant.
- Provide Post-It notes and pens or pencils.
- Place many books of widely varying size and weight (very small and thin to large, textbook style) on the table—up to about five books for each participant.
- Have access to a whiteboard or other display device. Write a list of possible feelings a stutterer might have regarding his or her stuttering: embarrassment, fear, shame, frustration, resignation, anger, hopelessness, guilt.
- At the beginning and end of the meeting, ask someone to read the Welcoming Words and Closing Words (*Appendix E*).

GOALS

1. To explore "baggage" that accumulates with stuttering.
2. To discuss the pros and cons of disclosing "baggage."

THE MEETING

WELCOMING WORDS

ICEBREAKER

Ask participants to choose up to three feelings they have about their stuttering from the list on the board, and write each one on a Post-It note. Then ask them to take each feeling, choose a book from the table (which symbolizes how much weight they feel from that emotion), and put the books in their bag. Have everyone hang their bag around their neck.

INDIVIDUAL GOALS

Ask each one in attendance (stutterers, facilitators, visitors) to identify a personal goal for the meeting, and share it with the group. Inform them that, at the end of the meeting, they will be reminded of their goals and have an opportunity to evaluate themselves. (If necessary, prompt ones who are having difficulty choosing a goal with some examples, like those in Appendix G.)

ACTIVITY

(Announce that participation in any activity is strictly voluntary. Everyone should join only those exercises with which they feel comfortable.) (Tell participants that they may remove the bags from around their necks!)

1. Hand out the Play-Doh, and instruct participants to choose a few emotions from the list on the board, and make a small object to symbolize that emotion. The Play-Doh figures do not have to actually represent the emotions in any real visual way; they just need to represent the emotions in the mind of the participant.

2. After having a few minutes to create the figures, have the group sit in a close circle. Tell participants that they will be asked to non-verbally hand some of their figurines to other participants in the circle, in a way that symbolizes how willing or unwilling they are in real life to share their personal burdens with others. Participants may hand out all of their burdens, some of them, or none, whichever best represents how they share personal feelings in their lives. Allow a few seconds for each participant in turn to share or not share their symbolic burdens.

3. Invite discussion of personal baggage, and how easy or hard it is to unload. How heavy was each person's bag of books? How did it feel to unload baggage in the activity, or to have someone else share their baggage? What does it take in real life for each person to share their baggage with others?

TAKEAWAY LESSONS

Encourage participants to share what stands out for them, or what they may have learned about themselves, their issues, and each other.

CONSIDER:

1. We all have baggage or leftover feelings from past hurts.

2. While some of our baggage probably should remain undisclosed, to the extent we can unburden ourselves from baggage frees us to a) put it behind us and b) reduce its negative effects on significant others.

3. Stuttering baggage often increases from young childhood to late adolescence when negative emotions associated with stuttering are not resolved.

4. A support group may be the best place to unburden ourselves of some of our stuttering baggage.

INDIVIDUAL GOAL EVALUATIONS

Ask participants to go back to the goals they stated at the beginning of the meeting, and grade themselves on a scale from 1 to 10. They may share their grades with the group if they choose.

CLOSING WORDS

"A time comes in your life when you realize you can't make any more excuses for yourself."

56. SUCCESS AND FAILURE IN ACHIEVING GOALS

PREPARATION

- Have available bottles of water or a large glass and a pitcher of drinking water.
- At the beginning and end of the meeting, ask someone to read the Welcoming Words and Closing Words (*Appendix E*).

GOAL

1. To explore some of the factors that may be related to why people fail or succeed in achieving goals.

THE MEETING

WELCOMING WORDS

ICEBREAKER

Inform the participants that drinking several glasses of water a day is recommended for adults. For those participants who are up to the challenge, ask them to drink a full bottle or glass of water without stopping. Ask them if this would be easy for them to do a few times every day. (*Or see Appendix A.*)

INDIVIDUAL GOALS

Ask each one in attendance (stutterers, facilitators, visitors) to identify a personal goal for the meeting, and share it with the group. Inform them that, at the end of the meeting, they will be reminded of their goals and have an opportunity to evaluate themselves. (If necessary, prompt ones who are having difficulty choosing a goal with some examples, like those in Appendix G.)

ACTIVITY

(Announce that participation in any activity is strictly voluntary. Everyone should join only those exercises with which they feel comfortable.)

1. Ask attendees to think of a self-improvement goal they have achieved, after first failing at it more than once. After time to think, have people share their experiences.

2. Ask each one to tell what they believe was different when they finally achieved the goal, and why they may have failed before. Allow discussion of the comments.

3. Ask each person to think of a goal they would currently like to accomplish that they would be comfortable sharing with the group. After sharing all the goals, ask each person to share where they stand with that goal, whether they have a good plan, whether they are part of the way there, and what factors may be helping or hurting the effort.

4. Ask people to react to the discussions, and share anything they may have heard that might help them in the future.

TAKEAWAY LESSONS

Encourage participants to share what stands out for them, or what they may have learned about themselves, their issues, and each other.

CONSIDER:

1. Often, when we fail to achieve a goal, we have not taken account of its cost. In other words, the benefits did not outweigh the costs. "The road to h*?! is paved with good intentions."

2. Achieving most self-improvement goals or changing something about our stuttering typically involves careful planning, improving in small steps, and sticking with small steps when motivation wanes.

INDIVIDUAL GOAL EVALUATIONS

Ask participants to go back to the goals they stated at the beginning of the meeting, and grade themselves on a scale from 1 to 10. They may share their grades with the group if they choose.

CLOSING WORDS

57. FACING PHONE ANXIETY

PREPARATION

- Prepare a list of phone calls for participants to make. These could be local businesses to call and ask for their hours, availability or details of a product or service, etc. Choose places that would routinely expect to get calls such as these. Print the list, or write it down for participants to read.
- At the beginning and end of the meeting, ask someone to read the Welcoming Words and Closing Words (*Appendix E*).

GOALS

1. To explore the emotions surrounding making phone calls to strangers.
2. To allow participants to practice making phone calls and then to discuss the experience.

THE MEETING

WELCOMING WORDS

ICEBREAKER

Answer the question "What would you do with your appearance in order to impress someone?" (*Or see Appendix A.*)

INDIVIDUAL GOALS

Ask each one in attendance (stutterers, facilitators, visitors) to identify a personal goal for the meeting, and share it with the group. Inform them that, at the end of the meeting, they will be reminded of their goals and have an opportunity to evaluate themselves. (If necessary, prompt ones who are having difficulty choosing a goal with some examples, like those in Appendix G.)

ACTIVITY

(Announce that participation in any activity is strictly voluntary. Everyone should join only those exercises with which they feel comfortable.)

1. Hand participants the list of phone calls for them to pass around and read. Ask for volunteers willing to make one of the calls.

156 | *In the Company of Friends*

2. After everyone who chose to make a call has done so, ask for discussion of what was the caller's feelings, characteristics of the stuttering (if the call was done by a stutterer), and the listener's reaction.

3. Invite participants to tell of a time they had an especially difficult phone conversation or a time when stuttering on the phone led to a bad consequence. Ask for any strategies individual stutterers have found successful for them in these situations.

TAKEAWAY LESSONS

Encourage participants to share what stands out for them, or what they may have learned about themselves, their issues, and each other.

CONSIDER:

1. Using the telephone is often especially difficult for stutterers because past failures have occurred due to the nature of telephone conversations: we must respond immediately on cue with no delay, we must respond with only a few word options (e.g., "Hello"), and we cannot show the listener that we are having difficulty.

2. Leaving recorded messages on voice mail also poses special difficulty for many of us.

3. For many of us, gains made in other speaking situations often do not generalize to the phone, so stuttering fears associated with the telephone must be confronted specifically.

4. With continued practice, telephone fears can be greatly reduced.

INDIVIDUAL GOAL EVALUATIONS

Ask participants to go back to the goals they stated at the beginning of the meeting, and grade themselves on a scale from 1 to 10. They may share their grades with the group if they choose.

CLOSING WORDS

58. OVERCOMING OBSTACLES TO BEING AUTHENTIC

PREPARATION

- Have a rock song with a regular beat bookmarked on your computer.
- Have access to a whiteboard or other display device.
- Have markers, and large Post-It notes or paper and tape.
- At the beginning and end of the meeting, ask someone to read the Welcoming Words and Closing Words (*Appendix E*).

GOALS

1. To discuss some of the behaviors that can prevent anyone from presenting an authentic self to the public.
2. To share ideas for avoiding these behaviors and presenting a more true self-image.

THE MEETING

WELCOMING WORDS

ICEBREAKER

Play the pre-selected song, and ask participants to stand up and show off their best dance moves, all at the same time. (*Or see Appendix A.*)

INDIVIDUAL GOALS

Ask each one in attendance (stutterers, facilitators, visitors) to identify a personal goal for the meeting, and share it with the group. Inform them that, at the end of the meeting, they will be reminded of their goals and have an opportunity to evaluate themselves. (If necessary, prompt ones who are having difficulty choosing a goal with some examples, like those in Appendix G.)

ACTIVITY

(Announce that participation in any activity is strictly voluntary. Everyone should join only those exercises with which they feel comfortable.)

1. Write the word *authenticity* on the whiteboard, and under it write *the real you*. Introduce the topic. Ask participants to write words or phrases on Post-It notes

that mean or symbolize authenticity. Ask them to read and paste their Post-It notes on the left side of the whiteboard.

2. Next, ask participants to write, on Post-It notes, actions or attitudes that might keep a person from being authentic. As they read these obstacles to authenticity, have them paste them to the right side of the board. Point out that the Post-It notes on the right prevent a person from honest interaction with others.

3. Invite participants to come to the board one at a time and tell how one of the right-sided obstacles has prevented them from showing their true selves to others, either for a one-time experience or as a continual issue. Encourage stutterers to include experiences with stuttering. Continue, if possible, until all the notes are removed.

4. Ask anyone who cares to comment to propose a strategy going forward that will prevent any of the obstacles listed from interfering with their showing their true selves.

TAKEAWAY LESSONS

Encourage participants to share what stands out for them, or what they may have learned about themselves, their issues, and each other.

CONSIDER:

1. Being authentic means different things to different people but implies being ourselves, being natural, and being honest.

2. Having control over or managing our stuttering can make us feel, and appear to others, more authentic.

3. Learning to accept our stuttering is vital to being authentic.

INDIVIDUAL GOAL EVALUATIONS

Ask participants to go back to the goals they stated at the beginning of the meeting, and grade themselves on a scale from 1 to 10. They may share their grades with the group if they choose.

CLOSING WORDS

59. CHOOSING OR NOT CHOOSING A NEW PATH

PREPARATION

- Have access to a whiteboard or other display device.
- At the beginning and end of the meeting, ask someone to read the Welcoming Words and Closing Words (*Appendix E*).

GOALS

1. To explore previous and current choices made regarding stuttering.
2. To explore reasons for changing and not changing.

THE MEETING

WELCOMING WORDS

ICEBREAKER

Ask the attendees to imagine they are driving around a huge parking lot looking for a place to park, and finally they see one at the same time another driver does. What would each person do? (*Or see Appendix A.*)

INDIVIDUAL GOALS

Ask each one in attendance (stutterers, facilitators, visitors) to identify a personal goal for the meeting, and share it with the group. Inform them that, at the end of the meeting, they will be reminded of their goals and have an opportunity to evaluate themselves. (If necessary, prompt ones who are having difficulty choosing a goal with some examples, like those in Appendix G.)

ACTIVITY

(Announce that participation in any activity is strictly voluntary. Everyone should join only those exercises with which they feel comfortable.)

1. Ask the group to think of an important life issue. Encourage stutterers to use stuttering. Ask everyone to think of one or two situations where they made some adjustments and the outcome was positive. The issue was present, but they handled it successfully. Ask, "What adaptations or strategies did you use to achieve

the successful outcome?" "How did you adapt to find success?" Allow time for discussion.

2. Ask participants to think of one or two situations in which the way they handled the situation—their adaptations and strategies—had a neutral effect, that is, not making the situation significantly better or worse. Allow time for discussion.

3. Next, ask participants to think of one or two negative times, when the way they handled the issue made the situation worse. Allow time for discussion.

4. Finally, ask the group to discuss why we tend to stick with adjustments that are not optimal for us in certain situations. Why don't we do the things we know will make the situation better? When we do manage to do the right thing, what is it that helps us do it? Have someone write some of the key words or phrases from the discussion.

TAKEAWAY LESSONS

Encourage participants to share what stands out for them, or what they may have learned about themselves, their issues, and each other.

CONSIDER:

1. We tend to persist in strategies, both for successful and unsuccessful outcomes.

2. Often, we expect different results from the same strategies. Einstein is credited with saying, "The definition of insanity is doing the same thing over and over again, but expecting different results."

3. Even so, if we are unable to do anything about our stuttering, it is not helpful to feel guilty or hopeless about management strategies that have not worked well.

INDIVIDUAL GOAL EVALUATIONS

Ask participants to go back to the goals they stated at the beginning of the meeting, and grade themselves on a scale from 1 to 10. They may share their grades with the group if they choose.

CLOSING WORDS

60. UNDERSTANDING THE STAGES OF CHANGE

PREPARATION

- At the beginning and end of the meeting, ask someone to read the Welcoming Words and Closing Words (*Appendix E*).

GOALS

1. To examine a formal model of the stages of making a change.
2. To consider the relevance of the model to our individual experiences.

THE MEETING

WELCOMING WORDS

ICEBREAKER

Ask participants what they would choose if they were given a willpower pill that only works on one area or activity. (*Or see Appendix A.*)

INDIVIDUAL GOALS

Ask each one in attendance (stutterers, facilitators, visitors) to identify a personal goal for the meeting, and share it with the group. Inform them that, at the end of the meeting, they will be reminded of their goals and have an opportunity to evaluate themselves. (If necessary, prompt ones who are having difficulty choosing a goal with some examples, like those in Appendix G.)

ACTIVITY

(Announce that participation in any activity is strictly voluntary. Everyone should join only those exercises with which they feel comfortable.)

1. Explain a five-step Stages of Change model and briefly summarize each of the stages.

    » Pre-contemplation: unaware of a need for change or no intention of making a change.

    » Contemplation: aware of a need for change and considering the possibility of changing.

» Preparation: ready for change and intend to take action to change.

» Action: beginning to modify specific behaviors, the environment, or both.

» Maintenance: beginning to stabilize new behaviors or thinking.

2. Ask participants to think of a change, regarding a problem or difficult issue but not involving stuttering, they have made in or for themselves in which they have experienced all five stages. If a participant cannot think of a problem in which all five stages were involved, ask him/her to pick one in which some change occurred. Next, have them, one at a time, share with the group their thinking and actions for all five stages.

3. Invite discussion of the similarities and differences or of the special issues faced in certain changes (e.g., the "changeability" of the problem or unavoidable interruptions in the process, etc.).

TAKEAWAY LESSONS

Encourage participants to share what stands out for them, or what they may have learned about themselves, their issues, and each other.

CONSIDER:

1. Serious change to solve or alleviate a difficult problem is rarely automatic; it requires dedication, focus, and energy.

2. Inevitably, events or circumstances will interrupt any smooth progression from one stage to the next, which may require returning to an earlier stage for some time.

INDIVIDUAL GOAL EVALUATIONS

Ask participants to go back to the goals they stated at the beginning of the meeting, and grade themselves on a scale from 1 to 10. They may share their grades with the group if they choose.

CLOSING WORDS

61. MAKING NEW CHANGES IN STUTTERING

PREPARATION

- Have access to a whiteboard or other display device.
- At the beginning and end of the meeting, ask someone to read the Welcoming Words and Closing Words (*Appendix E*).

GOALS

1. To evaluate preliminary or ongoing plans to change something about one's stuttering.
2. To explore ways to overcome obstacles that present themselves in making changes.

THE MEETING

WELCOMING WORDS

ICEBREAKER

Ask participants to describe the worst tattoo they have seen. (*Or see Appendix A.*)

INDIVIDUAL GOALS

Ask each one in attendance (stutterers, facilitators, visitors) to identify a personal goal for the meeting, and share it with the group. Inform them that, at the end of the meeting, they will be reminded of their goals and have an opportunity to evaluate themselves. (If necessary, prompt ones who are having difficulty choosing a goal with some examples, like those in Appendix G.)

ACTIVITY

(Announce that participation in any activity is strictly voluntary. Everyone should join only those exercises with which they feel comfortable.)

1. Announce that this meeting is about making changes. Change is often described with a five-step model: pre-contemplation, contemplation, preparation, action, and maintenance, but this meeting will consider only the middle three: contemplation, preparation, and action. Contemplation is the stage in which someone recognizes that a change would be good but does not have any specific plan. Preparation is the

stage of thinking about what would be necessary to make the change, how it could be done, and when the person wants to do it. Action is the time of taking steps and working on change.

2. Ask stuttering participants to talk about a change they have thought about making, or plan to make, or are in the process of making. Nonstuttering participants should select a difficult problem or issue, which they believe they should change. What is the needed change? What stage are they in and how did they get to this point? What are the obstacles to moving on to the next step? Obstacles for each person can be written on the whiteboard.

3. One at a time, for each participant, ask the participants if anyone has a suggestion (which may or may not be followed) to help him or her overcome the obstacles.

4. Ask if this discussion has possibly motivated anyone to move ahead through the three steps. If so, invite them to share.

TAKEAWAY LESSONS

Encourage participants to share what stands out for them, or what they may have learned about themselves, their issues, and each other.

CONSIDER:

1. Intentional change, to be successful, requires our careful thought and counting the cost in terms of time, energy, and focus.

2. Obstacles that occur during our efforts to make lasting change in stuttering can be emotional, physical, cultural, motivational, etc.

3. Considering the five-step model, Stages of Change, the process of making new changes will likely be more easily understood.

INDIVIDUAL GOAL EVALUATIONS

Ask participants to go back to the goals they stated at the beginning of the meeting, and grade themselves on a scale from 1 to 10. They may share their grades with the group if they choose.

CLOSING WORDS

62. FORMING LONG-TERM HABITS TO ACCOMPLISH GOALS

PREPARATION

- Have access to a whiteboard or other display device.
- At the beginning and end of the meeting, ask someone to read the Welcoming Words and Closing Words (*Appendix E*).

GOALS

1. To determine the next, optimal goal for dealing with stuttering.
2. To consider new habits that must be adopted to achieve this goal.

THE MEETING

WELCOMING WORDS

ICEBREAKER

Ask participants how they fill their plates at a family-style dinner when food is passed around, and then how do they proceed to eat the food? (*Or see Appendix A.*)

INDIVIDUAL GOALS

Ask each one in attendance (stutterers, facilitators, visitors) to identify a personal goal for the meeting, and share it with the group. Inform them that, at the end of the meeting, they will be reminded of their goals and have an opportunity to evaluate themselves. (If necessary, prompt ones who are having difficulty choosing a goal with some examples, like those in Appendix G.)

ACTIVITY

(Announce that participation in any activity is strictly voluntary. Everyone should join only those exercises with which they feel comfortable.)

1. On the whiteboard, list some positive activities, such as flossing daily, taking the stairs instead of the elevator, getting enough sleep, staying organized, drinking plenty of water, etc. Ask participants to help compile the list. Ask participants to share one of these activities that they do not do as regularly as they would like. Why not? List the reasons on the board.

2. Pose the question, "What do you need to do to get the results that you want?"

3. Ask the stutterers, "What is the next good step you could take in order to better deal with your stuttering?" Ask others to talk about another goal that has proven elusive.

4. Invite discussion of what habits or practices everyone could cultivate in order to move toward the goal. List these beneficial steps on the whiteboard.

TAKEAWAY LESSONS

Encourage participants to share what stands out for them, or what they may have learned about themselves, their issues, and each other.

CONSIDER:

1. Change typically involves adopting new habits. "If you keep on doing what you've always done, you'll keep on getting what you've always got."

2. Establishing habits can be difficult, but they are important for taking the next step in accomplishing a goal.

INDIVIDUAL GOAL EVALUATIONS

Ask participants to go back to the goals they stated at the beginning of the meeting, and grade themselves on a scale from 1 to 10. They may share their grades with the group if they choose.

CLOSING WORDS

63. SETTING SHORT-TERM GOALS

PREPARATION

- Decide whether there will be a follow-up session at a future meeting, and the date. Participants will set short-term goals during this meeting, so a scheduled future meeting to discuss progress might be useful.
- Provide paper and pens or pencils.
- At the beginning and end of the meeting, ask someone to read the Welcoming Words and Closing Words (*Appendix E*).

GOALS

1. To discuss how to set and meet a specific short-term goal.
2. To set a short-term goal, share it with group members, and make a specific plan to accomplish it and measure success.

THE MEETING

WELCOMING WORDS

ICEBREAKER

Announce that this meeting is about the necessity of creating specific, concrete steps to achieve a goal. Ask the group to consider what they would need to do in order to survive for one week in the woods or the desert. Their ideas should be specific, and should involve as little equipment and as few supplies as necessary.

INDIVIDUAL GOALS

Ask each one in attendance (stutterers, facilitators, visitors) to identify a personal goal for the meeting, and share it with the group. Inform them that, at the end of the meeting, they will be reminded of their goals and have an opportunity to evaluate themselves. (If necessary, prompt ones who are having difficulty choosing a goal with some examples, like those in Appendix G.)

ACTIVITY

(Announce that participation in any activity is strictly voluntary. Everyone should join only those exercises with which they feel comfortable.)

1. Ask everyone in attendance—stutterers and nonstutterers—to think of a goal which, in an ideal world, they could accomplish in the next two weeks or so. Allow some time for thinking.

2. Ask participants to write the goal on a sheet of paper, and then think about and write down a) a few small steps that would result in accomplishing the goal, b) a specific way they could monitor their own adherence to the plan, c) what reinforcement they could give themselves as a reward for progress, d) someone they could tell about the plan and who would keep them accountable by asking them about their progress, and e) the most likely stumbling blocks to accomplishing the goal. Suggest that stutterers set a goal relating to their stuttering or their reaction to it. Allow a few minutes.

3. Ask each participant to share what they have written.

4. Ask the group to comment on the goals and plans: Were goals and procedures realistic? Were the reinforcement and monitoring plans doable and appropriate? Is the process of writing like this a helpful exercise?

5. If a follow-up meeting is scheduled, announce that a later meeting will follow up on these goals, and the date. Ask participants to keep the papers they wrote at this meeting and to bring them to the meeting.

TAKEAWAY LESSONS

Encourage participants to share what stands out for them, or what they may have learned about themselves, their issues, and each other.

CONSIDER:

1. Our short-term goals should be very specific and measurable.

2. It is important to plan ahead. Making a plan will increase the likelihood of achieving our goals.

3. Having a set plan on paper allows us to better self-evaluate and adjust our plan to reach our goal.

INDIVIDUAL GOAL EVALUATIONS

Ask participants to go back to the goals they stated at the beginning of the meeting, and grade themselves on a scale from 1 to 10. They may share their grades with the group if they choose.

CLOSING WORDS

"It makes you realize that after you reach your goal, you're not finished. It's always ongoing. The hardest part is when you first start, the first step."

64. GIVING UP THE IDEA OF BEING "NORMAL"

PREPARATION

- Prepare a list of role-play scenarios for everyone in attendance such as the following (*or adaptations from Appendix D*):
    - » At a restaurant, asking the waiter to take back undercooked or cold food.
    - » Calling a plumber because the sink faucet is spraying water.
    - » Trying to talk to a classmate in the next seat on the first day of class.
    - » At a coffee shop, asking about the new drinks while there's a long line behind you.
    - » In a department store, describing a piece of clothing you saw in a magazine and liked.
    - » Meeting a professor after you filled out a computerized answer sheet wrong and got an F on the test.
    - » At the grocery store, asking another customer where they found a cake they have in their cart.
- At the beginning and end of the meeting, ask someone to read the Welcoming Words and Closing Words (*Appendix E*).

GOALS

1. To explore the idea that nothing is "normal," and embrace differences.
2. To explore new ways of presenting oneself as a stutterer.

THE MEETING

WELCOMING WORDS

ICEBREAKER

Ask participants to, as a group, enter the closest elevator, press every button, and then ride from the top floor down to the first while facing the back wall of the elevator. Do not turn around when the elevator door opens or when someone enters.

If no elevator is available, pair the participants and ask them to walk around outside the meeting room for five minutes while holding a short rope between them—a rope which would be visible to everyone they pass. When they return, ask everyone to describe how this exercise made them feel. (*Or see Appendix A.*)

INDIVIDUAL GOALS

Ask each one in attendance (stutterers, facilitators, visitors) to identify a personal goal for the meeting, and share it with the group. Inform them that, at the end of the meeting, they will be reminded of their goals and have an opportunity to evaluate themselves. (If necessary, prompt ones who are having difficulty choosing a goal with some examples, like those in Appendix G.)

ACTIVITY

(Announce that participation in any activity is strictly voluntary. Everyone should join only those exercises with which they feel comfortable.)

1. Ask everyone to define "normal" in one or two sentences. Then, from all the definitions, invite a brief discussion of what normal is.

2. Ask why people are reluctant or afraid to be different from normal.

3. Ask everyone in attendance to name something about their speech, which they believe others notice. For stutterers this will be stuttering; others should choose some aspect of their speech.

4. Have each person talk through one of the role-play scenarios, with someone else acting as the other person in the conversation. The person acting out the scenario should exaggerate the speech characteristic they identified, and the other person should respond in an unhelpful (but not mean) way.

5. Repeat the scenarios, but this time the person acting out the scenario should inform, with humor, the other person about their speech characteristic.

6. Invite discussion of how everyone felt while role-playing, and of how a person might increase their acceptance and reduce the desire to be normal.

TAKEAWAY LESSONS

Encourage participants to share what stands out for them, or what they may have learned about themselves, their issues, and each other.

CONSIDER:

1. "Normal" is a slippery concept; yet, we typically strive as much as possible to appear normal. Of course, if no one tried to be normal, the world would be chaotic; however, trying to be normal when we cannot creates lots of problems for us.

2. Ironically, much of the time, we are striving not to be judged as abnormal by others just as they are striving not to be judged abnormal by us.

3. Many of our negative emotions related to stuttering are derived from our beliefs that if we cannot talk normally or like normal, fluent people, we will be judged negatively.

4. In fact, we who stutter cannot be normal with respect to speech fluency, just as short people cannot be normal with respect to height.

5. A healthy decision to reject further attempts to be normal in our speech releases us from a great deal of unnecessary worry and may even result in increased fluency.

INDIVIDUAL GOAL EVALUATIONS

Ask participants to go back to the goals they stated at the beginning of the meeting, and grade themselves on a scale from 1 to 10. They may share their grades with the group if they choose.

CLOSING WORDS

> "I know I won't be fluent overnight, if ever. I don't get frustrated with myself like I used to. I feel like I've gotten a lot better at being patient, ever since I started coming to the sessions."

65. LIFE PRIORITIES AND CHANGE

PREPARATION

- Make copies of the "Personal Priority Checklist" (*Appendix F*), at least twice as many as the expected number of participants.
- Have access to a whiteboard or other display device.
- At the beginning and end of the meeting, ask someone to read the Welcoming Words and Closing Words (*Appendix E*).

GOALS

1. To identify desired changes in attitudes or priorities, and to examine the associated changes necessary to accomplish them.

2. To apply the same ideas and insights to issues surrounding stuttering and other concrete issues.

THE MEETING

WELCOMING WORDS

ICEBREAKER

Invite discussion of the proper way to put toilet paper on the roller and why. (*Or see Appendix A.*)

INDIVIDUAL GOALS

Ask each one in attendance (stutterers, facilitators, visitors) to identify a personal goal for the meeting, and share it with the group. Inform them that, at the end of the meeting, they will be reminded of their goals and have an opportunity to evaluate themselves. (If necessary, prompt ones who are having difficulty choosing a goal with some examples, like those in Appendix G.)

ACTIVITY

(Announce that participation in any activity is strictly voluntary. Everyone should join only those exercises with which they feel comfortable.)

1. Distribute the "Personal Priority Checklist" and ask participants to fill it out. Announce that these checklists will not be shared with the group or with anyone else, except for parts the participants choose to share.

2. Distribute another copy of the checklist, and ask participants to fill it out with the answers they hope to have in five years.

3. Ask participants to share one or two items in the list that changed between the two time frames, and whether their hope was that it become more important or less. Have someone list these on the whiteboard.

4. Ask participants who shared a desired change to talk about what other changes will be necessary in order for the desired change to occur. Allow the group to respond and discuss.

5. Ask participants to identify a long-term goal relating to stuttering or communication—or, for nonstutterers, another troubling issue. Invite them to share how they would like the issue to improve and to identify some of the specific, associated changes that would be needed in order to help accomplish the goal.

6. Invite discussion of the similarities or differences between specific goals and desires, and more general and abstract life changes.

TAKEAWAY LESSONS

Encourage participants to share what stands out for them, or what they may have learned about themselves, their issues, and each other.

CONSIDER:

1. To embark on a self-improvement journey, we should identify the problems we wish to alleviate first, being very honest with ourselves.

2. Intentional long-term goals will facilitate changes in priorities and overcoming problems in our lives, while wishful thinking may not be effective.

3. Writing out short-term goals will assist us in accomplishing our long-term goals, either with stuttering or something more general.

INDIVIDUAL GOAL EVALUATIONS

Ask participants to go back to the goals they stated at the beginning of the meeting, and grade themselves on a scale from 1 to 10. They may share their grades with the group if they choose.

CLOSING WORDS

66. STUTTERING JOURNEYS OF CHANGE

PREPARATION

- Have a whiteboard or other display device ready, with a number of horizontal lines, each labeled at the left and right with "A" and "Z." Have colored markers available.
- At the beginning and end of the meeting, ask someone to read the Welcoming Words and Closing Words (*Appendix E*).

GOALS

1. To identify personal, major changes made in life.
2. To determine what motivates personal changes.
3. To explore change as a process.

THE MEETING

WELCOMING WORDS

ICEBREAKER

Ask two volunteers to stand up and advertise a caffeinated Coca-Cola. One person will focus on the negative outcome of not buying the product (you will be sleepy, dull, distracted, bored, lethargic, sluggish, etc.) while the other person will focus on the positive benefits of buying it (you will be alert, full of energy, productive, etc.). Then ask everyone which advertising technique used appealed to them more. (*Or see Appendix A.*)

INDIVIDUAL GOALS

Ask each one in attendance (stutterers, facilitators, visitors) to identify a personal goal for the meeting, and share it with the group. Inform them that, at the end of the meeting, they will be reminded of their goals and have an opportunity to evaluate themselves. (If necessary, prompt ones who are having difficulty choosing a goal with some examples, like those in Appendix G.)

ACTIVITY

(Announce that participation in any activity is strictly voluntary. Everyone should join only those exercises with which they feel comfortable.)

1. Ask each person to think of a recent important change they have made in their lives, or are in the process of making, and share it with the group. It should be something major, like relocating, changing an important relationship or job, or undertaking a new activity.

2. Have each one identify the change, and what prompted them to make the change. Invite discussion of what factors cause people to make a change.

3. Have each person write their first name initial above the top line drawn across the whiteboard indicating where they believe they are with the change, with A representing not even starting, and Z representing successful completion of the change and being satisfied with the results. Ask them to briefly explain why they placed their initial where they did.

4. Ask the stutterers to talk about the first time they came to the group, what prompted them to come, and what they hoped to achieve in the group.

5. Have the stutterers come to the board and, each on their own line with a different-colored marker, write a "1" above where they were with their stuttering and their acceptance or management of it when they first came to the group, a "2" where they are now, and a "3" where they expect to end up. Have each one comment briefly on why he or she placed the numbers where they did.

TAKEAWAY LESSONS

Encourage participants to share what stands out for them, or what they may have learned about themselves, their issues, and each other.

CONSIDER:

1. Every time we make a significant change, we must be ready for change. And, very likely, we are either avoiding a negative or trying to achieve a positive.

2. Change is a process, and we all have our own unique journey.

3. We have moving targets. We might start out with a change in mind, but upon realizing things about that change, we might move back or forward in the process.

4. Support from others can assist us in defining what we want to change and proceeding to make the change.

5. Change happens when preparation meets opportunity.

INDIVIDUAL GOAL EVALUATIONS

Ask participants to go back to the goals they stated at the beginning of the meeting, and grade themselves on a scale from 1 to 10. They may share their grades with the group if they choose.

CLOSING WORDS

"Hearing other people's experiences helps. It gives me more of an acceptance instead of pretending I don't stutter. I acknowledge it more and it is easier to deal with."

67. RESISTING CHANGE

PREPARATION

- Provide paper and pens or pencils.
- At the beginning and end of the meeting, ask someone to read the Welcoming Words and Closing Words (*Appendix E*).

GOALS

1. To better understand why we resist making desired changes.
2. To experience how to overcome resistance by setting a specific, attainable goal for change.

THE MEETING

WELCOMING WORDS

ICEBREAKER

Ask everyone what they would do if they were at a restaurant in Thailand thinking they had ordered chicken wings but were served chicken feet. (*Or see Appendix A.*)

INDIVIDUAL GOALS

Ask each one in attendance (stutterers, facilitators, visitors) to identify a personal goal for the meeting, and share it with the group. Inform them that, at the end of the meeting, they will be reminded of their goals and have an opportunity to evaluate themselves. (If necessary, prompt ones who are having difficulty choosing a goal with some examples, like those in Appendix G.)

ACTIVITY

Announce that participation in any activity is strictly voluntary. Everyone should join only those exercises with which they feel comfortable.)

1. Ask each person in attendance to tell about someone—not necessarily by name—with whom they feel comfortable confiding personal matters and who they believe gives good advice and guidance.

2. Ask each one to briefly tell about a change they would like to make in their lives, but have been unsuccessful doing. Stutterers are encouraged to choose a change related to stuttering.

3. Ask each one to place themselves in their trusted confidante's shoes and to give the advice they think that person might give.

4. Ask why anyone might resist that advice. Follow up with all the reasons we might resist good advice.

5. Ask each participant to think of a small step they can make toward accomplishing a desired change. It should be something that can be done immediately, in the coming week, and something that can be objectively judged on whether it has been done or not. Ask people to write down the step, and how they will be able to tell whether it has been done or not. Participants may share their ideas with the group, or not.

TAKEAWAY LESSONS

Encourage participants to share what stands out for them, or what they may have learned about themselves, their issues, and each other.

CONSIDER:

1. Some resistance to new ideas and behaviors is a necessary self-protection trait of all humans. But too much resistance leads us to question or even dread new ideas and behaviors.

2. We tend to resist good advice for the same reason we resist change in general. It may be outside of our comfort zone. It may require a new persona with which we are simply so unfamiliar that it seems like too big of a step. We may not like our adjustments, but they are the only ones we have.

3. Ideally, we should constantly monitor ourselves to "resist unnecessary resistance to change." Perhaps our minds should be like parachutes: they only function when they are open.

INDIVIDUAL GOAL EVALUATIONS

Ask participants to go back to the goals they stated at the beginning of the meeting, and grade themselves on a scale from 1 to 10. They may share their grades with the group if they choose.

CLOSING WORDS

68. COST VERSUS BENEFIT OF SPEECH THERAPY

PREPARATION

- At the beginning and end of the meeting, ask someone to read the Welcoming Words and Closing Words (*Appendix E*).
- Have access to a whiteboard or other display device.

GOALS

1. To discuss the pros and cons of speech therapy.
2. To consider what long-term effects might be associated with either continuing or discontinuing therapy.

THE MEETING

WELCOMING WORDS

ICEBREAKER

Ask participants to think of the most valuable thing they own and to tell the group what it is. Then, tell them to imagine that they found a magic lamp from which a genie appeared to grant them one wish. But, here's the catch: They must give up that prized possession in order for this wish to come true. Would they trade their most valued item for something else? If so, what would it be? (*Or see Appendix A.*)

INDIVIDUAL GOALS

Ask each one in attendance (stutterers, facilitators, visitors) to identify a personal goal for the meeting, and share it with the group. Inform them that, at the end of the meeting, they will be reminded of their goals and have an opportunity to evaluate themselves. (If necessary, prompt ones who are having difficulty choosing a goal with some examples, like those in Appendix G.)

ACTIVITY

(Announce that participation in any activity is strictly voluntary. Everyone should join only those exercises with which they feel comfortable.)

1. Ask someone to make notes on the whiteboard. Divide the whiteboard horizontally into halves, and label the top half "Continue." Divide this "Continue" section into

two columns, and label them "Costs" and "Benefits." Have the group discuss the pluses and minuses of continuing (or starting) speech therapy, and list them on the board.

2. Label the bottom half of the board "Discontinue," divided into "Cost" and "Benefit," and have the group discuss the pluses and minuses of discontinuing (or never starting) speech therapy. List them on the board.

3. Ask participants to imagine what their lives may be like in five years and to discuss what differences, if any, continuing or discontinuing therapy might make.

TAKEAWAY LESSONS

Encourage participants to share what stands out for them, or what they may have learned about themselves, their issues, and each other

CONSIDER:

1. With all potential changes, positive or negative, there are costs and benefits to take into account.

2. Considering continuing or starting speech therapy for stuttering, we are well advised to discern if what we have to give up is worth what we want to get. The same is true for deciding whether to discontinue or never start speech therapy.

INDIVIDUAL GOAL EVALUATIONS

Ask participants to go back to the goals they stated at the beginning of the meeting, and grade themselves on a scale from 1 to 10. They may share their grades with the group if they choose.

CLOSING WORDS

69. UNDERSTANDING "COMFORT ZONES"

PREPARATION

- Supply paper and pens or pencils.
- Use of a whiteboard or other display is helpful.
- Draw a Comfort Zone Model to hand out to participants; be prepared to explain and discuss it (*Appendix F*).
- At the beginning and end of the meeting, ask someone to read the Welcoming Words and Closing Words (*Appendix E*).

GOALS

1. To gain a better understanding of comfort zones and to discuss how to use this understanding as a tool for self-improvement.
2. To identify a specific short-term goal for expanding our comfort zones.

THE MEETING

WELCOMING WORDS

ICEBREAKER

Ask participants to write a generic compliment to another person on a piece of paper. After everyone has written a compliment, crumple the papers and have a "snowball fight" by throwing the crumpled paper around the room. Following, each participant will pick up a "snowball," and compliment the person next to them using what's written on the paper. (*Or see Appendix A.*)

INDIVIDUAL GOALS

Ask each one in attendance (stutterers, facilitators, visitors) to identify a personal goal for the meeting, and share it with the group. Inform them that, at the end of the meeting, they will be reminded of their goals and have an opportunity to evaluate themselves. (If necessary, prompt ones who are having difficulty choosing a goal with some examples, like those in Appendix G.)

ACTIVITY

(Announce that participation in any activity is strictly voluntary. Everyone should join only those exercises with which they feel comfortable.)

1. Distribute the Comfort Zone Model drawings, briefly explain its parts, and begin a discussion. Prompt for discussion of topics such as how different participants have different comfort zones, how comfort zones vary over time, how different situations or moods can affect comfort-zone boundaries, and why activity too far outside the zone is not productive.

2. Ask participants to share some things that are a little outside their personal comfort zones—things they can usually do without a problem, but that they need to talk themselves into. Have one of the participants divide the whiteboard in half, and write some of the responses on one side. Allow discussion of the various responses and why participants believe they may be uncomfortable with these actions. Discuss how participants might benefit from deliberately doing these things, rather than doing them only when necessary.

3. Repeat the above for actions farther outside the comfort zones of participants—things they can do, but with much hesitation or anxiety. Record some of these on the other side of the board. Again, discuss why these things are uncomfortable and how doing them by choice rather than necessity may be beneficial.

TAKEAWAY LESSONS

Encourage participants to share what stands out for them, or what they may have learned about themselves, their issues, and each other.

CONSIDER:

1. We all automatically and immediately create and then stay in our comfort zones. For example, we sit in the same seat after choosing one randomly the first time.

2. Moving out of our comfort zone involves discomfort, which can range from a vague feeling of unease to terror.

3. Growth, through experience, inevitably involves facing anxiety but results in expanding our comfort zones such that we can live life more fully.

INDIVIDUAL GOAL EVALUATIONS

Ask participants to go back to the goals they stated at the beginning of the meeting, and grade themselves on a scale from 1 to 10. They may share their grades with the group if they choose.

CLOSING WORDS

70. EXPANDING OUR "COMFORT ZONE"

PREPARATION

- A whiteboard or other display device is helpful.
- Draw a Comfort Zone Model to hand out to participants; be prepared to explain and discuss it (*Appendix F*).
- Provide paper and pens or pencils for the group.
- At the beginning and end of the meeting, ask someone to read the Welcoming Words and Closing Words (*Appendix E*).

GOALS

1. To gain insight through examining the concept of a "comfort zone" and applying it to challenging stuttering situations.
2. To promote desensitization by challenging participants to attempt to expand their own comfort zones.

THE MEETING

WELCOMING WORDS

ICEBREAKER

Ask those in attendance to share their "control freak" characteristics—what areas in life they feel the need to control, or areas of not being in control that bother them. (*Or see Appendix A.*)

INDIVIDUAL GOALS

Ask each one in attendance (stutterers, facilitators, visitors) to identify a personal goal for the meeting, and share it with the group. Inform them that, at the end of the meeting, they will be reminded of their goals and have an opportunity to evaluate themselves. (If necessary, prompt ones who are having difficulty choosing a goal with some examples, like those in Appendix G.)

ACTIVITY

(Announce that participation in any activity is strictly voluntary. Everyone should join only those exercises with which they feel comfortable.)

1. Draw the "Comfort Zone" model on a whiteboard or other device. Introduce the idea that personal growth does not happen when we stay in our familiar and safe place. It also does not happen if we attempt something completely outside our experience. Personal growth comes from purposely going a little outside our comfort zone, which can build on the abilities we have and expand them.

2. Invite discussion of the comfort zone concept. What is a comfort zone? Why does the diagram say there is no personal growth if we go far outside the zone?

3. Ask participants to listen to some scenarios and rate them on a scale of 1 to 10, with 1 being well within the comfort zone and 10 being far out of it. Have everyone jot their answers on paper, to refer to later. Read the scenarios:

   » Interviewing for a job.
   » Calling a store and asking about their hours or a product special.
   » Leaving a message on a stranger's answering machine.
   » Talking to your pet.
   » Talking with your family or friends.
   » Talking with a friend about your stutter.
   » Giving a toast at a wedding as a maid of honor or best man.
   » Striking up a conversation with a stranger sitting next to you in a class or meeting.
   » Inviting someone on a date.
   » Asking your teacher for more time to give a timed speech in class.

4. Remind the group of the idea that the opportunity for growth is greatest just outside the comfort zone, and ask each participant which of the scenarios would be the most appropriate for achieving a little or moderate amount of growth. Which activities would be so far out of the comfort zone that they would not be growth opportunities?

5. Ask anyone who chooses to participate to do something in the "growth area" a little outside his or her comfort zone. Some possibilities are:

   » Call a store and ask when they close.
   » Call a store and ask about a specific item or special.
   » Leave a message on an answering machine.
   » Call a hotel and ask about the rates to hold a meeting with 40 attendees.
   » Call a utility company or closed store and use the automatic answering machine system.

> » Give an impromptu speech.
>
> » Sing a song.

6. Ask participants to think about something in the growth area they can do in the coming week, related to anything they do—school, communication, jobs, relationships, physical activity, etc. Invite anyone to share their ideas.

TAKEAWAY LESSONS

Encourage participants to share what stands out for them, or what they may have learned about themselves, their issues, and each other.

CONSIDER:

1. Expanding our comfort zone always involves discomfort and anxiety.

2. Expanding our comfort zone should generally be in small steps (with tolerable anxiety), but sometimes a very large risk of anxiety or fear can result in a large expansion of our comfort zone. It's like learning to swim at greater and greater depths of a pool versus jumping into the deep end.

3. Growth, through experience, inevitably involves facing anxiety but results in expanding our comfort zones such that we can live life more fully.

4. Our comfort zones ordinarily continue to expand throughout life but can become constricted after various physical or psychological wounds.

INDIVIDUAL GOAL EVALUATIONS

Ask participants to go back to the goals they stated at the beginning of the meeting, and grade themselves on a scale from 1 to 10. They may share their grades with the group if they choose.

CLOSING WORDS

"If you never mention something, it becomes unmentionable."

71. PRACTICE AND COMFORT ZONES

PREPARATION

- At the beginning and end of the meeting, ask someone to read the Welcoming Words and Closing Words (*Appendix E*).

GOALS

1. To practice speaking to the group and to discuss the anxiety surrounding public speaking.

2. To examine repetition of an uncomfortable task as a strategy for expanding comfort zones.

THE MEETING

WELCOMING WORDS

ICEBREAKER

Ask participants to respond to this scenario: You are on vacation with a good friend and decide to visit a beach you heard about. When you get there, you find out it's a nude beach. (*Or see Appendix A.*)

INDIVIDUAL GOALS

Ask each one in attendance (stutterers, facilitators, visitors) to identify a personal goal for the meeting, and share it with the group. Inform them that, at the end of the meeting, they will be reminded of their goals and have an opportunity to evaluate themselves. (If necessary, prompt ones who are having difficulty choosing a goal with some examples, like those in Appendix G.)

ACTIVITY

(Announce that participation in any activity is strictly voluntary. Everyone should join only those exercises with which they feel comfortable.)

1. Inform the group that all stutterers who choose to participate will be making a short impromptu speech. After a minute, ask each one to write down how much anxiety they expect to feel during the speech, with 1 being no anxiety and 10 being a crippling amount.

2. Ask for volunteers to speak for 60 to 90 seconds on learning to drive, learning to swim, or learning to take public transportation.

3. After all the speeches, ask participants to rate how much anxiety they felt during their speeches and to compare it with the amount they wrote down at the beginning of the activity.

4. Invite stutterers to give another speech to speak for 60 to 90 seconds on a book or movie that bothered or troubled them, a social situation that is not pleasant for them, or a necessary routine or household chore they usually procrastinate on.

5. Ask stutterers to rate their anxiety a third time and to report any change in their comfort level.

6. Ask if any stutterers would like to do a third speech on another of the previous topics. If so, let them do so, rate their comfort levels, and report any changes.

7. Introduce or review the topic of comfort zones. Explain the desirability of consciously working to expand them. Ask if the experience of giving two speeches in a brief period can be indicative of how to expand people's comfort zones.

TAKEAWAY LESSONS

Encourage participants to share what stands out for them, or what they may have learned about themselves, their issues, and each other.

CONSIDER:

1. We often find that massed practice—or doing similar difficult situations over and over—weakens anxiety, at least temporarily.

2. Practicing public speaking can be very helpful in expanding our comfort zones in that widely feared activity.

3. Becoming more comfortable speaking publicly, with limited preparation, opens doors for us in the future.

INDIVIDUAL GOAL EVALUATIONS

Ask participants to go back to the goals they stated at the beginning of the meeting, and grade themselves on a scale from 1 to 10. They may share their grades with the group if they choose.

CLOSING WORDS

72. STUTTERING BEHAVIORS AND STUTTERING EMOTIONS: THE CHICKEN OR THE EGG?

PREPARATION
- Supply paper and pens or pencils.
- Make copies of the model of the Interaction of Thoughts, Feelings & Actions image (*Appendix F*),
- At the beginning and end of the meeting, ask someone to read the Welcoming Words and Closing Words (*Appendix E*).

GOAL
1. To examine the relationships between behaviors and emotions.

THE MEETING

WELCOMING WORDS

ICEBREAKER
Tell the participants to imagine they live in a society where one's ability to sign their name beautifully is highly regarded, and failure to be able to do that signals inferiority. Ask everyone to pair up and assign themselves person A and person B. A is to start signing his or her name, repeatedly, down the page and to resist any interference. After a few signatures, B is to intermittently bump A's arm as he or she writes. After doing this for a few minutes, ask the participants to change roles.* Briefly discuss their behaviors and their feelings as they tried to write neatly. (*Or see Appendix A.*)

INDIVIDUAL GOALS
Ask each one in attendance (stutterers, facilitators, visitors) to identify a personal goal for the meeting, and share it with the group. Inform them that, at the end of the meeting, they will be reminded of their goals and have an opportunity to evaluate themselves. (If necessary, prompt ones who are having difficulty choosing a goal with some examples, like those in Appendix G.)

---

* This activity is from colleague J. Scott Yaruss, PhD.

ACTIVITY

(Announce that participation in any activity is strictly voluntary. Everyone should join only those exercises with which they feel comfortable.)

1. Ask the nonstutterers to think of a troubling thing that they do, which they are willing to share with the group. If they need help getting started, give some examples, like being extremely shy, overspending, being impatient in traffic, procrastinating, etc. Explain that they will be discussing some aspects of this issue, while the stutterers will be talking about stuttering.

2. Ask each person to take a sheet of paper, and make two columns. On one side list specific behaviors—things people do that can be observed—associated with stuttering or other issues. On the other side, list feelings or emotions that accompany the behaviors.

3. Ask participants to share what they have written.

4. Discuss the relationship between behaviors and emotions. Could one exist without the other? For example, could somebody stutter (or be shy, or overspend, etc.) without it bringing up feelings and emotions? If you could somehow reduce the feelings and emotions surrounding an issue, would the behavior become less serious or less frequent?

TAKEAWAY LESSONS

Encourage participants to share what stands out for them, or what they may have learned about themselves, their issues, and each other.

CONSIDER:

1. Beginning stuttering in young children can occur without any noticeable awareness and, hence, no emotion; however, it can also be associated with extreme awareness in young children.

2. In older children and adults, occasional stuttering can also occur without any particular negative emotions, but, most of the time, stuttering is clearly associated with various emotions, such as embarrassment, fear, humiliation, frustration, or annoyance.

3. From sharing with others, confronting our fears, expanding our comfort zones, etc., we can reduce the strength of many negative emotions. Often, though not necessarily, this reduces the behavioral symptoms of stuttering.

4. Reducing our stuttering typically has a noticeable positive effect on our negative emotions. Research has shown, however, that our self-concepts change slower than

our behavior so, unless we continue to work on our avoidances and fears, they tend to come back.

INDIVIDUAL GOAL EVALUATIONS

Ask participants to go back to the goals they stated at the beginning of the meeting, and grade themselves on a scale from 1 to 10. They may share their grades with the group if they choose.

CLOSING WORDS

"As an introvert who stutters, learning ways to express myself with less pressure allowed me to be at ease in new situations."

73. ACKNOWLEDGING A PROBLEM

PREPARATION

- Supply paper and pens or pencils.
- At the beginning and end of the meeting, ask someone to read the Welcoming Words and Closing Words (*Appendix E*).

GOALS

1. To acknowledge positives and negatives about yourself.
2. To evaluate how it feels to comment on someone else's problems, and how it feels to have someone else comment on yours.
3. To realize there is comfort in knowing that someone else feels the same way you do.

THE MEETING

WELCOMING WORDS

ICEBREAKER

Ask people how they would respond if a friend asks their opinion on a bad haircut or hair-dye job. (*Or see Appendix A.*)

INDIVIDUAL GOALS

Ask each one in attendance (stutterers, facilitators, visitors) to identify a personal goal for the meeting, and share it with the group. Inform them that, at the end of the meeting, they will be reminded of their goals and have an opportunity to evaluate themselves. (If necessary, prompt ones who are having difficulty choosing a goal with some examples, like those in Appendix G.)

ACTIVITY

(Announce that participation in any activity is strictly voluntary. Everyone should join only those exercises with which they feel comfortable.)

1. Have each one present write three to five positives about themselves on one piece of paper, and three to five negatives on another.

2. Have each one share their list of positives with the group.

3. Have each one circle one of the negatives on their list. It should be a major negative, and stutterers should choose one which relates in some way to their stuttering if possible. Divide the group into pairs, avoiding pairing people who know each other well. Have everyone trade their negative lists with their partner.

4. Ask each one to imagine that their partner's circled negative is their own, and comment on it the way they would like someone else to comment.

5. Invite discussion of how it felt to hear someone else's perspective on a problem. What was surprising, or what did anyone learn?

TAKEAWAY LESSONS

Encourage participants to share what stands out for them, or what they may have learned about themselves, their issues, and each other.

CONSIDER:

1. It can be comforting to know that someone else would want the same reaction or comments if they were in our shoes.

2. We all want nonjudgmental acceptance and respect.

INDIVIDUAL GOAL EVALUATIONS

Ask participants to go back to the goals they stated at the beginning of the meeting, and grade themselves on a scale from 1 to 10. They may share their grades with the group if they choose.

CLOSING WORDS

74. ACKNOWLEDGING THE ELEPHANT IN THE ROOM

PREPARATION

- Ahead of time, prepare name tags with the following labels:
    - » wearing an eye patch
    - » arm in a sling
    - » glasses with one lens missing
    - » black eye
    - » nose bleeding
    - » one finger missing
    - » extreme sweating
    - » very bad haircut
    - » large rip in clothes
    - » Band-Aid on forehead
    - » neck brace
    - » large scar on face
    - » severe limp
    - » using an electronic voice generator to talk
- At the beginning and end of the meeting, ask someone to read the Welcoming Words and Closing Words (*Appendix E*).

GOALS

1. To explore the benefits of acknowledging unpleasant issues that people have, such as stuttering.
2. To consider the additional benefits of humor in acknowledging unpleasant issues.

THE MEETING

WELCOMING WORDS

ICEBREAKER

Ask everyone which of the seven Disney Snow White dwarfs best represents them and why—Grumpy, Sleepy, Bashful, Doc, Sneezy, Dopey, or Happy. If none of the seven seems appropriate, people are free to make up an eighth one. (*Or see Appendix A.*)

INDIVIDUAL GOALS

Ask each one in attendance (stutterers, facilitators, visitors) to identify a personal goal for the meeting, and share it with the group. Inform them that, at the end of the meeting, they will be reminded of their goals and have an opportunity to evaluate themselves. (If necessary, prompt ones who are having difficulty choosing a goal with some examples, like those in Appendix G.)

ACTIVITY

(Announce that participation in any activity is strictly voluntary. Everyone should join only those exercises with which they feel comfortable.)

1. Have the group sit in a circle. Distribute the name tags with the conditions on them. Tell the group to imagine they are attending a club meeting for the first time, a club they have been very eager to join. Ask each one to stand, introduce themselves, and explain their obvious condition in a serious way.

2. Have everyone pass their name tag to the person on their left. Have everyone stand, introduce themselves, and explain their condition with a humorous explanation.

3. Have everyone remove the name tags. Ask everyone to introduce themselves and explain that they stutter. Nonstutterers in the group should stutter on purpose. Everyone should decide whether to explain their stuttering seriously, humorously, or with some blend of the two.

4. Ask the stutterers and nonstutterers to comment on the introductions of the other group. Ask everyone to discuss the use of serious or humorous language in discussing the "elephant in the room."

TAKEAWAY LESSONS

Encourage participants to share what stands out for them, or what they may have learned about themselves, their issues, and each other.

CONSIDER:

1. The "elephant in the room" is the issue that everyone cannot help but notice or focus on but that no one mentions for fear of hurting or embarrassing someone.

2. Stuttering is sometimes not mentioned in a stutterer's home, and the more it is not mentioned, the more "unmentionable" it becomes.

3. The old advice to stuttering children to "ignore it and it will go away" is not true.

4. When the "elephant in the room" is named or acknowledged, the tension in the entire room often evaporates.

5. If a person with a noticeable issue is psychologically ready, using a little self-deprecating humor can be an extremely effective way to reduce the tension such that the issue fades into the background.

INDIVIDUAL GOAL EVALUATIONS

Ask participants to go back to the goals they stated at the beginning of the meeting, and grade themselves on a scale from 1 to 10. They may share their grades with the group if they choose.

CLOSING WORDS

"Coming to group helps me throughout the week. If something happens, it gives me a place to vent about it... to relate to people who have the same problem. It helps to take a breath and realize it's okay."

75. FEELING OUT OF CONTROL WHEN STUTTERING

PREPARATION

- Have available a package of small chocolate candies.
- Have available a blindfold.
- Prepare index cards or slips of paper with simple tasks to do in or near the meeting area, such as going to the water fountain and getting a drink, turning a light off and on, moving a chair from one place to another, locking and unlocking a door, etc.
- At the beginning and end of the meeting, ask someone to read the Welcoming Words and Closing Words (*Appendix E*).

GOALS

1. To discuss, in general, the feeling surrounding lack of control.
2. To explore thoughts and feelings associated with being out of control with stuttering.

THE MEETING

WELCOMING WORDS

ICEBREAKER

Ask those in attendance to each take a piece of chocolate candy and eat it slowly. Ask each person to describe what chocolate tastes like without using the word "chocolate." (*Or see Appendix A.*)

INDIVIDUAL GOALS

Ask each one in attendance (stutterers, facilitators, visitors) to identify a personal goal for the meeting, and share it with the group. Inform them that, at the end of the meeting, they will be reminded of their goals and have an opportunity to evaluate themselves. (If necessary, prompt ones who are having difficulty choosing a goal with some examples, like those in Appendix G.)

ACTIVITY

(Announce that participation in any activity is strictly voluntary. Everyone should join only those exercises with which they feel comfortable.)

1. Ask participants to form pairs.

2. One at a time, have pairs of participants come to the front. Blindfold one of them, and hand the other one of the tasks you have written. The person without the blindfold is to talk the blindfolded one through accomplishing the task, without touching them or telling them what the task is.

3. After the exercise, ask participants to describe their feelings while performing a task blindfolded. Expand the conversation to include the usual feelings or emotions accompanying situations in which people have no control, and what, if anything, can be done to lessen the negative feeling of being out of control.

4. Expand the discussion to stuttering and include the feeling of being out of control during moments of stuttering. Ask stuttering participants to share their own unique experience of being out of control during stuttering. Suggest they highlight specific situations in which lack of control caused strong feelings, and how they coped with the feelings, or realized later how they might have handled the situation better.

TAKEAWAY LESSONS

Encourage participants to share what stands out for them, or what they may have learned about themselves, their issues, and each other.

CONSIDER:

1. Perhaps the only common experience of all stutterers is a temporary feeling of being out of control as they speak, even though it can manifest in many different ways. We know what it feels like although we cannot describe it completely to a nonstutterer.

2. Most people do not like feeling out of control. Emotions that quickly become associated with loss of control can range from surprise, to mild annoyance or frustration, to panic.

3. Much of what happens in speech therapy is learning strategies to prevent the loss of control we experience or to regain it once it occurs. Stutterers vary in their abilities to achieve these goals.

INDIVIDUAL GOAL EVALUATIONS

Ask participants to go back to the goals they stated at the beginning of the meeting, and grade themselves on a scale from 1 to 10. They may share their grades with the group if they choose.

CLOSING WORDS

76. IF YOU REALLY KNEW ME

PREPARATION

- Bring a bag of marshmallows to the meeting.
- At the beginning and end of the meeting, ask someone to read the Welcoming Words and Closing Words (*Appendix E*).

GOALS

1. To consider how we would like others to see us.
2. To explore what factors may be preventing us from presenting our true selves to others.

THE MEETING

WELCOMING WORDS

ICEBREAKER

Announce that this meeting is about the barriers that prevent us from communicating important facts about ourselves. Pass around the marshmallows, and have everyone take four of them. Have each person, one at a time, put as many marshmallows in his/her mouth as possible and say something important about themselves, which they would want other people to know.

INDIVIDUAL GOALS

Ask each one in attendance (stutterers, facilitators, visitors) to identify a personal goal for the meeting, and share it with the group. Inform them that, at the end of the meeting, they will be reminded of their goals and have an opportunity to evaluate themselves. (If necessary, prompt ones who are having difficulty choosing a goal with some examples, like those in Appendix G.)

ACTIVITY

(Announce that participation in any activity is strictly voluntary. Everyone should join only those exercises with which they feel comfortable.)

1. Ask the stutterers, and any nonstutterers who wish to participate, to share one or two things about themselves, which they wish more people knew. These should be

about who they are, their abilities or personal traits, or other important factors in their lives that not many people know about.

2. Ask participants to discuss what factors—stuttering or otherwise—may be preventing them from presenting themselves as they would like to and why stuttering may make it harder for others to see their true selves.

3. Invite participants to share any thoughts on what they could do to make it easier to present themselves as they would like to be seen. Ask them about the difference between this and bragging.

TAKEAWAY LESSONS

Encourage participants to share what stands out for them, or what they may have learned about themselves, their issues, and each other.

CONSIDER:

1. Stuttering often does—but need not—interfere with presenting ourselves as we would like to be seen.

2. Whereas people argue whether or not being called a "stutterer" versus "a person who stutters" makes a difference, when we truly can see ourselves as a person who just happens to stutter, then we can focus on our strengths and assets without "over-compensating."

3. Presenting ourselves in a positive way is not the same as bragging.

INDIVIDUAL GOAL EVALUATIONS

Ask participants to go back to the goals they stated at the beginning of the meeting, and grade themselves on a scale from 1 to 10. They may share their grades with the group if they choose.

CLOSING WORDS

77. DISCLOSING STUTTERING

PREPARATION

- Gather several items for participants to "sell." These could be ordinary objects found in the room—coffee cup, hat, scissors, chair, etc.—or ordinary items brought in.
- Label four index cards, each with one of the disclosure strategies:
    » disclose initially
    » disclose only after it becomes obvious
    » disclose with humor
    » do not disclose
- On other index cards, write one of these conditions:
    » extreme perspiration
    » shaky or squeaky voice
    » extreme blushing
    » eye twitch
    » hand or head tremors
    » extreme stiff neck
    » nose bleed
- At the beginning and end of the meeting, ask someone to read the Welcoming Words and Closing Words (*Appendix E*).

GOALS

1. To explore the forms and ramifications of not disclosing stuttering.
2. To encourage acceptance of stuttering by disclosing it.

THE MEETING

WELCOMING WORDS

ICEBREAKER

Ask participants if there is anything unusual they always carry in their purses, wallets, backpacks, or bags. (*Or see Appendix A.*)

INDIVIDUAL GOALS

Ask each one in attendance (stutterers, facilitators, visitors) to identify a personal goal for the meeting, and share it with the group. Inform them that, at the end of the meeting, they will be reminded of their goals and have an opportunity to evaluate themselves. (If necessary, prompt ones who are having difficulty choosing a goal with some examples, like those in Appendix G.)

ACTIVITY

(Announce that participation in any activity is strictly voluntary. Everyone should join only those exercises with which they feel comfortable.)

1. Inform the group that each person will be making a one- to two-minute sales pitch, selling one of the ordinary objects on the table. Also, stutterers will be secretly instructed to deal with their stutter in one of four ways: disclose at the start of their talk that they stutter, disclose it only after stuttering occurs, disclose it using humor, or do not disclose it at all. Nonstutterers will be given an imaginary condition instead of stuttering.

2. Ask for a stutterer to volunteer to go first. Shuffle the four disclosure cards, and hand them one. The stutterer will choose a product to sell, and make a one- or two-minute sales pitch, using the disclosure strategy on the card. After the talk, ask the listeners whether they could tell which strategy the speaker was using, and how effectively they did it. Repeat for every stutterer who chooses to participate.

3. If time allows, ask the nonstutterers to take a turn. Hand them a disclosure card, and also a condition card. They are to sell their product, and disclose or not disclose their condition according to their disclosure card. Ask the listeners how well the speaker handled his or her disclosure assignment.

4. Invite discussion of whether to disclose stuttering or another noticeable condition, and how to do it. What factors affect how anyone decides to handle this? How important is it to do it appropriately for the situation?

TAKEAWAY LESSONS

Encourage participants to share what stands out for them, or what they may have learned about themselves, their issues, and each other.

CONSIDER:

1. Disclosure often reduces our anticipatory anxiety and, therefore, stuttering itself.

2. There are many ways we can disclose sensitive personal attributes.

3. In some cases it may not be necessary to disclose our shortcomings. However, if we choose not to disclose, we may run the risk of being a less successful communicator in the long run.

4. Sometimes by not mentioning or disclosing something, we only make the situation more uncomfortable.

INDIVIDUAL GOAL EVALUATIONS

Ask participants to go back to the goals they stated at the beginning of the meeting, and grade themselves on a scale from 1 to 10. They may share their grades with the group if they choose.

CLOSING WORDS

"Don't waste your energy just trying to fight yourself. You're going to lose every time you fight your speech. It's a snowball effect. Face your fears. It has taught me to be patient and made me a much stronger person."

78. MONITORING ACCESSORY OR SECONDARY BEHAVIORS

PREPARATION

- Be prepared to define accessory behaviors, found in the glossary in Appendix H.
- Have a list of impromptu speaking topics ready from Appendix B.
- At the beginning and end of the meeting, ask someone to read the Welcoming Words and Closing Words (*Appendix E*).

GOALS

1. To understand the origin and use of accessory or secondary behaviors stutterers might use.
2. To experience stuttering without these behaviors.

THE MEETING

WELCOMING WORDS

ICEBREAKER

Invite participants to say a few sentences about themselves, but not to use the word "my." (*Or see Appendix A.*)

INDIVIDUAL GOALS

Ask each one in attendance (stutterers, facilitators, visitors) to identify a personal goal for the meeting, and share it with the group. Inform them that, at the end of the meeting, they will be reminded of their goals and have an opportunity to evaluate themselves. (If necessary, prompt ones who are having difficulty choosing a goal with some examples, like those in Appendix G.)

ACTIVITY

(Announce that participation in any activity is strictly voluntary. Everyone should join only those exercises with which they feel comfortable.)

1. Introduce the session's main theme: to explore stuttering without accessory or secondary behaviors or crutches. Each stutterer will identify, if possible, any acces-

sory behavior that he or she uses. Nonstuttering guests will be asked to fake a mild stutter and will be assigned the imaginary accessory behavior of using fillers such as "um," "like," or "you know" at any point.

2. Assign everyone a "monitoring partner" who will monitor his or her partner's accessory behaviors during a short speaking task. Inform stutterers that if they stutter, they should try to repeat or prolong the first syllable as tension-free as they can. They should try not to use the accessory behavior and, at the same time, resist the temptation to end the stutter as soon as possible. If any stuttering group member feels more comfortable using a therapy strategy, they may do so, as long as they try to stutter easily and concentrate on not using the accessory behavior. Each group member will then be asked to choose two very short impromptu speaking topics to talk about in front of the group. After speaking on both topics, the monitoring partner will then provide at least one statement of positive feedback and one of constructive criticism.

3. Ask group members to discuss the activity as follows: Why do stutterers use accessory behaviors? How did they feel concentrating on not doing the accessory behavior. Did it affect their stuttering in any way? How easy was it to monitor the accessory behavior and still communicate? What did they learn during the process?

4. Each group member will rate and discuss their success decreasing secondary behaviors and using "easy stuttering."

TAKEAWAY LESSONS

Encourage participants to share what stands out for them, or what they may have learned about themselves, their issues, and each other.

CONSIDER:

1. Accessory behaviors are typically learned, consciously or unconsciously, as ways to reduce the occurrence or severity of stuttering. Typically, they lose their effectiveness over time and often become incorporated into the stutter, thus making it worse.

2. By identifying and monitoring them, we can usually eliminate accessory behaviors, providing we are willing to accept a more overt form of stuttering.

3. Listeners often prefer overt, simple stuttering to stuttering that appears to be the result of trying to hide it.

INDIVIDUAL GOAL EVALUATIONS

Ask participants to go back to the goals they stated at the beginning of the meeting, and grade themselves on a scale from 1 to 10. They may share their grades with the group if they choose.

CLOSING WORDS

"For me, the key to fluency is in quitting trying not to stutter. Once I did this, my speech became much more fluent."

79. IMPROVING EYE CONTACT

PREPARATION

- At the beginning and end of the meeting, ask someone to read the Welcoming Words and Closing Words (*Appendix E*).
- Prepare index cards or slips of paper with different eye-contact techniques from Appendix C.

GOALS

1. To discuss and explore different eye-contact possibilities.
2. To gain experience in changing one's usual eye contact with listeners.

THE MEETING

WELCOMING WORDS

ICEBREAKER

Ask participants to describe a situation when they were mistaken for someone else and what they did. (*Or see Appendix A.*)

INDIVIDUAL GOALS

Ask each one in attendance (stutterers, facilitators, visitors) to identify a personal goal for the meeting, and share it with the group. Inform them that, at the end of the meeting, they will be reminded of their goals and have an opportunity to evaluate themselves. (If necessary, prompt ones who are having difficulty choosing a goal with some examples, like those in Appendix G.)

ACTIVITY

(Announce that participation in any activity is strictly voluntary. Everyone should join only those exercises with which they feel comfortable.)

1. Ask everyone to think of a recent routine, but annoying, experience they can talk about for a minute. If needed, give examples, like buying or trying to buy something, getting unwanted phone calls, cleaning up something at home, sitting in traffic, or a frustrating experience with a computer or other device.

2. Ask for a volunteer to turn to the person next to them and tell their brief story, as naturally as possible. Then, ask the partner to assume the speaker role and tell his or her story of annoyance in the same way.

3. Proceed around the room until everyone has shared a story with someone.

4. Ask each speaker to report on how effective they believe the eye contact was, during their time as speaker and listener.

5. Have each person draw a card or slip of paper, and tell their story again, and listen to their partner's story, using the listed eye contact technique.

6. Ask everyone to report their eye-contact instruction. Read any of the techniques that were not used by the group. Ask for discussion of which assigned eye-contact techniques were most distracting or irritating. Ask if anyone is aware of cultural differences in appropriate eye contact. Ask participants to think about their own usual eye contact and what could be improved.

TAKEAWAY LESSONS

Encourage participants to share what stands out for them, or what they may have learned about themselves, their issues, and each other.

CONSIDER:

1. Eye contact is an extremely important component in effective or ineffective communication in American culture.

2. A good way to learn about our eye contact is to talk to ourselves in a mirror for up to a half hour.

3. When our eye contact is too limited and we try to improve it, we will find ourselves staring as we learn a new habit. Such staring typically disappears after we learn better eye contact.

INDIVIDUAL GOAL EVALUATIONS

Ask participants to go back to the goals they stated at the beginning of the meeting, and grade themselves on a scale from 1 to 10. They may share their grades with the group if they choose.

CLOSING WORDS

80. EXPERIMENTING WITH FLUENCY SHAPING

PREPARATION

- Arrange to have a magazine or newspaper clipping available for everyone to read aloud.
- On slips of paper, write the following fluency shaping "targets": a) *Slow Rate*—speak very slowly, b) *Light Contact*—take a normal breath and begin speaking with as little tension as possible in the lips and tongue, c) *Easy Voice Onset*—begin speaking by letting a little air out like a slight /h/ sound on voiced sounds, and d) *"Continuous Phonation"*—speak while keeping your voice on longer than usual and running your words together without clear breaks between them. Be prepared to explain these fluency shaping targets from the glossary (*Appendix H*).
- Select a list of impromptu speaking topics from Appendix B.
- At the beginning and end of the meeting, ask someone to read the Welcoming Words and Closing Words (*Appendix E*).

GOALS

1. To experiment with fluency shaping targets.
2. To discuss fluency shaping as a treatment option available to stutterers.

THE MEETING

WELCOMING WORDS

ICEBREAKER

Ask everyone to write the following sentence on a sheet of paper in careful, neat cursive if they can: "Speaking with fluency shaping is a little like writing in cursive." Ask them to pass around their samples. (*Or see Appendix A.*)

INDIVIDUAL GOALS

Ask each one in attendance (stutterers, facilitators, visitors) to identify a personal goal for the meeting, and share it with the group. Inform them that, at the end of the meeting, they will be reminded of their goals and have an opportunity to evaluate themselves. (If necessary, prompt ones who are having difficulty choosing a goal with some examples, like those in Appendix G.)

ACTIVITY

(Announce that participation in any activity is strictly voluntary. Everyone should join only those exercises with which they feel comfortable.)

1. Explain that the session will focus on experimenting with "fluency shaping." Emphasize that the goal is not to advocate for these approaches or to help stuttering but to help everyone get a sense of how concentrating on speech in a deliberate, somewhat unnatural way can result in less stuttering.

2. Hand out the magazine or newpaper clippings to everyone and ask them, one at a time, to read aloud for about five sentences while following the instructions on the slip of paper. Before they begin reading, ask them to disclose their instructions to the group. Ask for clarification in advance if anyone is uncertain of what to do. Ask nonstutterers to follow the same instructions.

3. Invite individual sharing of what participants were asked to do. Were they able to change their speech by slowing down, using light contact, using easy voice onset, or "continuous phonation?" Was their stuttering affected during these trials? How did this exercise affect their sense of "control" in any way?

4. For anyone who wishes to try, hand out impromptu speaking topics and ask them to try their assigned target, or another target, while speaking for about 30–60 seconds. Ask them to report how successful they were and any other insights.

5. Ask stutterers who learned any of these fluency shaping strategies in individual speech therapy to share any experiences they have had in using them. Invite discussion of the extent to which they found the techniques useful.

TAKEAWAY LESSONS

Encourage participants to share what stands out for them, or what they may have learned about themselves, their issues, and each other.

CONSIDER:

1. Fluency shaping is a bit like singing speech. In almost all stutterers, no stuttering occurs when they sing. Singing uses the voice, articulators, and breathing differently than in normal spontaneous speech.

2. Fluency shaping is sometimes called a "speak more fluently" approach versus "stuttering modification," which can be called a "stutter more fluently" approach. In fluency shaping, the emphasis is not at all on the stuttering. If a stutterer can focus attention on the "targets" (or new ways of speaking in a slightly unnatural way), the stuttering often drops out.

3. Fluency shaping is a widely-used speech therapy strategy in stuttering. Common "targets" are *Slow Rate, Light Contact, Easy Voice Onset, and "Continuous Phonation"* (*See the glossary in Appendix H.*) Fluency shaping should be taught and practiced under the direction of a capable speech-language pathologist who is trained in its use because, if not taught well, the resulting speech can sound very unnatural or robotic. Or, the "targets" can become accessory behaviors.

INDIVIDUAL GOAL EVALUATIONS

Ask participants to go back to the goals they stated at the beginning of the meeting, and grade themselves on a scale from 1 to 10. They may share their grades with the group if they choose.

CLOSING WORDS

"I try to talk in cursive."

81. EXPERIMENTING WITH CONTROLLING OR CHANGING STUTTERING

PREPARATION

- Select a list of impromptu speaking topics from Appendix B and write them on slips of paper. On alternate slips of paper, add a type of stuttering, i.e., stutter as you usually do but longer, stutter with at least 5 repetitions of a beginning syllable (e.g., "li-li-li-li-li-li-li-like"), stutter with at least a 3-second prolongation on an initial syllable (e.g., "mmmmmmmmmmmmmmmmm[4 sec]maybe"), or stutter with a block of at least 3 seconds (e.g, "go----------------------------[4 sec tense silence]—ld").
- Have access to a whiteboard or other display device.
- At the beginning and end of the meeting, ask someone to read the Welcoming Words and Closing Words (*Appendix E*).

GOALS

1. To experiment with stuttering modification voluntary control techniques.
2. To explore and discuss stuttering modification as a treatment option available to stutterers in order to have more control over their stuttering.

THE MEETING

WELCOMING WORDS

ICEBREAKER

Ask participants to share what it takes for them to have the perfect night's sleep. (*Or see Appendix A.*)

INDIVIDUAL GOALS

Ask each one in attendance (stutterers, facilitators, visitors) to identify a personal goal for the meeting, and share it with the group. Inform them that, at the end of the meeting, they will be reminded of their goals and have an opportunity to evaluate themselves. (If necessary, prompt ones who are having difficulty choosing a goal with some examples, like those in Appendix G.)

ACTIVITY

(Announce that participation in any activity is strictly voluntary. Everyone should join only those exercises with which they feel comfortable.)

1. Explain that the session will focus on "controlling stuttering." Emphasize that the goal is not to help stuttering but to get a sense of what aspects of stuttering might be "controlled" or changed.

2. Hand out the slips of paper to everyone and ask them, one at a time, to talk about the topic while following the instructions on the other paper. If they do not stutter for real, have them fake a stutter on a word and try to follow the instructions. Ask in advance if anyone is uncertain of what to do and clarify. Ask nonstutterers to follow the same instructions while faking stuttering in a way they believe would be perceived as real stuttering.

3. Invite participants to share with the group what they were asked to do. Were they able to stutter for real in a different way? Were they able to fake stutter in a different way? How did this exercise affect their sense of "control" in any way?

4. Ask stutterers to share any experiences they have had in "controlling" or changing their actual stuttering (not their feelings or thoughts about it). Arrange for a volunteer to write these experiences or strategies on a whiteboard.

TAKEAWAY LESSONS

Encourage participants to share what stands out for them, or what they may have learned about themselves, their issues, and each other.

CONSIDER:

1. The form of our stuttering does and can change, and, although we typically cannot "stop stuttering," we can control or change the way that we stutter.

2. Controlling stuttering is a common speech therapy strategy. The most common "voluntary controls" are the stuttering modification techniques of cancellation, pull-out, and preparatory set. (*See the glossary in Appendix H.*) These strategies should be taught and practiced under the direction of a capable, speech-language pathologist who is trained in their use because, if not taught well, they can become ineffective accessory behaviors.

INDIVIDUAL GOAL EVALUATIONS

Ask participants to go back to the goals they stated at the beginning of the meeting, and grade themselves on a scale from 1 to 10. They may share their grades with the group if they choose.

CLOSING WORDS

"I have more confidence since I learned some controls of stuttering, and I'm not scared of interacting with people now."

82. WHEN A LOVED ONE DOES NOT UNDERSTAND

PREPARATION
- At the beginning and end of the meeting, ask someone to read the Welcoming Words and Closing Words (*Appendix E*).

GOALS
1. To appreciate how views of stuttering are influenced by the views of our family and close friends.
2. To explore ways to better react to loved-ones' misunderstandings.

THE MEETING

WELCOMING WORDS

ICEBREAKER
Ask people to talk about a funny or embarrassing time when they said or did the wrong thing and wished they could have a do-over. (*Or see Appendix A.*)

INDIVIDUAL GOALS
Ask each one in attendance (stutterers, facilitators, visitors) to identify a personal goal for the meeting, and share it with the group. Inform them that, at the end of the meeting, they will be reminded of their goals and have an opportunity to evaluate themselves. (If necessary, prompt ones who are having difficulty choosing a goal with some examples, like those in Appendix G.)

ACTIVITY
(Announce that participation in any activity is strictly voluntary. Everyone should join only those exercises with which they feel comfortable.)

1. Ask everyone to think of a situation when they were having an especially difficult time with stuttering (or another serious challenge), and someone they should have been able to count on for support and understanding let them down. This could be a family member, a close friend, or someone else in their inner circle of trust, who did not understand the situation or did not give the support they could have. Or it

could be a time when negativity or lack of understanding came as a surprise, from someone they did not expect to behave that way. Have each person in turn describe the situation, and tell how they reacted.

2. Ask everyone to think about the situation they just related and consider the following questions about it: Did anything in their own behavior or reactions make the situation worse? Do they have a better understanding now of what might have sparked the disappointing behavior of the other person? If they had it to do over, how would they act differently? Are they developing better techniques or deeper understanding, so they might be better able to handle this type of difficult situation in the future?

TAKEAWAY LESSONS

Encourage participants to share what stands out for them, or what they may have learned about themselves, their issues, and each other.

CONSIDER:

1. Listeners take their cues from us. If we're uncomfortable with our stuttering, it is likely that they will be too. By contrast, if we're okay with it, they likely will be too.

2. The people who really care about us will stick around. We need to learn to spend less time and energy with people who fail to support us.

3. Self-advocating and educating our family and friends about stuttering can help these people be more supportive of us.

INDIVIDUAL GOAL EVALUATIONS

Ask participants to go back to the goals they stated at the beginning of the meeting, and grade themselves on a scale from 1 to 10. They may share their grades with the group if they choose.

CLOSING WORDS

83. FRIENDS, FAMILY, AND STUTTERING

PREPARATION

- Bring to the meeting a number of items that some people particularly like, such as an athletic jersey, a labeled hat, a golf club, a tube of lipstick, a bike helmet, a novel, a computer, a guitar, etc.
- At the beginning and end of the meeting, ask someone to read the Welcoming Words and Closing Words (*Appendix E*).

GOALS

1. To understand the feelings or motivations of family members or friends who reacted in negative ways to those who stutter.
2. To reprocess old, negative messages from family and friends.

THE MEETING

WELCOMING WORDS

ICEBREAKER

Have members select an object from the table to symbolize one of their alter egos, in other words, a secondary or alternative personality. Ask them to explain. (*Or see Appendix A.*)

INDIVIDUAL GOALS

Ask each one in attendance (stutterers, facilitators, visitors) to identify a personal goal for the meeting, and share it with the group. Inform them that, at the end of the meeting, they will be reminded of their goals and have an opportunity to evaluate themselves. (If necessary, prompt ones who are having difficulty choosing a goal with some examples, like those in Appendix G.)

ACTIVITY

(Announce that participation in any activity is strictly voluntary. Everyone should join only those exercises with which they feel comfortable.)

1. Ask each stutterer to think of a family member or friend—or someone else who is or has been significant in their lives—who either now or in the past sometimes has/

had difficulty dealing with their stuttering. For nonstutterers, ask that they pick a troubling issue that someone has had difficulty accepting or dealing with.

2. Ask each one who is willing to participate to imagine that they are that person who has/had difficulty dealing with stuttering or another issue. Ask participants to imagine that the roles are reversed, and they are that person, speaking to themselves. Set up two chairs facing each other and let the participant (as the other person) talk to their imaginary self in the opposite chair. Begin speaking with "When you stutter …"

3. After everyone has had a turn, ask each participant to relate his/her experience talking to himself/herself in this way.

4. Next, if they are willing, ask the stutterers to repeat the imaginary dialogue, but this time, in the other chair as themselves and responding to what the person who did not deal with their stuttering probably thought or may have said.

5. Invite discussion of what we can and cannot do when others are not fully accepting of our differences.

TAKEAWAY LESSONS

Encourage participants to share what stands out for them, or what they may have learned about themselves, their issues, and each other.

CONSIDER:

1. Our self-perceptions of stuttering are affected by the views of others, especially when we were children.

2. Recognition of others' discomfort and bringing it up to family and friends can promote healing through open communication.

3. Some people may not even know they are sending negative messages regarding our stuttering and may stop immediately if we simply tell them.

INDIVIDUAL GOAL EVALUATIONS

Ask participants to go back to the goals they stated at the beginning of the meeting, and grade themselves on a scale from 1 to 10. They may share their grades with the group if they choose.

CLOSING WORDS

84. HANDLING NEW SITUATIONS AND NEW PEOPLE

PREPARATION

- At the beginning and end of the meeting, ask someone to read the Welcoming Words and Closing Words (*Appendix E*).

GOALS

1. To share strategies participants use in potentially stressful communication situations and to discuss their effectiveness.

2. To improve abilities to meet new people in large groups.

THE MEETING

WELCOMING WORDS

ICEBREAKER

Ask participants what they did and what they felt when they thought someone was waving at them but then discovered that the person was waving at someone behind them. (*Or see Appendix A.*)

INDIVIDUAL GOALS

Ask each one in attendance (stutterers, facilitators, visitors) to identify a personal goal for the meeting, and share it with the group. Inform them that, at the end of the meeting, they will be reminded of their goals and have an opportunity to evaluate themselves. (If necessary, prompt ones who are having difficulty choosing a goal with some examples, like those in Appendix G.)

ACTIVITY

(Announce that participation in any activity is strictly voluntary. Everyone should join only those exercises with which they feel comfortable.)

1. Invite discussion of different strategies participants use when meeting a new person. What behaviors have worked well for them? What has not worked? Are there examples of a time when things went terribly wrong? Do people approach different situations in different ways, and if so, what factors make a difference?

2. Invite the same discussion as it applies to meeting people in a large group.

TAKEAWAY LESSONS

Encourage participants to share what stands out for them, or what they may have learned about themselves, their issues, and each other.

CONSIDER:

1. People, especially strangers, have different reactions toward our stuttering, primarily due to the fact that they are surprised or "taken aback" by the first appearance of stuttering.

2. We can learn a variety of effective strategies when meeting someone for the first time, e.g., acting in a confident manner (even if we don't feel confident), using humor, using fluency-enhancing strategies that have been helpful in the past, and trying not to focus only on negative outcomes.

3. If a conversational partner is insincere or disrespectful, we can deal with the situation most effectively by being assertive and honest about our stuttering and our feelings.

INDIVIDUAL GOAL EVALUATIONS

Ask participants to go back to the goals they stated at the beginning of the meeting, and grade themselves on a scale from 1 to 10. They may share their grades with the group if they choose.

CLOSING WORDS

85. "SPEED DATING" AND STUTTERING

PREPARATION

- This session would be particularly appropriate when a number of stutterers and nonstuttering guests are likely to be present. Based on the number present, decide how much time will be allotted to the "speed dating" activity, in order to leave time for discussion after it.
- Arrange to have one movable chair for each participant.
- At the beginning and end of the meeting, ask someone to read the Welcoming Words and Closing Words (*Appendix E*).

GOALS

1. To practice get-acquainted conversation, both trivial and a little serious.
2. To share the emotions provoked by the exercise.

THE MEETING

WELCOMING WORDS

ICEBREAKER

Ask participants to share a personal story about a time in which they did something outrageous or completely out of character. (*Or see Appendix A.*)

INDIVIDUAL GOALS

Ask each one in attendance (stutterers, facilitators, visitors) to identify a personal goal for the meeting, and share it with the group. Inform them that, at the end of the meeting, they will be reminded of their goals and have an opportunity to evaluate themselves. (If necessary, prompt ones who are having difficulty choosing a goal with some examples, like those in Appendix G.)

ACTIVITY

(Announce that participation in any activity is strictly voluntary. Everyone should join only those exercises with which they feel comfortable.)

1. Introduce the concept of "speed dating," or getting acquainted with a stranger and "putting your best foot forward" in a very short period of time. This most likely will not be for getting a date but to meet lots of people quickly, network in business, or screen applicants for a job.

2. Arrange enough pairs of chairs facing each other for all the participants with as much space as is practical between the groups. Ask participants to stand. Choose half of the group, and tell them they are the "sitters," and ask them to each sit facing an empty chair. Tell the remaining half of the group that they are the "movers," and will be briefly talking to a sitter and then moving on to another sitter. Explain that the movers will sit facing a sitter, and introduce themselves in the best possible light for a minute, then they will switch roles and the sitter will talk for a minute. At the end of the two minutes, the movers will all stand and move on to another sitter to repeat the exercise. Begin the exercise, and in each round allow about a minute for the first speaker, then call out "switch speakers." After about another minute, call out "switch partners."

3. After half the activity time is up, stop the exercise, have everyone stand, and divide the group again into sitters and movers, with some different members in each of these. Explain that, this time, each participant will tell about a time he or she was embarrassed at their behavior or disappointed in themselves.

4. After the exercise, move the chairs back into discussion formation and talk about the experience. Which of the two kinds of conversation was more fun, more uncomfortable, and more satisfying? For the stutterers, was there a difference in stuttering or fluency between the two halves of the exercise? Did the stutterers disclose their stuttering, and if so, how?

TAKEAWAY LESSONS

Encourage participants to share what stands out for them, or what they may have learned about themselves, their issues, and each other.

CONSIDER:

1. Whereas "speed dating" activities are popular in our culture, they can be extremely stress-inducing for fluent speakers and for stutterers.

2. When we need to make a good impression quickly, verbal skills become very important.

3. We typically do better in "speed dating" activities if we disclose our stuttering early. Beyond that, other communication skills are important, such as good eye contact and pleasant demeanor.

INDIVIDUAL GOAL EVALUATIONS

Ask participants to go back to the goals they stated at the beginning of the meeting, and grade themselves on a scale from 1 to 10. They may share their grades with the group if they choose.

CLOSING WORDS

"When I first started stuttering 10 years ago, I had a lot of people there trying to throw in their advice and trying to support me. But what helped me the most was listening to the stories of other people who stuttered."

86. REDUCING AUDIENCE PRESSURE

PREPARATION

- Prepare two sets of index cards, with a topic for a short speech on each one. Make enough of each set for the largest number of people likely to attend. On one set, write neutral topics, and on the other set, controversial topics that require careful thought and are likely to evoke strong emotion in the audience or even start an argument. *(For some topics, see Appendix B.)*
- At the beginning and end of the meeting, ask someone to read the Welcoming Words and Closing Words *(Appendix E)*.

GOALS

1. To practice public speaking in a fun and safe environment.
2. To explore how topic difficulty can affect stuttering.

THE MEETING

WELCOMING WORDS

ICEBREAKER

Ask participants to explain what they would do in the following scenario. "You are with several friends at a restaurant. You have not decided what you want to order and everyone is waiting on you. You earlier told the waitress to start with the others, but they have ordered and it is now your turn. You still are not sure what you want." *(Or see Appendix A.)*

INDIVIDUAL GOALS

Ask each one in attendance (stutterers, facilitators, visitors) to identify a personal goal for the meeting, and share it with the group. Inform them that, at the end of the meeting, they will be reminded of their goals and have an opportunity to evaluate themselves. (If necessary, prompt ones who are having difficulty choosing a goal with some examples, like those in Appendix G.)

ACTIVITY

(Announce that participation in any activity is strictly voluntary. Everyone should join only those exercises with which they feel comfortable.)

1. Inform the participants that each of them will be making two brief speeches. They will be handed a topic, then given a few seconds to think before making a speech of approximately 60–90 seconds. Discussion will follow, after all the speeches are over.

2. Ask for volunteers, or call on participants to take turns making a speech. As each participant comes to the front, hand him or her a card from the first set. Pass out cards to everyone, and ask them to appear very interested in topics and all speakers.

3. Repeat the exercise, handing out topics from the second set. Pass out cards to everyone asking them to be very unsupportive of the speaker and to show nonverbal disagreement with what he/she is saying.

4. Ask for discussion of the stress level the speakers experienced before the speeches began and during the two speeches. Was there any difference in stuttering or normal speech disfluencies (e.g., "uhs," "ums," "likes" or "you knows") when the topics were more difficult? What other factors make a difference in giving speeches, both during this meeting and in general?

TAKEAWAY LESSONS

Encourage participants to share what stands out for them, or what they may have learned about themselves, their issues, and each other.

CONSIDER:

1. Difficulty or controversy surrounding various topics may or may not make a difference in our stuttering in public speaking situations.

2. If an audience is generally not responding positively, it can be helpful to find a person with "kind eyes" and talk only to that person.

3. Practice may not make us perfect, but practice will make us better public speakers.

INDIVIDUAL GOAL EVALUATIONS

Ask participants to go back to the goals they stated at the beginning of the meeting, and grade themselves on a scale from 1 to 10. They may share their grades with the group if they choose.

CLOSING WORDS

87. MANAGING TIME PRESSURE

PREPARATION

- (Optional) Have donuts for the group, to be handed out during the activity.
- At the beginning and end of the meeting, ask someone to read the Welcoming Words and Closing Words (*Appendix E*).

GOALS

1. To become aware of situations often associated with time pressure.
2. To recognize and explore the usefulness of strategies that might be effective when confronting time pressure.

THE MEETING

WELCOMING WORDS

ICEBREAKER

What is your morning routine? What would it be like if you overslept and had only 5 minutes to get ready? (*Or see Appendix A.*)

INDIVIDUAL GOALS

Ask each one in attendance (stutterers, facilitators, visitors) to identify a personal goal for the meeting, and share it with the group. Inform them that, at the end of the meeting, they will be reminded of their goals and have an opportunity to evaluate themselves. (If necessary, prompt ones who are having difficulty choosing a goal with some examples, like those in Appendix G.)

ACTIVITY

(Announce that participation in any activity is strictly voluntary. Everyone should join only those exercises with which they feel comfortable.)

1. Ask participants to, one at a time, take a donut (or imagine they have a donut, if none are available), stand in front of the group, and take exactly one minute to explain to the judges in a donut competition why theirs deserves the prize. The leader will say "STOP" after one minute. (Participants may eat their donuts after their presentation.)

2. Have each one talk about how they did in their presentation, including one thing they did well and one thing they could have done better.

3. Ask each person to think of a social situation in which they faced time pressure. Examples might be answering a question in class, introducing themselves to a stranger, ordering food in a drive-thru, meeting a new boss, or explaining how to do something. Invite discussion of how the situation went, and how it could have been handled better.

TAKEAWAY LESSONS

Encourage participants to share what stands out for them, or what they may have learned about themselves, their issues, and each other.

CONSIDER:

1. Time pressure is a fact of life, and when it is there, our stuttering may get worse. A healthy dose of self-acceptance is helpful when this happens.

2. Strategies such as deliberate pausing or planning can help in time-pressured situations.

3. The more times we enter time-pressured situations, the more opportunities we have to manage them more effectively.

INDIVIDUAL GOAL EVALUATIONS

Ask participants to go back to the goals they stated at the beginning of the meeting, and grade themselves on a scale from 1 to 10. They may share their grades with the group if they choose.

CLOSING WORDS

88. BUILDING CONFIDENCE

PREPARATION

- Write down the names and phone numbers of several local hotels or motels. Get at least as many as there will be people at the meeting. Write down the details of a fictional room reservation—an arrival and departure date, number of beds needed, etc.
- Have access to a whiteboard or other display device.
- At the beginning and end of the meeting, ask someone to read the Welcoming Words and Closing Words (*Appendix E*).

GOALS

1. To consider how confidence can improve our daily living.
2. To identify strategies to promote self-confidence.

THE MEETING

WELCOMING WORDS

ICEBREAKER

Ask the group what they would do if they accepted a dare to jump in a lake naked, but when they got out of the lake they noticed their clothes were gone. (*Or see Appendix A.*)

INDIVIDUAL GOALS

Ask each one in attendance (stutterers, facilitators, visitors) to identify a personal goal for the meeting, and share it with the group. Inform them that, at the end of the meeting, they will be reminded of their goals and have an opportunity to evaluate themselves. (If necessary, prompt ones who are having difficulty choosing a goal with some examples, like those in Appendix G.)

ACTIVITY

(Announce that participation in any activity is strictly voluntary. Everyone should join only those exercises with which they feel comfortable.)

1. Ask each person to rate their confidence level on a scale from 1 to 10 if they were required to make a phone call to a local business, and briefly explain why they gave themselves that rating.

2. Have each person in the group call a hotel or motel and ask if a room is available for the dates listed. Decide whether they will make the calls one at a time with the others observing, or make the calls at the same time. After the calls, ask each person to comment on how their call went and their anxiety level.

3. Tell the group that they will be making a second call, and ask them to rate their confidence level again on the 1–10 scale and comment on their rating. Ask the group to discuss how their confidence level changed as they thought about the second call, and why. Then, inform the group that this second call will not in fact be made, but was brought up as a starting point for conversation.

4. Ask the group what confidence means. List key words from the responses on a whiteboard or other display medium, if available, or on paper.

5. Ask the nonstutterers to think of an insecurity or personal issue that creates anxiety or low self-esteem. Ask the group to discuss how confidence relates to stuttering or to another issue for nonstutterers.

6. Ask if anyone has advice for someone who wants to increase their self-confidence.

TAKEAWAY LESSONS

Encourage participants to share what stands out for them, or what they may have learned about themselves, their issues, and each other.

CONSIDER:

1. As we grow in various skills, our confidence improves.

2. Increasing our self-confidence can improve our daily living and our life satisfaction.

3. The more confident we become, the less we worry about stuttering; therefore, we could potentially stutter less.

INDIVIDUAL GOAL EVALUATIONS

Ask participants to go back to the goals they stated at the beginning of the meeting, and grade themselves on a scale from 1 to 10. They may share their grades with the group if they choose.

CLOSING WORDS

89. HANDLING HOLIDAY STRESS

PREPARATION

- At the beginning and end of the meeting, ask someone to read the Welcoming Words and Closing Words (*Appendix E*).

GOALS

1. To explore concerns about anticipated holiday stress.
2. To consider strategies for coping with stuttering-related holiday stress.

THE MEETING

WELCOMING WORDS

ICEBREAKER

Ask participants to explain how they typically do their gift shopping, such as for Christmas, Hanukkah, an anniversary, or a birthday. (*Or see Appendix A.*)

INDIVIDUAL GOALS

Ask each one in attendance (stutterers, facilitators, visitors) to identify a personal goal for the meeting, and share it with the group. Inform them that, at the end of the meeting, they will be reminded of their goals and have an opportunity to evaluate themselves. (If necessary, prompt ones who are having difficulty choosing a goal with some examples, like those in Appendix G.)

ACTIVITY

(Announce that participation in any activity is strictly voluntary. Everyone should join only those exercises with which they feel comfortable.)

1. Ask everyone in attendance to think of an issue—other than stuttering—that causes them trouble or anxiety during the holidays and to share it with the group.

2. Ask participants to share any strategies they have found, which help or do not help, in trying to cope with this issue.

3. Ask stutterers whether their stuttering causes any extra anxiety or difficulty during the holidays and what they do to cope with it.

TAKEAWAY LESSONS

Encourage participants to share what stands out for them, or what they may have learned about themselves, their issues, and each other.

CONSIDER:

1. Whereas most people enjoy the holidays, some people find it a very stressful time.

2. Our stuttering may get better or worse during holiday festivities.

3. Discussing holiday stress may either reduce its negative effect on stuttering, or it may help in making sense of negative effects after the holidays are over.

INDIVIDUAL GOAL EVALUATIONS

Ask participants to go back to the goals they stated at the beginning of the meeting, and grade themselves on a scale from 1 to 10. They may share their grades with the group if they choose.

CLOSING WORDS

90. STAYING THE COURSE TO MAINTAIN GAINS IN STUTTERING

PREPARATION
- Have access to a whiteboard or other display device.
- On half of the whiteboard, write the following list of goals. (The other half of the board is for ideas, which will be generated during the meeting.)
  » become a nonsmoker after previous heavy smoking
  » maintain a healthy weight after being overweight
  » maintain a healthy diet
  » having organized finances after serious financial problems
  » maintaining a lifestyle of exercising regularly
  » keeping a clean house long term
  » drinking moderately or not at all after previous excessive drinking
  » saving money regularly throughout one's earning career after previous failure to do so
- At the beginning and end of the meeting, ask someone to read the Welcoming Words and Closing Words (*Appendix E*).

GOALS
1. To understand that maintaining a new habit or life change requires continued effort.
2. To explore different possible reactions to failure or relapse.
3. To discuss various strategies for maintenance, including which may be more effective for different people or situations.

THE MEETING

WELCOMING WORDS

ICEBREAKER
Ask participants to share a personal goal or resolution they have set, but which did not last very long. (*Or see Appendix A.*)

INDIVIDUAL GOALS

Ask each one in attendance (stutterers, facilitators, visitors) to identify a personal goal for the meeting, and share it with the group. Inform them that, at the end of the meeting, they will be reminded of their goals and have an opportunity to evaluate themselves. (If necessary, prompt ones who are having difficulty choosing a goal with some examples, like those in Appendix G.)

ACTIVITY

(Announce that participation in any activity is strictly voluntary. Everyone should join only those exercises with which they feel comfortable.)

1. Explain that making a major life change is difficult, but assume you have done that. Now, how are we to maintain those gains? A wide range of obstacles face anyone who's trying to maintain a life change, depending on the change, the individual, and one's life circumstances.

2. Refer to the list of goals on the board. Introduce the goals one at a time and invite discussion of obstacles that might be likely to face people with each goal as they try to maintain their gains. Next, ask what strategies might be useful in facing these obstacles and maintaining focus. (If ideas are not forthcoming, suggest possibilities like: partner/family/friends not supportive, stressful life events, fear of failure, fear of negative secondary consequences, significant commitment required, or embarrassment at acknowledging the goal.) List the maintenance techniques on the open side of the board. Allow a few minutes for participants to react to each of the goals.

3. Ask the participants to think about maintaining any gains they have achieved regarding their stuttering or their feelings about it. Nonstutterers should consider any other communication issues. Add any new maintenance goal to the list on the whiteboard, and ask for any additional obstacles.

4. Ask the stutterers what strategies or techniques they have used to overcome the obstacles relating to their stuttering.

TAKEAWAY LESSONS

Encourage participants to share what stands out for them, or what they may have learned about themselves, their issues, and each other.

CONSIDER:

1. Making any significant life change is difficult. Yet, even when successful, maintaining the gains requires overcoming different problems with different solutions.

2. Regression, back-sliding, or relapse are facts of life in managing most major life changes, including those related to stuttering. One reason for this is that our self-concepts change much more slowly than our behavior.

3. Maintaining gains in stuttering poses some special obstacles related to the nature of stuttering, such as its inherent variability and its genetic nature.

INDIVIDUAL GOAL EVALUATIONS

Ask participants to go back to the goals they stated at the beginning of the meeting, and grade themselves on a scale from 1 to 10. They may share their grades with the group if they choose.

CLOSING WORDS

"I started coming 3 ½ years ago when I was a freshman in college. I realized I needed to make a change with my speech."

91. PROS AND CONS OF "QUICK FIXES" FOR STUTTERING

PREPARATION

- Have available a box of Tic-Tacs, a package of Laffy Taffy, a box of saltine crackers, bottles of water, and a timer.
- At the beginning and end of the meeting, ask someone to read the Welcoming Words and Closing Words (*Appendix E*).

GOALS

1. To explore the pros and cons of "quick fixes" for stuttering and another problem.
2. To gain insight into reasons why various quick-fix strategies for stuttering are adopted.

THE MEETING

WELCOMING WORDS

ICEBREAKER

Give everyone a bottle of water and a Tic-Tac. Ask them to swallow the Tic-Tac like a pill, rather than chewing it. (*Or see Appendix A.*)

INDIVIDUAL GOALS

Ask each one in attendance (stutterers, facilitators, visitors) to identify a personal goal for the meeting, and share it with the group. Inform them that, at the end of the meeting, they will be reminded of their goals and have an opportunity to evaluate themselves. (If necessary, prompt ones who are having difficulty choosing a goal with some examples, like those in Appendix G.)

ACTIVITY

(Announce that participation in any activity is strictly voluntary. Everyone should join only those exercises with which they feel comfortable.)

1. Tell the group to assume that three different pills will eliminate stuttering (or for the nonstutterers, narcolepsy), but each pill would eliminate the condition for a

different period of time. The three pills that reduce stuttering (or narcolepsy) represent different risk-benefit ratios. One needs to be taken four-times-a-day, another twice-a-day, and the third once-a-week. Each of them has potential side effects; the four times a day pill could cause dry mouth, the twice a day pill could cause fluid retention and weight gain, and the once a week pill could cause Parkinson-like shakiness or tremors.

2. Now ask each group member to choose which pill they would take for their stuttering or narcolepsy. After they choose, the leader will explain that this will be an ongoing activity throughout the session. Each member will be asked to "take your pill" when necessary. There are different foods to consume as a representation of the different pills: Tic-Tacs (not chewed but taken with water), Laffy Taffy (eaten as quickly as possible), and crackers (eaten quickly without water). Those who chose the four-times-a-day pill would have to swallow a Tic-Tac every 5 minutes, when indicated by the leader (use timer). Choosers of the twice-a-day pill would have to eat two Laffy Taffys as fast as possible every 10 minutes. Lastly, those who chose a once-a-week pill will have to eat four saltine crackers (with no water), one after another, every 15 minutes.

3. At this point, members may change their pill but are reminded that it is not so much about the pills' type and quantity, but more about taking them when they are told.

4. Ask the participants to imagine the following scenario: "You have been chosen to be a groomsman or a bridesmaid at a close friend's wedding. You were given three tasks to complete throughout the day of the wedding. The tasks were a) to get everyone organized for a group photo, b) to call the limousine company and give the driver directions on how to get to the chapel because they are late, and c) to give a toast at the wedding reception." One at a time, ask participants to explain how they would accomplish each of these tasks. As participants explain what they would do, every five minutes, say, "Take your pill." Participants must take a Tic-Tac, eat two Laffy Taffys, or eat four crackers, according to the schedule.

5. After 30–45 minutes, inform the group that they have now finished taking their "pills," which they chose earlier. Ask each group member to address why they would or would not take a "pill," with the same "schedule and 'side effects,'" that would reduce narcolepsy. If so, in what situations would they take it? Then, ask the same question in relation to stuttering.

6. Invite any further discussion of anyone's experience searching for or trying a quick fix for stuttering.

TAKEAWAY LESSONS

Encourage participants to share what stands out for them, or what they may have learned about themselves, their issues, and each other.

CONSIDER:

1. The popular press, internet, and social media regularly feature or promote quick fixes for stuttering, but they typically only provide temporary relief, similar to the immediate fluency many of us experience when we read aloud with another person. While some of the medications, devices, and techniques could potentially reduce our stuttering, often the side effects (or cost in time, money, and effort) are worse than the benefits.

2. Businesses often prey on stutterers seeking cures. Unfortunately, there is no "pill" or quick fix for stuttering.

3. Continuously searching for a quick fix for stuttering can take away from our personal growth and identity.

INDIVIDUAL GOAL EVALUATIONS

Ask participants to go back to the goals they stated at the beginning of the meeting, and grade themselves on a scale from 1 to 10. They may share their grades with the group if they choose.

CLOSING WORDS

"When I started, I just wanted to do anything to get rid of my stutter."

92. UNDERSTANDING RELAPSE

PREPARATION

- Have access to a whiteboard or other display device.
- At the beginning and end of the meeting, ask someone to read the Welcoming Words and Closing Words (*Appendix E*).

GOALS

1. To examine the factors that could cause stutterers to slip back from their fluency level.
2. To share individual experiences relating to relapse.

THE MEETING

WELCOMING WORDS

ICEBREAKER

Ask participants to report their last New Year's resolution and whether they kept it. (*Or see Appendix A.*)

INDIVIDUAL GOALS

Ask each one in attendance (stutterers, facilitators, visitors) to identify a personal goal for the meeting, and share it with the group. Inform them that, at the end of the meeting, they will be reminded of their goals and have an opportunity to evaluate themselves. (If necessary, prompt ones who are having difficulty choosing a goal with some examples, like those in Appendix G.)

ACTIVITY

(Announce that participation in any activity is strictly voluntary. Everyone should join only those exercises with which they feel comfortable.)

1. Introduce the topic of stuttering relapse, a slipping back or return to worse stuttering after achieving a greater degree of fluency. It is the opposite of maintaining one's gains.

2. Ask participants to share a time when they really wanted to accomplish something, but were unable to stick with it to completion.

3. Ask the group to share some of the reasons they believe they were unable to stick with their plans. Have someone list these reasons, in a few words each, on the whiteboard. Encourage the group to discuss which factors they thought were most important.

4. Ask stutterers to talk about times when they had a relapse in stuttering or when stuttering got much worse than it had been for some time. Ask if they are aware of why the relapse occurred, and if so, to add those reasons to the list on the whiteboard.

5. Invite discussion on relapse of stuttering. As they discuss this, have them compare the reasons for stuttering relapse with those listed on the board.

6. Have the group consider which of the reasons on the list are applicable or are not applicable to stuttering relapse, and what additional factors need to be added as especially relevant to stuttering.

TAKEAWAY LESSONS

Encourage participants to share what stands out for them, or what they may have learned about themselves, their issues, and each other.

CONSIDER:

1. Relapse in stuttering can be a frightening experience.

2. Relapse in stuttering does not happen to everyone, but it happens quite often. We are advised to be aware of the reality and likelihood of relapse.

3. Many speech-language pathologists are unaware—or perhaps afraid—of relapse in their stuttering clients. Therefore, it is not uncommon for them never to mention relapse.

4. There are many reasons for relapse. A few of them are

   » We do not have sufficient skills to remain stutter-free in all kinds of life situations.

   » As we become successful in managing stuttering, little stutters go unnoticed and are thereby "reinforced." This may occur for a while, but, suddenly, we find ourselves stuttering as much as ever.

   » We sometimes have the suspicion that we are destined for failure, so we fail to take the necessary risk in self-disclosure to adopt a new identity as a more fluent speaker.

- » Our old fears tend to come back with time and lead us to a new cycle of avoidance.
- » We may have difficulty adjusting to a new identity. "We feel like unwelcome strangers to ourselves."
- » We may just get weary of worrying about our speech and would rather stutter.

INDIVIDUAL GOAL EVALUATIONS

Ask participants to go back to the goals they stated at the beginning of the meeting, and grade themselves on a scale from 1 to 10. They may share their grades with the group if they choose.

CLOSING WORDS

"Some days will be good, and some will be bad."

93. CREATING A "RETURN-FROM-RELAPSE" PLAN

PREPARATION

- At the beginning and end of the meeting, ask someone to read the Welcoming Words and Closing Words (*Appendix E*).

GOALS

1. To consider past relapses in stuttering and to think about each individual's keys to preventing or recovering from relapses.

2. To construct individual plans to use in case of relapses.

THE MEETING

WELCOMING WORDS

ICEBREAKER

Ask participants what is the first thing they would say without thinking when something unbelievable happens. (*Or see Appendix A.*)

INDIVIDUAL GOALS

Ask each one in attendance (stutterers, facilitators, visitors) to identify a personal goal for the meeting, and share it with the group. Inform them that, at the end of the meeting, they will be reminded of their goals and have an opportunity to evaluate themselves. (If necessary, prompt ones who are having difficulty choosing a goal with some examples, like those in Appendix G.)

ACTIVITY

(Announce that participation in any activity is strictly voluntary. Everyone should join only those exercises with which they feel comfortable.)

1. Introduce the topic of stuttering relapse, a slipping back or return to worse stuttering after achieving a greater degree of fluency. It is the opposite of maintaining one's gains.

2. Ask participants to share what they did to achieve their most fluent level and what one or two basic techniques were keys to their progress.

3. Ask for discussion of relapses, times when participants fell back from a level of fluency they had already reached, and whether these times were triggered by failure to observe the basics each participant discussed earlier.

4. Like a crash diet from a physician, ask each stutterer to begin a one-week "return-from-relapse" plan if they ever find themselves in a relapse. It should be written and placed in a safe but locatable place in the event it becomes needed. Remembering their own individual basics, each person should construct a plan for each day that will take them through their entire previous therapy process from beginning to end in a greatly shortened, but intensive, step-by-step way. For each day, it should list the practice tasks; the number, kind, and location of conversation partners; the criteria for moving to the next step; and a daily reward for completion.

5. Ask participants to think back to their previous therapy and to write down the first day's assignment then share it with the group. Encourage them to finish it as soon as possible but before the next support group meeting.

TAKEAWAY LESSONS

Encourage participants to share what stands out for them, or what they may have learned about themselves, their issues, and each other.

CONSIDER:

1. Relapse may or may not occur, but if it does, it can be a frightening experience for which we are typically unprepared and, at the time, incapable of thinking rationally about. Talking about it in the support group can give us courage to confront a relapse.

2. Stuttering relapses are least likely to persist if they are confronted within a few days or weeks.

3. A "return-from-relapse" plan, ready to institute, provides the best way for us to "grit our teeth" and plunge purposely into rediscovering what worked for us in speech therapy. Given our frame of mind, it is best not to think about what happened but to do what the plan says to do, that is, to go back to the basics.

4. Re-experiencing the doing of the basics often takes us immediately back to the sense of control we lost in our relapse.

5. If we cannot get ourselves out of our relapse, it is wise for us to consult with a professional who can help us.

INDIVIDUAL GOAL EVALUATIONS

Ask participants to go back to the goals they stated at the beginning of the meeting, and grade themselves on a scale from 1 to 10. They may share their grades with the group if they choose.

CLOSING WORDS

"I will continue to use all the tools that I have acquired here, and, if I move to a new place, I would try to find a local NSA chapter there to join."

94. BEING REALISTIC ABOUT CHALLENGES

PREPARATION

- Have access to a whiteboard or other display device.
- Have available a few raw eggs and hard-boiled eggs.
- At the beginning and end of the meeting, ask someone to read the Welcoming Words and Closing Words (*Appendix E*).

GOALS

1. To consider reasonable and unreasonable fears related to challenges.
2. To share experiences with the result of unrealistic fears.

THE MEETING

WELCOMING WORDS

ICEBREAKER

Divide the participants into pairs and ask them to toss an egg back and forth while, after each successful toss and catch, backing up one step. This should continue until someone drops or breaks the egg. Demonstrate with a volunteer using a raw egg (in a place where it is easy to clean up), but, without disclosing it, distribute hard-boiled eggs to the members. (*Or see Appendix A.*)

INDIVIDUAL GOALS

Ask each one in attendance (stutterers, facilitators, visitors) to identify a personal goal for the meeting, and share it with the group. Inform them that, at the end of the meeting, they will be reminded of their goals and have an opportunity to evaluate themselves. (If necessary, prompt ones who are having difficulty choosing a goal with some examples, like those in Appendix G.)

ACTIVITY

(Announce that participation in any activity is strictly voluntary. Everyone should join only those exercises with which they feel comfortable.)

1. Ask those in attendance to think of a challenge they are facing, or expect to face in the future, and which they do not mind sharing. Invite stutterers to consider a speaking situation that involves stuttering. After a minute for reflection, invite people to briefly describe the challenging situation.

2. Ask people to imagine and tell the worst possible result from their challenging situation.

3. Next, ask them to imagine and tell the best possible outcome.

4. Finally, ask them to give their opinion of the most likely outcome.

5. Invite discussion of why we so often dwell on the negative possibilities, instead of the positive or the realistic possibilities. Ask a volunteer to write the reasons on the whiteboard.

TAKEAWAY LESSONS

Encourage participants to share what stands out for them, or what they may have learned about themselves, their issues, and each other.

CONSIDER:

1. In challenging situations, we typically find it easier to think of possible failures than possible successes.

2. Our negative thinking often makes a challenging situation worse or much more prolonged.

3. Once we have decided that we must face a challenging situation involving stuttering, it is best to not delay. In addition to "getting it behind us," we often find that it was not as bad as we had imagined.

INDIVIDUAL GOAL EVALUATIONS

Ask participants to go back to the goals they stated at the beginning of the meeting, and grade themselves on a scale from 1 to 10. They may share their grades with the group if they choose.

CLOSING WORDS

95. FINDING RESILIENCE

PREPARATION

- Provide paper and pens or pencils for the participants.
- At the beginning and end of the meeting, ask someone to read the Welcoming Words and Closing Words (*Appendix E*).

GOALS

1. To identify and discuss major life obstacles not related to stuttering.
2. To find meaning in our life obstacles and appreciate the value of resilience.
3. To explore how we can find resilience through everyday life with regards to hindering aspects of stuttering.

THE MEETING

WELCOMING WORDS

ICEBREAKER

Ask those in attendance to imagine they will be sent to a pleasant deserted island where food and water and comfort are not a problem, but there is no way to leave or to communicate with the outside world. What is the one item each one would want to bring? (*Or see Appendix A.*)

INDIVIDUAL GOALS

Ask each one in attendance (stutterers, facilitators, visitors) to identify a personal goal for the meeting, and share it with the group. Inform them that, at the end of the meeting, they will be reminded of their goals and have an opportunity to evaluate themselves. (If necessary, prompt ones who are having difficulty choosing a goal with some examples, like those in Appendix G.)

ACTIVITY

(Announce that participation in any activity is strictly voluntary. Everyone should join only those exercises with which they feel comfortable.)

1. Ask everyone to think of an extremely difficult experience that they have faced in life. This could be something like the death of a loved one, a divorce, an illness, an injury, a natural disaster, or being the victim of a crime. Advise everyone to choose an experience they would not mind discussing. Ask them to think about the experience, what they learned from it, and how they got through it.

2. Ask people to share what meaning they have found, if any, in their difficult experience. If anyone has not found any meaning, share that as well.

3. Ask the group to imagine that some unforeseeable catastrophe in the near future means that everyone's current job or life situation will no longer exist. Everyone will need to retrain for an entirely new job or reinvent their lives in some way. Ask each participant to discuss how he or she might cope with such a challenge. What sort of support—internal or external—might possibly help anyone power through such a difficult time?

4. Summarize some of the coping tools the group has mentioned, and say to the stutterers that people in the group have imagined a terrible challenge but have decided that they do have the resources to meet those challenges. Ask the group to share ways they might generalize the discussion of resilience to apply to the issue of stuttering.

TAKEAWAY LESSONS

Encourage participants to share what stands out for them, or what they may have learned about themselves, their issues, and each other.

CONSIDER:

1. We often find that we have resilience, of which we were not even aware, to survive and even prevail in very difficult situations.

2. Support from others can be extremely helpful in crises, especially when we are not coping well.

3. Viktor Frankl (psychiatrist, author, and Holocaust survivor) wrote that intolerable suffering can be transformed into tolerable sacrifice when it has meaning or a greater purpose.

INDIVIDUAL GOAL EVALUATIONS

Ask participants to go back to the goals they stated at the beginning of the meeting, and grade themselves on a scale from 1 to 10. They may share their grades with the group if they choose.

CLOSING WORDS

96. REDUCING SOCIAL IMPEDIMENTS FROM STUTTERING

PREPARATION

- Provide slips of paper and pens or pencils, and a disposable cup or other small container for each one in attendance. Provide markers for participants to write their names on their cups. If the cups cannot be written on, provide Post-It notes to use as labels.
- At the beginning and end of the meeting, ask someone to read the Welcoming Words and Closing Words (*Appendix E*).

GOALS

1. To increase insight and desensitization to stuttering by exploring relationships and the effects that stuttering may have on them.
2. To compare individual versus group appraisals of stuttering's impediment to effective group communication.

THE MEETING

WELCOMING WORDS

ICEBREAKER

Have each person write or put his or her name on a cup. Place slips of paper and pens or pencils where everyone can reach them. Pass the cups around and have everyone write something—complimentary, humorous, or whatever—about each person, and place it in his or her cup. Have people take turns reading the comments in their cup to the group. (*Or see Appendix A.*)

INDIVIDUAL GOALS

Ask each one in attendance (stutterers, facilitators, visitors) to identify a personal goal for the meeting, and share it with the group. Inform them that, at the end of the meeting, they will be reminded of their goals and have an opportunity to evaluate themselves. (If necessary, prompt ones who are having difficulty choosing a goal with some examples, like those in Appendix G.)

ACTIVITY

(Announce that participation in any activity is strictly voluntary. Everyone should join only those exercises with which they feel comfortable.)

1. Hand out the cups, and (if not already done) have everyone write or paste their name on it. Ask everyone to think of a serious issue in their lives that has caused them considerable difficulty or pain. Encourage stutterers to use stuttering as the issue. Have everyone share their issue with the group and briefly comment on why they chose it. Ask everyone to imagine they are part of a committee where they will be working closely with strangers for several weeks to create an important report. Ask everyone to write down a score on a slip of paper, on a scale from 1 to 100, for how much they believe their issue will affect their work in the committee.

2. Ask everyone to take a slip of paper for each of the others in the group, and write down on a scale of 1 to 100 how much they think that person's work on the committee would be affected by their issue, plus an honest and positive comment. Pass the cups around, and have everyone put these scores and comments in that person's cup.

3. Ask participants to read the comments, and share some of the results if they choose to do so, including how their self-assessed scores compare with those of the others, and what about the scores or comments they found surprising. After the discussion, announce that the papers will not be collected; participants may keep them or throw them away.

TAKEAWAY LESSONS

Encourage participants to share what stands out for them, or what they may have learned about themselves, their issues, and each other.

CONSIDER:

1. Our stuttering is often perceived as an impediment to making a serious difference in important verbal communications.

2. Yet, evidence from others often indicates that our stuttering need not limit our ability to make important contributions to important communications.

INDIVIDUAL GOAL EVALUATIONS

Ask participants to go back to the goals they stated at the beginning of the meeting, and grade themselves on a scale from 1 to 10. They may share their grades with the group if they choose.

CLOSING WORDS

97. STUTTERING IN CONVERSATIONS WHEN BEING EVALUATED

PREPARATION

- At the beginning and end of the meeting, ask someone to read the Welcoming Words and Closing Words (*Appendix E*).

GOALS

1. To explore the dynamics of a get-acquainted scenario.
2. To consider different strategies for managing stuttering in these situations.

THE MEETING

WELCOMING WORDS

ICEBREAKER

Invite people to share what person, living or dead, they would like, or would have liked to, spend an hour with, and why. (*Or see Appendix A.*)

INDIVIDUAL GOALS

Ask each one in attendance (stutterers, facilitators, visitors) to identify a personal goal for the meeting, and share it with the group. Inform them that, at the end of the meeting, they will be reminded of their goals and have an opportunity to evaluate themselves. (If necessary, prompt ones who are having difficulty choosing a goal with some examples, like those in Appendix G.)

ACTIVITY

(Announce that participation in any activity is strictly voluntary. Everyone should join only those exercises with which they feel comfortable.)

1. Divide the group into pairs. As much as possible, pair people who do not know each other well. Ask participants to imagine they are trying to "fix up" a friend, and want to get to know a little about the other person to see if he or she might be a match for the friend. They will have about ten minutes to talk. Send the pairs into different rooms or areas.

2. After about ten minutes, reconvene. Invite discussion of how the exercise went and what role stuttering played. Ask how stuttering usually affects interaction with unfamiliar people in a conversation involving evaluating people and what strategies can be used to deal with it.

3. Invite the group to think of other situations that involve carrying on conversations that have a definite purpose of evaluating others or being evaluated.

TAKEAWAY LESSONS

Encourage participants to share what stands out for them, or what they may have learned about themselves, their issues, and each other.

CONSIDER:

1. A history of stuttering often has left us with less flexible communication skills than those of nonstutterers.

2. In order to feel confident and be successful in serious conversations that involve evaluating people, we typically must reach a level of acceptance of our stuttering.

INDIVIDUAL GOAL EVALUATIONS

Ask participants to go back to the goals they stated at the beginning of the meeting, and grade themselves on a scale from 1 to 10. They may share their grades with the group if they choose.

CLOSING WORDS

98. UNDERSTANDING STUTTERING STEREOTYPES

PREPARATION

- Supply paper and pens or pencils for the group.
- Bring several pictures of different people, with as much diversity as possible in clothing, appearance, expression, etc.
- At the beginning and end of the meeting, ask someone to read the Welcoming Words and Closing Words (*Appendix E*).

GOALS

1. To gain insight into ways our negative thinking limits us.
2. To discuss ways to change public attitudes toward stuttering.

THE MEETING

WELCOMING WORDS

ICEBREAKER

Hold up the pictures one at a time, and ask the group to speculate on the person—what kind of job they have, family life, personality, etc. (*Or see Appendix A.*)

INDIVIDUAL GOALS

Ask each one in attendance (stutterers, facilitators, visitors) to identify a personal goal for the meeting, and share it with the group. Inform them that, at the end of the meeting, they will be reminded of their goals and have an opportunity to evaluate themselves. (If necessary, prompt ones who are having difficulty choosing a goal with some examples, like those in Appendix G.)

ACTIVITY

(Announce that participation in any activity is strictly voluntary. Everyone should join only those exercises with which they feel comfortable.)

1. Invite the group to discuss stereotypes in a general way for a few minutes. Prompt if necessary with questions such as: When we meet someone, what observations

do we use in order to make assumptions about them? Is the process of stereotyping people ever useful? Is it possible to view others with no stereotyping at all?

2. Ask everyone to respond to a few statements by writing on paper whether they believe the statement is true or false. They should rate each statement on a five-point scale, with a rating of 1 if they believe the statement is completely false, and 5 if they believe it is completely true. Tell the group to just write their responses for now, and there will be discussion afterward. Read each statement and pause briefly while participants write their responses:

   » People think stutterers are seen as less attractive than other people.
   » People think stutterers are dumb.
   » People get impatient with stutterers.
   » People don't want to hear what stutterers have to say.
   » People feel sorry for stutterers.

3. One statement at a time, have participants reveal their agreement or disagreement, and allow discussion.

TAKEAWAY LESSONS

Encourage participants to share what stands out for them, or what they may have learned about themselves, their issues, and each other.

CONSIDER:

1. Stereotyping others is a fact of life.

2. We often make assumptions about what people think about us, but it's up to us to decide what we do about it or if we internalize that information.

3. Learning accurate information about stuttering can help reduce negative public stereotypes or stigma regarding stuttering, but this is especially so when people can interact with stutterers on a personal level, as in a stuttering support group.

INDIVIDUAL GOAL EVALUATIONS

Ask participants to go back to the goals they stated at the beginning of the meeting, and grade themselves on a scale from 1 to 10. They may share their grades with the group if they choose.

CLOSING WORDS

99. INTERACTING WITH NONSTUTTERERS

PREPARATION

- This plan would be especially appropriate when a number of nonstuttering guests are likely to be present.
- At the beginning and end of the meeting, ask someone to read the Welcoming Words and Closing Words (*Appendix E*).

GOALS

1. To share some of the ways stutterers interact with nonstutterers at a first meeting.
2. To consider the pros and cons of talking about stuttering with first acquaintances.

THE MEETING

WELCOMING WORDS

ICEBREAKER

Ask participants to tell about an unusual ability or hidden talent they have. (*Or see Appendix A.*)

INDIVIDUAL GOALS

Ask each one in attendance (stutterers, facilitators, visitors) to identify a personal goal for the meeting, and share it with the group. Inform them that, at the end of the meeting, they will be reminded of their goals and have an opportunity to evaluate themselves. (If necessary, prompt ones who are having difficulty choosing a goal with some examples, like those in Appendix G.)

ACTIVITY

(Announce that participation in any activity is strictly voluntary. Everyone should join only those exercises with which they feel comfortable.)

1. Ask the nonstutterers in attendance, "When you meet someone who stutters, what do you wish the person would tell you about his or her stuttering?"
2. Ask the stutterers to discuss the following questions and any other questions that come up during the discussion. How much do you usually tell someone about your

stuttering the first time you meet them? How does what you tell them vary with different situations? What is the most common question people ask you about your stuttering? Do you like talking about stuttering? Does anyone ever ask for too much information?

3. Ask the nonstutterers, one by one, what new things they learned from the session.

TAKEAWAY LESSONS

Encourage participants to share what stands out for them, or what they may have learned about themselves, their issues, and each other.

CONSIDER:

1. Most nonstutterers are quite curious about our stuttering and enjoy hearing about what we think about our stuttering. Most of them, too, view such disclosures as a very positive thing.

2. Some of us are comfortable answering questions about our stuttering; some of us are not. This inevitably creates a problem for nonstuttering listeners, because they don't want to be offensive, by and large. So even if we prefer not to talk much about our stuttering, it makes communication with nonstutterers easier for everyone if we acknowledge our stuttering and then simply let them know if we care to talk more about it.

INDIVIDUAL GOAL EVALUATIONS

Ask participants to go back to the goals they stated at the beginning of the meeting, and grade themselves on a scale from 1 to 10. They may share their grades with the group if they choose.

CLOSING WORDS

100. EDUCATING OTHERS ABOUT STUTTERING

PREPARATION

- Consider using this plan when a number of nonstuttering visitors will be present.
- Provide paper and pens or pencils for the nonstutterers in attendance.
- At the beginning and end of the meeting, ask someone to read the Welcoming Words and Closing Words (*Appendix E*).

GOALS

1. To practice putting the experience of stuttering into words.
2. To discuss how we might effectively tell strangers what they may want to know about stuttering.

THE MEETING

WELCOMING WORDS

ICEBREAKER

Read the following scenario to the participants. "You live in a society where left-handed people are excluded. They are clearly looked down on, and it is a stigma. This stigma is as bad as having HIV/AIDS was in the early years of its "discovery." Assume you are left-handed and are going to be one of several lefties in a YouTube national broadcast about left-handers." In 30 seconds or less, tell us what you would say. (*Or see Appendix A.*)

INDIVIDUAL GOALS

Ask each one in attendance (stutterers, facilitators, visitors) to identify a personal goal for the meeting, and share it with the group. Inform them that, at the end of the meeting, they will be reminded of their goals and have an opportunity to evaluate themselves. (If necessary, prompt ones who are having difficulty choosing a goal with some examples, like those in Appendix G.)

ACTIVITY

(Announce that participation in any activity is strictly voluntary. Everyone should join only those exercises with which they feel comfortable.)

1. Tell stutterers in the group that in a few minutes they will be giving a brief talk on their own experience with stuttering. They should try to include when they started stuttering, any ideas they may have on what causes it, how it feels to stutter, how they would like others to react to stuttering, and anything else they would like to share. Ask nonstutterers to take a few minutes to think of questions they have regarding stuttering, and write them down.

2. After allowing a few minutes for preparation, ask stutterers to give their talk.

3. Ask nonstutterers for their reactions to the presentations, and to ask the stutterers any unanswered questions they may have on their lists.

TAKEAWAY LESSONS

Encourage participants to share what stands out for them, or what they may have learned about themselves, their issues, and each other.

CONSIDER:

1. Telling our stories of stuttering is one of the best ways to educate the nonstuttering majority about stuttering.

2. When we are open about our stuttering, it is virtually always perceived as a positive thing and can help put us at ease.

3. Nonstutterers are almost always extremely interested in hearing stutterers' stories.

INDIVIDUAL GOAL EVALUATIONS

Ask participants to go back to the goals they stated at the beginning of the meeting, and grade themselves on a scale from 1 to 10. They may share their grades with the group if they choose.

CLOSING WORDS

101. STUTTERING IN MOVIES AND TELEVISION

PREPARATION

- At the beginning and end of the meeting, ask someone to read the Welcoming Words and Closing Words (*Appendix E*).

GOALS

1. To share stories of stutterers depicted in television and movies.

2. To consider how stuttering in film and television reflects the reality of stuttering and the erroneous stereotype of stutterers.

THE MEETING

WELCOMING WORDS

ICEBREAKER

Ask people to name a television show, past or present, they know is not really that good, but they enjoy watching it anyway. (*Or see Appendix A.*)

INDIVIDUAL GOALS

Ask each one in attendance (stutterers, facilitators, visitors) to identify a personal goal for the meeting, and share it with the group. Inform them that, at the end of the meeting, they will be reminded of their goals and have an opportunity to evaluate themselves. (If necessary, prompt ones who are having difficulty choosing a goal with some examples, like those in Appendix G.)

ACTIVITY

(Announce that participation in any activity is strictly voluntary. Everyone should join only those exercises with which they feel comfortable.)

1. Ask participants—stutterers and nonstutterers—to talk about stutterers they have seen in television shows or movies. If necessary, prompt with *A Fish Called Wanda, My Cousin Vinny, Rocket Man, The King's Speech,* or other movies featuring stuttering.

2. Ask for discussion of what the characters are like, other than stuttering. How do they relate to other people? What physical mannerisms do they have? What is their usual attitude? How do these characters conform or not conform to some of the usual stereotypes people have about stutterers?

TAKEAWAY LESSONS

Encourage participants to share what stands out for them, or what they may have learned about themselves, their issues, and each other.

CONSIDER:
1. Most stutterers in films are used to feature weak, introverted, fearful, or psychologically maladjusted individuals.

2. A few movies show stutterers in a strong role, such as *Rocket Man* and *The King's Speech*.

3. Given that most people know very little about stuttering, public attitudes toward stuttering are likely a reflection of what people see in films or television.

INDIVIDUAL GOAL EVALUATIONS

Ask participants to go back to the goals they stated at the beginning of the meeting, and grade themselves on a scale from 1 to 10. They may share their grades with the group if they choose.

CLOSING WORDS

102. STUTTERING IN THE MEDIA

PREPARATION

- A computer and monitor are needed.
- Invite some nonstutterers to the meeting.
- Before the meeting, locate a few videos of stuttering in the media that feature actual stutterers and actor stutterers in real situations, which show stuttering in both a negative and positive light (readily available on YouTube). Prepare to show these at the meeting, by bookmarking the locations, copying them into a file, or some other way.
- Provide paper and pens or pencils.
- At the beginning and end of the meeting, ask someone to read the Welcoming Words and Closing Words (*Appendix E*).

GOALS

1. To discuss how stutterers and stuttering are portrayed in movies and television.
2. To explore how stutterers and nonstutterers understand stuttering differently, and what nonstutterers need to know about stuttering.

THE MEETING

WELCOMING WORDS

ICEBREAKER

Ask participants which television reality show they would most like to be on. (*Or see Appendix A.*)

INDIVIDUAL GOALS

Ask each one in attendance (stutterers, facilitators, visitors) to identify a personal goal for the meeting, and share it with the group. Inform them that, at the end of the meeting, they will be reminded of their goals and have an opportunity to evaluate themselves. (If necessary, prompt ones who are having difficulty choosing a goal with some examples, like those in Appendix G.)

ACTIVITY

(Announce that participation in any activity is strictly voluntary. Everyone should join only those exercises with which they feel comfortable.)

1. Announce that you will be showing several short videos of stuttering from the media, and ask everyone in attendance to jot down a few reactions as they watch. Play the videos.

2. Ask any nonstutterers, if present, to discuss the videos: How could you tell the people stuttered? If the sound were turned off, would you be able to tell, and if so, how? Could you see a difference in the actual stutterers and the actors? What do you think was going on in the minds of the actual stutterers?

3. Repeat the above for the stutterers.

4. Ask the following questions: How are stutterers—both real and fictional—portrayed in the media? Has portrayal of stuttering affected social attitudes toward stuttering positively or negatively?

TAKEAWAY LESSONS

Encourage participants to share what stands out for them, or what they may have learned about themselves, their issues, and each other.

CONSIDER:

1. Videos often feature stuttering on internet sites as something humorous, much like spectacular falls or accidents. Other videos feature stutterers as weak, introverted, fearful, or psychologically maladjusted individuals.

2. With careful searches, videos prepared by people who stutter, support groups, or speech-language pathologists can be found that portray stuttering and stutterers in a positive light.

3. Given that most people (even some stutterers) know very little about stuttering, public attitudes toward stuttering are likely a reflection of what people see in print, in videos/movies, and on social media.

INDIVIDUAL GOAL EVALUATIONS

Ask participants to go back to the goals they stated at the beginning of the meeting, and grade themselves on a scale from 1 to 10. They may share their grades with the group if they choose.

CLOSING WORDS

103. IDENTIFYING BETTER COMMUNICATION SKILLS

PREPARATION

- Have access to a whiteboard or other display device.
- At the beginning and end of the meeting, ask someone to read the Welcoming Words and Closing Words (*Appendix E*).

GOALS

1. To identify attributes of a good communicator.
2. To think about flaws in our own communication styles.
3. To discover practical ways to improve our communication skills.

THE MEETING

WELCOMING WORDS

ICEBREAKER

Say to someone, "Welcome to the red carpet! I love your outfit! Let me be the first to congratulate you on winning an Academy Award." Ask everyone to turn to the person to their left, introduce him or her to the crowd, and explain what award he or she won. The crazier the better! (*Or see Appendix A.*)

INDIVIDUAL GOALS

Ask each one in attendance (stutterers, facilitators, visitors) to identify a personal goal for the meeting, and share it with the group. Inform them that, at the end of the meeting, they will be reminded of their goals and have an opportunity to evaluate themselves. (If necessary, prompt ones who are having difficulty choosing a goal with some examples, like those in Appendix G.)

ACTIVITY

(Announce that participation in any activity is strictly voluntary. Everyone should join only those exercises with which they feel comfortable.)

1. Ask everyone in attendance to think of one person they think of as a really good communicator. After a pause for thinking, ask participants to tell who their good

communicator is and what specific attributes seem to make him or her good. Have someone list these attributes on the whiteboard.

2. Ask participants to share what aspects of their own communication foster good communication. Then ask them to share aspects that prevent them from being a better communicator.

3. Ask participants to identify any specific, concrete communication skills they could realistically try to improve. How might they do that?

TAKEAWAY LESSONS

Encourage participants to share what stands out for them, or what they may have learned about themselves, their issues, and each other.

CONSIDER:

1. Being aware of what is perceived as good communication can help us analyze and improve our own communication skills.

2. If we have stuttered for many years, we may have been so concerned about the stuttering that we understandably did not focus on being better communicators.

3. Stuttering need not define our communication effectiveness because some excellent communicators and public speakers also stutter.

INDIVIDUAL GOAL EVALUATIONS

Ask participants to go back to the goals they stated at the beginning of the meeting, and grade themselves on a scale from 1 to 10. They may share their grades with the group if they choose.

CLOSING WORDS

104. ENCOURAGING AND DISCOURAGING SOCIAL INTERACTIONS

PREPARATION

- Provide paper and pens or pencils.
- Have access to a whiteboard or other display device.
- This meeting requires internet access and a monitor large enough for the group to see. Before the meeting, find five or six videos of diverse people talking, preferably ordinary-looking people speaking on non-controversial topics. Bookmark the internet locations, or copy the videos into a file for playback.
- At the beginning and end of the meeting, ask someone to read the Welcoming Words and Closing Words (*Appendix E*).

GOALS

1. To explore the communication styles of different speakers.
2. To discuss what factors make people more inviting or less inviting to interact with socially.

THE MEETING

WELCOMING WORDS

ICEBREAKER

Ask participants to imagine the following scenario: It is the first day of class or your first visit to a new church, and you arrive early to make sure that you get a good seat. The next thing you know, somebody approaches you and asks if you could move because you are in the seat that they like to sit in. What would you say or do in this situation? (*Or see Appendix A.*)

INDIVIDUAL GOALS

Ask each one in attendance (stutterers, facilitators, visitors) to identify a personal goal for the meeting, and share it with the group. Inform them that, at the end of the meeting, they will be reminded of their goals and have an opportunity to evaluate themselves. (If necessary, prompt ones who are having difficulty choosing a goal with some examples, like those in Appendix G.)

ACTIVITY

(Announce that participation in any activity is strictly voluntary. Everyone should join only those exercises with which they feel comfortable.)

1. Announce that the group is going to watch videos of different people talking. The content of the clips is not important. Instead, participants should think about how likely they would be to want to start a conversation with that person if they met in some social setting. Ask them to rate the likelihood they would definitely not want to talk to the person on a scale of 1–10, with 1 meaning not at all and 10 meaning they would very much like to.

2. Show the videos one at a time, and after each, ask participants to tell what rating they gave the person, and why.

3. Ask participants to think of time when they were sure that a stranger simply wanted to meet and talk to them. What do they think was responsible for that?

4. Ask participants to think of a time when they wanted to talk with someone in a non-mandatory situation. Explain what happened, good or bad.

5. Invite discussion of some of the ways people may unintentionally encourage or discourage strangers from wanting to meet them.

TAKEAWAY LESSONS

Encourage participants to share what stands out for them, or what they may have learned about themselves, their issues, and each other.

CONSIDER:

1. Stuttering can and does play a role in our non-mandatory social interactions.

2. The less our stuttering affects our social-interaction decisions, the more fully we can enjoy social interactions. This does not mean that we must be out-going people, but stuttering does not need to be the reason we fail to interact with others.

INDIVIDUAL GOAL EVALUATIONS

Ask participants to go back to the goals they stated at the beginning of the meeting, and grade themselves on a scale from 1 to 10. They may share their grades with the group if they choose.

CLOSING WORDS

105. CONVERSATION SKILLS AND STUTTERING

PREPARATION

- At the beginning and end of the meeting, ask someone to read the Welcoming Words and Closing Words (*Appendix E*).

GOALS

1. To gain insight into what it means to be a good conversationalist.
2. To consider ways to improve conversational skills.

THE MEETING

WELCOMING WORDS

ICEBREAKER

Announce that everyone in the group has met an important goal. One at a time, have participants stand up and introduce the person on their left, and announce what imaginary accomplishment they have achieved. (*Or see Appendix A.*)

INDIVIDUAL GOALS

Ask each one in attendance (stutterers, facilitators, visitors) to identify a personal goal for the meeting, and share it with the group. Inform them that, at the end of the meeting, they will be reminded of their goals and have an opportunity to evaluate themselves. (If necessary, prompt ones who are having difficulty choosing a goal with some examples, like those in Appendix G.)

ACTIVITY

Announce that participation in any activity is strictly voluntary. Everyone should join only those exercises with which they feel comfortable.)

1. Ask everyone to think of someone—not a close friend—who is really easy to talk to. After a minute for everyone to think, ask each one to explain why they chose this person.

2. Next, ask everyone to think of someone who is a good communicator. This may be

the same person mentioned before. Ask each one to explain why this person is a good communicator.

3. Ask everyone to think of some other people, those who are not easy to talk with or are not effective communicators, and share some of the characteristics that make them not as good as the examples discussed earlier.

4. Ask everyone, stutterers and nonstutterers, to identify some habits they may have, which may sometimes make them less effective at communication or less fun to talk with. For stutterers, ask how often their awareness of stuttering makes them less than ideal communicators, such as saying as little as possible or ending a conversation as quickly as possible, and how this might be perceived by the other person in the conversation.

5. Finally, ask everyone to identify some way that—stuttering aside—they could be better at conversing and communicating.

TAKEAWAY LESSONS

Encourage participants to share what stands out for them, or what they may have learned about themselves, their issues, and each other.

CONSIDER:

1. Whereas stuttering can and often does result in our not being the best conversationalist or communicators that we can be, it does not need to do that.

2. In its simplest form, stuttering simply means that it takes a little longer to say what we want to say.

3. Some excellent and even famous communicators happen to stutter.

INDIVIDUAL GOAL EVALUATIONS

Ask participants to go back to the goals they stated at the beginning of the meeting, and grade themselves on a scale from 1 to 10. They may share their grades with the group if they choose.

CLOSING WORDS

106. GESTURES AND BODY LANGUAGE

PREPARATION

- Video recording equipment and viewing equipment (e.g., a large screen), which can be seen by the group, is needed. Choose a spot next to a door for speakers to stand and be recorded, and set up the equipment to record the speakers.
- Arrange a nearby room or hallway for participants to wait while others are being video recorded.
- Prepare index cards with the following scenarios, which speakers will tell the owner of a dog—for which they had agreed to pet-sit for two weeks—when the owner comes to pick up the dog:
    » The dog loves it here. Would you consider letting me keep the dog permanently?
    » I really liked the dog, but it chewed up and ruined our new couch.
    » I really could not stand the dog. It barked all night and growled at me when I tried to stop it.
    » The dog died.
    » The dog got very sick, and I had to take it to a vet. It is well now, but you owe me $1200.
    » The dog ran off right after you left, and it took 10 days to find it. The dog did lose a lot of weight.
- At the beginning and end of the meeting, ask someone to read the Welcoming Words and Closing Words (*Appendix E*).

GOALS

1. To explore the role of gestures and body language in communication.
2. To consider gestures and body language apart from their related verbal communication.

THE MEETING

WELCOMING WORDS

ICEBREAKER

Ask the participants, if they were told to make a face, without thinking about it, what face would they make. (*Or see Appendix A.*)

INDIVIDUAL GOALS

Ask each one in attendance (stutterers, facilitators, visitors) to identify a personal goal for the meeting, and share it with the group. Inform them that, at the end of the meeting, they will be reminded of their goals and have an opportunity to evaluate themselves. (If necessary, prompt ones who are having difficulty choosing a goal with some examples, like those in Appendix G.)

ACTIVITY

(Announce that participation in any activity is strictly voluntary. Everyone should join only those exercises with which they feel comfortable. However, if someone does not wish to be video recorded, an option would be to whisper so no one will hear any of what they say, and discover if that makes a difference.)

1. Announce that everyone will be making a short, roughly one-minute video. These need to be made in private, so those waiting will go to another location (specify) and you will call them in, one at a time. Instruct those who have been recorded to say absolutely nothing about the video experience!

2. As participants come in, read the following, "You agreed to be a pet-sitter for a very close friend's dog for two weeks while he/she was on vacation. The friend just rang your doorbell and is hoping to pick up the dog. Based on what happened on this card, I want you to respond after your friend says, 'Hi.' Ready? Let's record."

3. After all the participants have carried out the task, ask them to come to the room to watch the video you recorded. Announce that the theme of the session is gestures and body language so you will play the videos with no sound.

4. After each person's video, pause the playback and ask what the speaker's scenario was. Then ask for everyone to compliment the speaker on some aspect of body language that was related to the scenario or not. The speaker is simply to listen and not respond, even with a "thank you."

5. Invite discussion of the role of gestures and body language in the total communication act. What percentage of communication is verbal and nonverbal? What does this tell us about the importance of stuttering to one's total communication?

TAKEAWAY LESSONS

Encourage participants to share what stands out for them, or what they may have learned about themselves, their issues, and each other.

CONSIDER:

1. Authorities have indicated that our body language is more important than what we say in communication.

2. Even though we stutter, we can be effective communicators with gestures and body language.

INDIVIDUAL GOAL EVALUATIONS

Ask participants to go back to the goals they stated at the beginning of the meeting, and grade themselves on a scale from 1 to 10. They may share their grades with the group if they choose.

CLOSING WORDS

> "I never thought about my body language. I only focused on my stuttering."

107. COMMUNICATING NONVERBALLY IN SILENCE

PREPARATION

- At the beginning and end of the meeting, ask someone to read the Welcoming Words and Closing Words (*Appendix E*).

GOALS

1. To experience the presence of others when no speech is involved.

2. To discover ways to communicate without words.

THE MEETING

WELCOMING WORDS

ICEBREAKER

Ask everyone to imagine the following scenario: You are settling in for an eight-hour bus ride. The bus is completely full. The person next to you clearly wants to engage in a conversation, but you do not want to talk to him or her. What do you do? (*Or see Appendix A.*)

INDIVIDUAL GOALS

Ask each one in attendance (stutterers, facilitators, visitors) to identify a personal goal for the meeting, and share it with the group. Inform them that, at the end of the meeting, they will be reminded of their goals and have an opportunity to evaluate themselves. (If necessary, prompt ones who are having difficulty choosing a goal with some examples, like those in Appendix G.)

ACTIVITY

(Announce that participation in any activity is strictly voluntary. Everyone should join only those exercises with which they feel comfortable.)

1. Have everyone count off in threes or fours, so that they can be divided into a few small groups of three or four.

2. Ask each small group to move to a different part of the room and sit in a very small circle facing one another with chairs no further than two to three feet apart. Ask

them to decide which one of them is A, B, C, (and D). Ask the As to raise their hands. Instruct everyone that when you say "Start," A will be the "communicator" for 90 seconds and A's job is to simply communicate who he or she is to the other two or three people in his/her group, but to do so in complete silence. There will be no talking, laughing aloud, etc. After 90 seconds, you will say "Next," and that is the signal for B to be the "communicator." Proceed until everyone has been the "communicator" for 90 seconds, and then say "Stop."

3. Ask everyone in the small groups to start with A, and offer positive feedback or compliments on some aspect of A's nonverbal communication. Next, everyone will compliment B, and so on. As the compliments are being made, the recipients of the compliments are to acknowledge them nonverbally but to say or do nothing to thank the complimenters or to, in any way, deflect the compliments.

4. Invite everyone to come together and share with the group their reactions. How did they feel as silent "communicators"? How did they feel as silent "listeners"? How did they feel as the recipients of compliments? How did they feel as complimenters?

TAKEAWAY LESSONS

Encourage participants to share what stands out for them, or what they may have learned about themselves, their issues, and each other.

CONSIDER:

1. Nonverbal communication is very powerful, especially during silence.

2. In our society, silence is often feared. When we can learn to tolerate or enjoy silence, we can hone our nonverbal communication skills.

3. Many of us are prone to filtering out nonverbal or verbal, positive feedback for many reasons, e.g., not wishing to be the center of attention, feeling inferior, etc. We easily miss the "good stuff."

4. We who stutter are at no disadvantage at all in terms of communicating nonverbally.

INDIVIDUAL GOAL EVALUATIONS

Ask participants to go back to the goals they stated at the beginning of the meeting, and grade themselves on a scale from 1 to 10. They may share their grades with the group if they choose.

CLOSING WORDS

108. MAKING SMALL TALK

PREPARATION

- Arrange the meeting room before anyone arrives such that there is no place to sit down, where everyone can stand around, and with enough room to mingle and talk. Chairs can be turned against the walls.
- At the beginning and end of the meeting, ask someone to read the Welcoming Words and Closing Words (*Appendix E*).

GOALS

1. To become aware of the various reasons small talk group activities are arranged.
2. To explore ways to make small talk easier or more enjoyable and effective.

THE MEETING

WELCOMING WORDS

ICEBREAKER

Ask everyone to follow you to another room or hallway. There, announce that the group will take place in the regular room but that for a warm-up, you want all participants to imagine that no one is acquainted with anyone else and all of you are competing for just one, new, attractive job. As you walk back to our usual room, I want you to check out the people who are your competition and know that the others are checking you out too. (*Or see Appendix A.*)

INDIVIDUAL GOALS

Ask each one in attendance (stutterers, facilitators, visitors) to identify a personal goal for the meeting, and share it with the group. Inform them that, at the end of the meeting, they will be reminded of their goals and have an opportunity to evaluate themselves. (If necessary, prompt ones who are having difficulty choosing a goal with some examples, like those in Appendix G.)

ACTIVITY

(Announce that participation in any activity is strictly voluntary. Everyone should join only those exercises with which they feel comfortable.)

1. Have the meeting room arranged where participants can mingle, chat, and carry on several small conversations at once as they would in a "meet and greet" at a conference reception or a networking event. Tell everyone that when the exercise begins, they are to find another person and chat for three minutes. (If there is an odd number of participants, there will be one group of three.) At the end of three minutes, they will be prompted to end the conversation and begin with someone else. Everyone should make an effort to first speak with people they have not met before, or do not know well.

2. After several rounds of small talk, end the exercise and have the group sit down. Invite discussion of these questions:

    » Why are these "meet and greet" activities so common?

    » What part of this exercise was fun?

    » What aspects were stressful?

    » How do you usually do in real-life, small-talk situations?

    » Do you usually initiate contact or wait for someone else to make the first move?

    » Are you aware of any mistakes you sometimes make in these situations?

    » Who did you talk with in this exercise who was especially effective in small talk, or who used a small-talk technique you had not thought about before?

TAKEAWAY LESSONS

Encourage participants to share what stands out for them, or what they may have learned about themselves, their issues, and each other.

CONSIDER:

1. "Meet and greet" or "cocktail party" informal groups are very common ways for strangers to connect, network, socialize, strategize, problem-solve, etc.

2. Many of us, stutterers and nonstutterers, are uncomfortable in small-talk situations with strangers or slight acquaintances.

3. If we want to be able to participate and be influential in these groups, we need to identify and learn to change our communication impediments.

4. If/since we cannot change our stuttering, we need to disclose our stuttering effectively and adopt body language and other interaction strategies that promote effective communication.

INDIVIDUAL GOAL EVALUATIONS

Ask participants to go back to the goals they stated at the beginning of the meeting, and grade themselves on a scale from 1 to 10. They may share their grades with the group if they choose.

CLOSING WORDS

"Now I'm more confident and not as afraid of my stuttering."

109. MANAGING UNEXPECTED SOCIAL STRESS AND STUTTERING

PREPARATION

- This session may only be effective when there are at least one or two people present for the first time. Inform any other group leaders or facilitators about the meeting plan, to get their cooperation.
- At the beginning and end of the meeting, ask someone to read the Welcoming Words and Closing Words (*Appendix E*).

GOALS

1. To gain insight into various ways people socialize in an unstructured setting.
2. To consider ways to manage stuttering in unstructured social settings.

THE MEETING

WELCOMING WORDS

ICEBREAKER

Ask participants to explain how they would react if a person they have never met reaches out in a very forward way, to shake their hand before saying anything. (*Or see Appendix A.*)

INDIVIDUAL GOALS

Ask each one in attendance (stutterers, facilitators, visitors) to identify a personal goal for the meeting, and share it with the group. Inform them that, at the end of the meeting, they will be reminded of their goals and have an opportunity to evaluate themselves. (If necessary, prompt ones who are having difficulty choosing a goal with some examples, like those in Appendix G.)

ACTIVITY

(Announce that participation in any activity is strictly voluntary. Everyone should join only those exercises with which they feel comfortable.)

1. Announce that the group will be talking about an interesting topic. Suddenly, look at your phone and apologize to the group that you need to take care of something

right now, but you will be back in a few minutes. Ask them to please not leave and that you will conduct the meeting as soon as you come back. Leave the room.

2. Return to the room after about eight minutes. Tell them you told a "white lie" about having to leave. The meeting will be about what happened while you were gone.

3. Ask for discussion of what occurred while you were gone. Who initiated or participated in conversation, who sat and watched, who retreated into their phone or music? Who felt comfortable or uncomfortable? Were the "socializers" or the "hermits" more likely to be comfortable?

4. Ask participants to talk about their usual reaction to unexpected social situations. Do they mingle, or withdraw? Is everyone comfortable with their usual pattern, or does anyone believe they would benefit from trying to change their habits? What role does stuttering play?

TAKEAWAY LESSONS

Encourage participants to share what stands out for them, or what they may have learned about themselves, their issues, and each other.

CONSIDER:

1. Some of us are comfortable picking up conversations when there is an unexpected break in a routine involving communication; some of us are not.

2. We often avoid introducing ourselves to strangers in awkward situations because of stuttering, shyness, or discomfort.

3. Sometimes "communication leaders" in awkward situations may not plan to lead; they simply do not tolerate awkward silences well.

INDIVIDUAL GOAL EVALUATIONS

Ask participants to go back to the goals they stated at the beginning of the meeting, and grade themselves on a scale from 1 to 10. They may share their grades with the group if they choose.

CLOSING WORDS

110. BECOMING A BETTER PUBLIC SPEAKER

PREPARATION

- Video recording and viewing equipment is needed. Choose a spot for speakers to stand, and set up the equipment to record the speakers from the waist up.

- Prepare index cards or slips of paper with topics such as: one car my family had when I was young, the farthest from home I have ever traveled, my morning routine, one celebrity I believe I would be comfortable having a conversation with, how my clothes and shoes are organized in my home, one or two foods I could eat a surprising amount of, one very unimpressive skill I have or accomplishment I have achieved, one of the first movies I can remember seeing, etc.

- Prepare index cards or slips of paper with goals for effective speaking, such as: good eye contact, good posture, effective use of gestures and body language, varying speed (talking faster and slower at appropriate times), varying volume (louder and softer voice at appropriate times; not monotone), varying pitch (higher and lower voice at appropriate times; not monotone), effective beginning and end to the talk, and varying facial expressions appropriately.

- At the beginning and end of the meeting, ask someone to read the Welcoming Words and Closing Words (*Appendix E*).

GOALS

1. To identify some of the keys to effective public speaking.
2. To practice speaking in front of the group.

THE MEETING

WELCOMING WORDS

ICEBREAKER

Ask participants to explain, without using any gestures, how to button a button. (*Or see Appendix A.*)

INDIVIDUAL GOALS

Ask each one in attendance (stutterers, facilitators, visitors) to identify a personal goal for the meeting, and share it with the group. Inform them that, at the end of the meeting, they will be reminded of their goals and have an opportunity to evaluate themselves. (If necessary, prompt ones who are having difficulty choosing a goal with some examples, like those in Appendix G.)

ACTIVITY

(Announce that participation in any activity is strictly voluntary. Everyone should join only those exercises with which they feel comfortable.)

1. Announce that participants will be making a short speech and will be emphasizing one particular aspect of effective public speaking.

2. Have participants come forward, select a topic and a point of emphasis from the two sets of cards, and speak very briefly (one to two minutes).

3. After all of the speeches, read the list of speaking techniques.

4. Play the videos. Pause after each one, and discuss what the speaker did especially well, and what could be improved. Have the speaker tell what point he or she was trying to emphasize, and comment on the overall success of his or her own speech.

TAKEAWAY LESSONS

Encourage participants to share what stands out for them, or what they may have learned about themselves, their issues, and each other.

CONSIDER:

1. Stuttering may have limited us in acquiring skills of effective public speakers.

2. Many effective public speakers find it useful to record themselves giving a speech and then watching it for ways to improve.

3. Considering that some relatively severe stutterers have become national winners in the public speaking organization Toastmasters International, stuttering need not be a reason we cannot greatly improve our public speaking skills.

INDIVIDUAL GOAL EVALUATIONS

Ask participants to go back to the goals they stated at the beginning of the meeting, and grade themselves on a scale from 1 to 10. They may share their grades with the group if they choose.

CLOSING WORDS

111. MAXIMIZING ENJOYMENT DURING CONVERSATION

PREPARATION

- At the beginning and end of the meeting, ask someone to read the Welcoming Words and Closing Words (*Appendix E*).

GOALS

1. To examine how stuttering affects one's social interactions and conversation.

2. To discuss ways to make conversation more enjoyable.

THE MEETING

WELCOMING WORDS

ICEBREAKER

Ask participants what is the best or worst pickup line they have ever heard. (*Or see Appendix A.*)

INDIVIDUAL GOALS

Ask each one in attendance (stutterers, facilitators, visitors) to identify a personal goal for the meeting, and share it with the group. Inform them that, at the end of the meeting, they will be reminded of their goals and have an opportunity to evaluate themselves. (If necessary, prompt ones who are having difficulty choosing a goal with some examples, like those in Appendix G.)

ACTIVITY

(Announce that participation in any activity is strictly voluntary. Everyone should join only those exercises with which they feel comfortable.)

1. Ask each person present to tell about a recent conversation that was enjoyable—who it was with, what it was about, and what was the setting.

2. Ask participants to tell about a conversation that was not enjoyable.

3. Discuss what factors are most important in making a conversation pleasant or unpleasant.

4. Ask stutterers to what extent stuttering interferes with their ability to enjoy a conversation.

5. Invite discussion about what factors we can control and what practical steps we can take to promote more enjoyable conversations and fewer unpleasant ones.

TAKEAWAY LESSONS

Encourage participants to share what stands out for them, or what they may have learned about themselves, their issues, and each other.

CONSIDER:

1. Stuttering can limit our enjoyment of simply talking with others.

2. Our most enjoyable conversations are typically those when we forget about stuttering, and we feel unconditionally accepted.

3. Seeking out enjoyable conversations is especially useful for people who find talking difficult.

INDIVIDUAL GOAL EVALUATIONS

Ask participants to go back to the goals they stated at the beginning of the meeting, and grade themselves on a scale from 1 to 10. They may share their grades with the group if they choose.

CLOSING WORDS

APPENDICES

APPENDIX A: ICEBREAKERS

1. Ask people what kind of a person they would want to be seated beside on a long plane flight.

2. Invite members to tell a joke. Remind them that it must be appropriate.

3. Ask everyone to tell what is the best thing that has happened to them in the last week.

4. [Preparation: Have paper and pens or pencils available.] Have everyone in the group write the first sentence of a possible short story at the top of a piece of paper. Let everyone pass the paper to the person on his or her left, then write a sentence continuing the new story they now have. After several repetitions of this, have people read the stories to the group.

5. Ask people what they would need to do if they were at home and had three hours before a blizzard had expected to shut everyone in for a week.

6. Ask participants if there are any jobs that are not inherently bad but would be especially unpleasant for them.

7. Ask participants how or what they might eat if they get home very hungry, and no one is watching.

8. Ask participants what they would do if they were offered 20 million dollars, but to get it they would have to go five years without bathing, shaving, or cutting their hair.

9. Ask participants to imagine that someone is talking to them for too long and will not stop. Have people stand, one at a time, and demonstrate how they would nonverbally try to communicate that they need to go.

10. Have everyone stand and, all at the same time, use a pen or pencil to demonstrate, outside their mouths, how they brush their teeth.

11. [Preparation: Have index cards or paper on hand, and pens or pencils.] Ask everyone to write down a personal question they would like to ask someone else in the group. Shuffle the questions, place them face down, and have participants take turns picking up a question and answering it.

12. Ask participants if they have any waking-up habits that might surprise people to know.

13. Ask those in attendance how they respond when someone looks really familiar but they can't remember if or where they met before.

14. Ask participants what food they would choose if they had to eat the same thing every day, assuming their nutritional needs are already taken care of.

15. [Preparation: Bring several spices to the meeting, with their labels covered. Have them numbered.] Pass around the spices, and ask people to guess what they are.

16. [Preparation: Bring a package of bendable straws to the meeting.] Give each participant a few bendable straws, and allow a few minutes to do or make something with them.

17. Ask participants to stand and shake hands with some other people in a way they would not normally do.

18. Ask participants what they would be most annoyed or embarrassed by, if a very finicky visitor dropped by the house or apartment unexpectedly.

19. Ask participants what time they usually set their alarm for, and how they react to it—usually wake before the alarm, turn it off and get up, use the snooze button one or more times, etc.

20. Invite participants to tell about their favorite vacation or road trip.

21. Ask participants what famous person, past or present, they would like to be for a day, and why.

22. [Preparation: Have paper and pens or pencils on hand.] Pass out paper and pens or pencils, and ask participants to doodle in the way they usually do. After a few minutes, have each one show their doodles, and invite comments.

23. [Preparation: Bring plastic Easter eggs to the meeting.] See who is the best juggler. Award a "prize."

24. Ask people in attendance what was their dream job when they were young.

25. Ask participants to respond to this scenario: You and a friend you haven't seen in years decide to have dinner together near the holidays. Your friend surprises you with a gift of toilet paper and several packs of mustard. What would you say?

26. [Preparation: Have on hand two unbreakable cups, something to use as a blindfold, and a pitcher of water or access to a water fountain.] Have participants gather at one end of the room (or a hallway) with a table at the other end. Place an empty cup on the table. One at a time, blindfold the participants, hand them a cup of water, and instruct them to walk to the table, pour their water into the other cup, and walk back with it. Award a "prize" to the one who spills the least.

27. Have everyone stand up, pair up with another person, and stand close together

facing each other. At your signal, everyone is to intimidate their "opponent" using only eye contact (no sounds or body movements).

28. Move into the hall as a group and have participants one at a time walk down the hall and back. After all have returned to their seats, ask people to comment on how the others walked.

29. [Preparation: Have several sentences ready, of about the same length—funny sentences, quotations, items in the news, etc. Have access to a whiteboard.] Have participants one by one come to the whiteboard. Read a sentence to them, and ask them to write it in perfect cursive script.

30. [Preparation: Print pictures of people everyone will recognize—e.g., George Washington, Elvis, Mark Twain, Marilyn Monroe, Albert Einstein.] Place the picture face down. One at a time, have participants come forward, pick up a picture, and show it to the group without looking at it themselves. Let them ask "yes" or "no" questions to the group, and see who can identify their picture with the fewest hints.

31. [Preparation: Have a basketball available.] One by one, have participants dribble the basketball around the room, or down a hallway and back, then describe their thoughts while they were doing it.

32. Ask each one to share something they would really like to do but that would probably get them arrested.

33. Have participants sit in a circle with space in the middle, and take off their shoes and place them on the floor. Have everyone close their eyes. Mix up the shoes, putting two different ones in front of each participant. At your signal, everyone is to pick up the two shoes in front of them, and pass them to the left or right until they find their own and put them on. Eyes closed! No talking!

34. On an airplane, bus, train, etc., do you prefer to have a window or aisle seat and why?

35. Divide the group into two teams, and have each team line up. See which team can be the quickest to line up in different ways—alphabetically by last name, by age, alphabetically by the names of their high schools, by length of hair, etc.

36. Ask participants to tell about the most amusing or embarrassing picture ever taken of themselves.

37. Ask people what their favorite candy bar is and to describe what it tastes like.

38. Ask participants to imagine they are on a week-long car trip with a well-known person from sports, the media, politics, etc. Which celebrity do they imagine they could enjoy

the week with? Which celebrity would they want to leave behind at the first pit stop?

39. Ask people what movie sequel they would like to see made, and what might happen in it.

40. Ask those in attendance to discuss what they feel is the stupidest or most memorable commercial currently running on television or social media.

41. [Preparation: Take marshmallows and uncooked spaghetti noodles to the meeting, or miniature marshmallows and toothpicks.] Have participants pair up with a partner. Allow five minutes for each team to build the highest structure possible with the marshmallows and spaghetti or toothpicks. Award "prizes."

42. Ask everyone to tell a knock-knock joke.

43. Ask everyone to tell about the first music recording they remember hearing or buying.

44. Ask whether people would rather live 100 years in the future, or 100 years in the past, and why.

45. [Preparation: On a piece of paper, write several obscure words and their meanings from a dictionary.] One at a time, read the words to the group and ask them to either guess the meaning or invent one. Read the real definition.

46. Divide participants into pairs or groups of three or four. Allow a few minutes for the teams to list as many things as they can that they all have in common. Let them read their lists.

47. Ask members to describe one piece of clothing they own that would probably make people laugh.

48. Ask participants what food or foods they can eat an unreasonable amount of at one time.

49. Ask people to name one amazing invention they believe will happen in the next 20 years.

50. If you were arrested—or at least taken to the police station—what would you have been arrested for?

51. How much money would it take in order for you to shave your head? You aren't allowed to wear a wig or hat for roughly six months after. If your head is already shaven, how much money would it take for you to wear an ugly, itchy wig for six months?

52. Ask this "Would you rather?" question: Would you rather be invisible or able to read minds and why?

53. What is the "normal" way to take a shower?

54. What is one uncommon thing that you keep in your wallet/ purse?

55. A person is driving at an acceptable speed. They look in the rear-view mirror and see the car behind is riding too close to their back bumper. Who are you in this situation and what do you do?

56. Discuss a reoccurring dream that you have.

57. Pick a phobia that you would like to have based on its name? Give a brief explanation of your reasoning for your choice.

58. You are the owner of a big company. While conducting an interview, you set certain standards for the way your future employees present themselves. What do you consider a "dress code disaster" for an interview and in the workplace? Explain for both male and female employees.

59. "What is one traffic law that you never violate? Now, what would it take for you to violate this law and take the risk of getting a ticket?"

60. "Pick a card out of the pile; all cards have a picture of a food or drink on them. Describe the way you eat or drink the item on your card including what it tastes like, feels like in your mouth, and how it smells, but you cannot say the name of this item when describing it. Present clues to the group to help them guess which item of food or drink you are describing."

61. [Males] "What would you do if you were just introduced to a woman with a very low neckline and one button too many had come undone?" [Females] "What would you do if you were just introduced to a guy and his fly was unzipped?"

62. Ask participants if they like to make things. Like what? What about cleaning up afterwards?

63. Ask group members to describe their musical talents and skills (singing, dancing, instruments)—or lack there of.

64. Aside from driving, what is one place or situation where looking at your smart phone should be off limits? Why?

65. Talk your way out of a speeding ticket as one of the following people: Oprah Winfrey, Charles Manson, Clint Eastwood, Elvis, Marilyn Monroe, and Donald Trump.

66. Ask each participant, at random, to share how they whistle or how they whistle while they work—or play.

67. What is your preference, a cat or a dog? Why?

68. Have participants draw specific shapes on a sheet of paper by looking only in a mirror and not at the sheet of paper.

69. "You are at a round-table meeting and you spill an entire chocolate milkshake on your shirt. You cannot leave the meeting or get out of your seat for half an hour. What would you do?"

70. "What's your comfort food?"

71. Ask group members to think about a time when they were the last person in line to check out at the grocery store, and a new line opens up. Have group members share what they would do in that situation (e.g., let the person in front of them go because they've waited longer, simply get in the new line themselves, etc.).

72. The group members will imagine that they are going to be going on a bus tour at a new college they are considering attending. When getting on the bus, they realize that each seat already has one person in it. The person they sit with will be the person they are paired with for the rest of the all-day tour. Ask the group members to share who they would sit with and why.

73. The group member will ask members to write down answers to three personal questions (e.g., what is under your bed, what do you do when you run out of underwear, and what do you do when you drop food on the floor). Each member will have a bowl in the middle of the table with their name on the bottom, so no one will know which bowl belongs to which group member. Each person will wrinkle up their pieces of paper and toss them into three bowls. Then the group leader will distribute the bowls to their owners, each person will read the pieces of paper that are in their bowl, and they will attempt to match the answer with the person who wrote it.

74. What is the perfect way to enjoy your morning, afternoon, or evening coffee, tea, or favorite beverage?

75. Participants will take turns singing their addresses.

76. The participants will be paired and assigned an adjective. Each is given five pennies. Then they will be asked to make a facial expression that demonstrates the adjective. Each pair will be asked to maintain the facial expression for as long as they can. The first person to "break" their facial expression gives their pennies to their partner. The winners will be paired with each other, and the first to "break" their expression will give the winner their pennies. Eventually, one person will have all of the pennies and will be the winner.

77. If you walk into a crowded room, where do you stand? Why?

78. Each participant will be given a piece of paper and a pen/pencil and asked to draw a cat. After a few moments, the facilitator will ask the participants to change their drawing to a dog. Then, after a few more moments, the facilitator will change the drawing to a cow. Finally, the facilitator will tell the participants to change their drawing to a house. This will emphasize the need to be flexible and "roll with the punches."

79. The participants will be told to write down what they wanted to be when they grew up at the following ages: 5, 10, 15, 20 or now. Then they will take turns sharing with the group.

80. Describe how you swallow pills.

81. The members of the group will be given a scenario where they are invited to a group that some of their friends are in as well as people they don't know. For some reason, they arrive late to the group and are starving because they have not had time to eat all day. When they walk in the room everyone is gathered around the food table. They walk over and there is only one cookie left. What would they do?

82. Ask participants what they would do if I were to give them a shot in the arm right now. What would their reaction and routine be?

83. Have each member try to draw circles clockwise while twisting their foot counterclockwise.

84. How do you eat an apple?

85. Have you ever been snow or water skiing? Was it fun or not?

86. The members will go around the table and tell about an obnoxious prank they have done or seen.

87. Each member will share a description of a typical breakfast or a special breakfast.

88. Each member will share an irrational fear that they have.

89. "What sit-com, celebrity, or famous family is most like yours?"

90. Each member will discuss their perfect surprise birthday party.

91. Can you dribble a basketball, hit a baseball, or spike a volleyball? Describe the feeling, real or imagined.

92. Ask participants to share with the group what the first line of their personal ad or dating profile would say.

93. Name what type of animal you would want to be if you were reincarnated. Why?

94. Write your name upside down and backwards.

95. What was your favorite Halloween costume as a child or adult?

96. If you were stranded on a desert island and could only have one Thanksgiving food item to eat for the rest of your life, what would it be?

97. Each group member will tell the other group members what they would be for Halloween if time, money, or effort were no object and why they would pick this costume.

98. Each group member will explain how they go about holiday shopping.

99. Ask each group member to share his or her best or worst Valentine's Day gift.

100. Each member will tell the worst or funniest new year's resolution he/she has had or heard.

APPENDIX B: BRIEF SPEAKING OR ROLE PLAYING TOPICS

IMPROMPTU SPEAKING TOPICS

NEUTRAL AND EASY

1. Tell about your favorite TV show.
2. What time in history do you wish you could live in?
3. Name a place you would like to visit, and why.
4. Where do you see yourself in ten years?
5. If a visitor came to your hometown, what would you show them?
6. Describe your dream car.
7. Tell about a toy you remember from childhood.
8. Tell about the foods that you can easily eat too much of.

CONTROVERSIAL AND MORE DIFFICULT

1. Recycling should be mandatory for everyone.
2. Reality TV shows have negative effects on children.
3. Measles and other vaccinations should be mandatory for all children.
4. Athletes and celebrities are overpaid.
5. Global warming is the biggest threat to the environment today.
6. Public schools should operate year-round.
7. Fossil fuels should be taxed highly because these national resources are in danger of running out.

SPEAKING TOPICS (AS MONOLOGUES) OR ROLE-PLAYING SCENARIOS WHERE ANOTHER PERSON RESPONDS

RELATING INFORMATION

1. You are in a car insurance office because you have been in an accident. Explain to the agent how it happened.

2. You are having a yard sale and want to sell an expensive watch. Describe to a possible buyer the watch and its value.

3. You are at the customer service window of a grocery store to find out if they have all the snacks you need for a party you are giving. Explain to the person what you need.

4. You are at the check-in desk of your doctor's office because you have not been feeling well. Explain to the person what is wrong.

5. You are at a travel information booth on a state toll road because your car is not running properly and you want information about nearby repair service. Describe to the toll booth attendant what is wrong with your car.

6. You are at a rent-a-car desk and have been asked about your driving experience. Describe your experience to the agent.

7. You are at a shoe store looking for a pair of dress shoes. Explain to the clerk exactly what kind of shoes you want.

8. You are in the post office to send a package to a relative in the Army overseas. Describe to the post office worker where and how you want it sent.

9. You are at the florist to order flowers for your husband/wife (boyfriend/girlfriend). Explain to the owner what you want.

10. You are at an ice cream store and want a special ice cream concoction. Explain to the worker how to make it.

11. You are telephoning your dentist's secretary to make an appointment to have a filling replaced. Explain to the secretary the details of what you want to have done.

12. You are consulting a speech-language pathologist about your speech problem. Explain your problem to her.

13. You are at an employment agency applying for a part-time job on Saturdays. Explain your qualifications to the person in charge.

14. You are reporting to the boss that you lost $50.00 you collected on a part-time pizza delivering job. Explain to your boss what happened.

15. You are at the exit booth of a large parking lot because you cannot find your car. Describe what your car looks like to the attendant.

16. You're at the Apple store to inquire about why your Mac laptop won't turn on after you left it in your car all day.

17. You need a new desk for your office and go to IKEA to inquire about desk designs and prices. Explain what you like to a sales attendant.

ASKING QUESTIONS

1. You need to get rid of too many clothes in your closet that you never wear. Ask a neighbor who is planning a yard sale about selling your clothes there and how you should price them.

2. You are traveling in a mountain national park and stop at a visitor information booth to find out about overnight facilities. Ask about it.

3. You are taking a science course and do not understand weightlessness in space. Ask your teacher to explain it.

4. You are at the Internal Revenue office to find out if your specific travel expenses are deductible on your income tax. Ask the person about it.

5. You are at an ice cream store and want to understand differences between ice cream and frozen yogurt. Ask the server to explain it to you.

6. You are at the cashier's window at a bank to inquire about opening a new savings account. Ask the teller about the details.

7. You are at a rent-a-car desk to inquire about renting a car for a week. Ask the agent about the possibilities, prices, and regulations.

8. You are at a shoe store to find out if they carry your favorite kind of casual shoes. Ask the clerk if they do.

9. You are in the post office to find out about mailing perishable items like cake. Ask the clerk about it.

10. You are at a booth that is collecting for the United Way and want to find out about volunteer work with the organization. Ask the person about it.

11. You are at the florist shop to buy flowers for your husband/wife (boyfriend/girlfriend). Ask the owner about appropriate flower gifts.

12. You are at the checkout counter of a grocery store and want to know about leaving your groceries to pick them up later. Ask the check-out person about possibilities for such and reclaiming procedures.

13. You are telephoning your dentist's secretary to confirm an appointment and find out about bringing past X-rays. Ask the secretary about it.

14. You are at a travel information booth on a state toll road. Ask the toll booth operator directions and other pertinent travel information to the next large city.

15. You are at an employment agency inquiring about part-time jobs. Ask the person in charge about jobs that interest you and fit into your schedule.

16. You are at the entrance booth of a large parking lot where you plan to leave your car for several days. Ask the attendant about cost and safety.

17. You are in Macy's asking a customer service representative what they think your hard-to-buy-for friend might like. Ask the representative what he might recommend.

18. You've traveled to a national park and stop into a travel center to inquire about the best places to stay around the park through your trip. Ask the helper there about what you should see.

19. You are making a new recipe with lots of foreign foods and are visiting an ethnic grocery. Ask the shop stocker for help to find the obscure foods.

20. You are at a pet store to find the perfect toy for your new dog that seems to destroy everything it touches. Ask the worker for his opinion and recommendations.

21. You are staying at a hotel in a large city and cramming four extra people into your room. You need extra towels and blankets and go to the lobby. Ask the concierge for the towels and blankets as inconspicuously as you can.

22. You're new to the local university and cannot find the building where your first class is to be held. You stop a nearby person for help. Explain your situation and ask the person for help.

23. You are on a train from Denver to San Francisco and realize you purchased a ticket for the wrong day, though the train is already moving and the train is full, so you don't have a seat. You find a conductor. Ask her what you should do.

24. You want to try out a new dessert recipe but aren't sure what you'd like to make.

You go into a bakery to look around. Ask the baker for help in making a particular dessert you see.

25. You're lost in Boston. Ask a nearby person for directions on how to find the famous aquarium because your phone doesn't have a signal.

PERSUADING

1. You are in a car insurance office and have been involved in an accident. Convince the agent that your insurance premiums should not be raised.

2. You are selling an expensive watch at a yard sale. Convince the interested buyer to give you more money for it.

3. You are at the checkout counter of a grocery store and want boxes instead of paper bags for your groceries. Convince the check-out person to go call for someone to get boxes.

4. You are telephoning your dentist's secretary because you received a bill that you consider excessive. Convince the secretary that it is too much.

5. You are at the loan desk of the bank because you want credit to finance a new car. Convince the loan officer to extend you the credit.

6. You are at an airline's counter at the airport ready to leave for Florida on vacation and you find that your reservation has been cancelled. Convince the airline's agent to put you on the flight.

7. You are at a shoe store and are selling shoes. Convince a customer to buy low-heeled shoes.

8. You are working at the post office and a woman presents a poorly wrapped package to be sent across country. Convince her to take it home and rewrap it.

9. You are working at a booth collecting for the United Way and a potential donor approaches. Convince the person to donate.

10. You are working at an ice cream store and a customer refuses to pay for an ice cream sundae because she did not like it. Convince him to pay for it.

11. You are taking a science course and want to do a special reading project rather than taking the regular tests. Convince your teacher to permit you to do so.

12. You are at a toll booth on a state toll road and have lost your toll ticket. Convince the toll booth attendant not to fine you.

13. You are telephoning an acquaintance to come to a party you are giving. Convince the person to change previous plans and come to your party.

14. You are seeing a speech-language pathologist about your speech problem and she asks you to stutter to strangers. Convince her that you should not be required to do so.

15. You are consulting with your boss to ask for a raise on your part-time job. Convince your boss that you deserve a raise.

16. You want to go to an event and you want your close friend to go with you. Your friend does not want to go. The event means a lot to you, and you'd really like your friend to go. Convince your friend to go with you.

17. You've come into your favorite restaurant to inquire about hosting a private event there, although you know that's something they don't do often. Convince the hostess to permit you to hold the event.

18. You're at a department store to return a shirt that does not fit. Convince the sale clerk that you bought it from that store but you seem to have lost the receipt.

19. You're selling cookies for a bake sale for nonprofit organization and haven't had a lot of business yet. Convince a person walking by to try your favorite kind of cookie.

APPENDIX C: SPEAKER/LISTENER ROLES OR CHARACTERISTICS

SPEAKER/LISTENER ROLES

- Use a vacant expression while the speaker is talking. Look zoned out. Take long pauses before you talk.
- Make no eye contact with the speaker. Look behind one of their shoulders, not down. Talk to them as you usually might, but avoid any eye contact.
- Constantly interrupt the speaker.
- Act as though you have more important things to do. Constantly check your watch, rush the conversation, and give short answers.
- Laugh at inappropriate times at things that are not intended to be funny, as if you actually think that they are.
- Hold strong and uncomfortable eye contact as if you are peering into the soul of the speaker.
- You're tired and distracted. Yawn frequently and act bored. Find it hard to have anything to say.
- Be overly interested and curious. Get excited by irrelevant details. Comment excessively.
- Be as caring and interested as you can. Listen attentively to the speaker and respond appropriately.
- Walk away from the person without responding at all.
- Show surprise and embarrassment that the person is talking to you.

EYE CONTACT DIFFERENCES

- Make normal eye contact.
- Avoid eye contact (unintentional). Look around as though you don't even notice the person.
- Avoid eye contact (intentional). Avoid the person's sight as though you are embarrassed or guilty.
- Glance. Look at the person's eyes occasionally, for a very brief time. Look away immediately if the other person's eyes meet yours.
- Hookup. When your eyes meet, hold the contact for a second or two before looking away, as though the person is interesting to you.

- Stare. Look at the person's eyes constantly.
- Evaluation. Occasionally look for a second at different parts of the person.
- Squint occasionally.
- Close eyes occasionally. Use extra-long blinks.
- Blink excessively.
- Do not blink at all.
- Look down most of the time.
- Look up most of the time.
- Look at the top of the person's head.
- Keep your head tilted slightly back, so you are looking slightly down at the person.

APPENDIX D: PAIRED ROLE PLAYING SCENARIOS AND DEBATE TOPICS

PAIRED ROLE PLAYS WITH DIFFERENT LISTENER REACTIONS

Participants will play themselves in these scenarios. Paired partners will play the listener roles.

POSITIVE

- Talking about stuttering with a new friend who told you that you would make a good teacher.
- Talking on the phone with a romantic partner who said they actually like your stutter because it made you unique.
- Interacting at a conference with a work colleague from a different state who greatly admires your work.

NEUTRAL

- Interacting with some boys who came to where you are working but did not say one thing about your stuttering when it was particularly severe.
- Talking with a new friend who initially asked about stuttering but no longer seems to even notice it.
- Calling your regular dentist's office and arranging appointments with a receptionist who never reacts to your stuttering.

NEGATIVE

- Ordering a meal from a drive-through when the person mocks your stuttering.
- Explaining to a teacher that you need more time for a required speech because you stutter, and the teacher is very reluctant to give you more time.
- Being asked at a job interview about your stuttering by an interviewer who said he used to stutter but got over it by being yelled at in Army basic training.

PAIRED ROLE PLAYS WITH DIFFERENT WAYS OF ACKNOWLEDGING A SPEECH-RELATED SYMPTOM

ACKNOWLEDGING BY EXAGGERATING THE SYMPTOM (NEGATIVE PRACTICE)

The leader asks participants to respond to each scenario in paired role plays and then explains the following. The "stranger" (B) is to bring up the assigned speech characteristic with each "speech disordered" participant (A). A is to respond by exaggerating the speech characteristic as much as possible instead of minimizing it.

- **Situation:** You are on the phone with the plumber because your sink is overflowing with water and flooding your kitchen.
    - » A: You stutter on every word, even if interrupted.
    - » B: The plumber on the other line sounds frustrated and tries to talk over the stutterer.
- **Situation:** You are at a restaurant on a first date. You don't want to come across as needy, but your food is undercooked and cold, and you want to send it back to the kitchen.
    - » A: You speak with a very hoarse (raspy) voice.
    - » B: The waiter comments on the hoarse voice and appears concerned.
- **Situation:** You are asking the barista at Starbucks about the new fall drink menu, and there is a long line behind you.
    - » A: You stutter severely until the end of the order.
    - » B: The barista interrupts you several times even though you keep talking.
- **Situation:** You are at the mall seeking help from a store employee. You are trying to describe a shirt that you want to buy that you saw in a magazine.
    - » A: You mispronounce several sounds, such as "s" and "z" sounds.
    - » B: The employee says he cannot understand. He or she looks very puzzled and later annoyed.
- **Situation:** You studied all week for a test and thought you aced it, only to find out that you filled out your computerized scoring sheet completely wrong causing you to get an F. You schedule a meeting to talk it over with your professor.
    - » A: You do not come to the point but, instead, talk all around it.
    - » B: The professor is frustrated that you take so long trying to get your point across.
- **Situation:** You are at a brand new, huge grocery store and see an older person with a delicious looking cake in their cart. You ask them what it is and where they got it

from in the store.

> » A: You keep stuttering even when the person tries to fill in the word they think you are trying to say.
>
> » B: The person tries to guess and finish your words even though you do not stop stuttering.

- **Situation:** You are a new student at the local university and it's the first day of class. You sit down next to a person in class and try to muster the courage to start a conversation.
    > » A: You quietly and tentatively begin talking even though you are ordinarily a very shy, quiet person.
    >
    > » B: The person initially looks puzzled, but later asks, "What? Are you talking?" etc.

ACKNOWLEDGING BY USING HUMOR

The leader asks each participant to role play and respond to their scenario again, this time disclosing with humor, i.e., telling another person in a funny way.

- **Situation:** You're on the phone with the plumber because your sink is overflowing with water and flooding your kitchen.
    > » A: You stutter on several words. Then you tell the plumber, "This might mean I'll need you even worse."
    >
    > » B: The plumber initially seems to be frustrated. He later responds appropriately to the joke and proceeds.

- **Situation:** You are at a restaurant on a first date. You don't want to come across as needy, but your food is undercooked and cold, and you want to send it back to the kitchen.
    > » A: You speak with a very hoarse (raspy) voice. Later, you joke about your voice, telling your date that you probably sound like the food already burned your throat.
    >
    > » B: The waiter listens, smiles, and then accepts your voice.

- **Situation:** You are asking the barista at Starbucks about the new fall drink menu, and there is a long line behind you.
    > » A: You stutter severely until the end of the order. You then comment that you have a venti-sized stutter.
    >
    > » B: The barista looks very uncomfortable until the joke and then responds positively.

- **Situation:** You're at the mall seeking help from a store employee. You are trying to describe a shirt that you want to buy that you saw in a magazine.
    - » A: You mispronounce several sounds, such as "s" and "z" sounds. Later, you comment that it's only an "eth."
    - » B: The worker asks about your lisp, but then smiles and moves on after the answer.
- **Situation:** You studied all week for a test and thought you aced it, only to find out that you filled out your computerized scoring sheet completely wrong causing you to get an F. You schedule a meeting to talk it over with your professor.
    - » A: You tell the professor that she might want to get a drink before you start to talk to her because it's going to take a while. You do not come to the point but talk all around it.
    - » B: The professor listens with patience and possibly a little smile.
- **Situation:** You are at a brand new, huge grocery store and see an older person with a delicious looking cake in their cart. You ask them what it is and where they got it from in the store.
    - » A: You keep stuttering when the person tries to fill in the word they think you are trying to say, and during that, you smile with a little wink or twinkle in your eye.
    - » B: Listens after seeing A's smile.
- **Situation:** You are a freshman at the local university and it's the first day of class. You sit down next to a person in class and try to muster the courage to start a conversation.
    - » A: Tries even though he/she is ordinarily a very shy, quiet person. After the first failed attempt, A smiles and says that he/she doesn't ordinarily yell at people when first meeting them. Then he/she proceeds.
    - » B: Looks puzzled until the joke, but then responds in a friendly way.

DEBATE TOPICS

- Public schools should be closed every time it snows versus schools should be kept open, no matter what the weather.
- We should eat meat versus we should be vegetarians.
- Cameras should be installed that give automatic tickets to drivers running red lights versus cameras should not be installed.
- PCs are better versus Macs are better.

- Health insurance companies should mandate parenting classes for people expecting a baby versus prospective parents do not need anyone telling them how to parent.
- Online shopping would be better for everyone versus local shopping would be better for everyone.
- Beaches are the best vacation spots versus mountains are the best vacation spots.

APPENDIX E: WELCOMING WORDS AND CLOSING WORDS

WELCOMING WORDS

Welcome to the _____ Chapter of the National Stuttering Association. The National Stuttering Association is a nonprofit organization dedicated to bringing hope, dignity, support, education, and empowerment to children and adults who stutter, their families, and professionals through support, education, advocacy, and research.

If you are a person who stutters, or have a special interest in stuttering, you are welcome here. For the time we meet here, this room is a very special place.

- It is a place where we are accepted and supported;
- It is a place where we can relax and speak freely;
- It is a place where we can stutter openly without fear and embarrassment;
- It is a place where we can practice whatever speaking and communicating techniques with which we may feel comfortable.

Together, we will help each other and we will help ourselves to accept and cope with our stuttering, to build our self-confidence, and to improve our verbal communication skills to the best of our abilities.

We who stutter, and those who support and help us, are not alone. Together we are strong.*

Optional: Because this meeting is a safe place where participants can discuss personal matters in a supporting environment, everything said here must remain strictly confidential. Let us share the hope and encouragement we receive here with others, but keep all the details to ourselves.

CLOSING WORDS

May the spirit we have shared tonight help our speech in the coming weeks, until we meet again.

May we go forth gladly into speaking situations, without force or struggle, accepting ourselves regardless of our fluency, and listening always to the music of our voices.

We are not alone. Together we are strong.*

Optional: Please remember the confidential nature of this meeting. Take the help and encouragement with you, and leave the details behind.

---

* Included with permission of the National Stuttering Association.

APPENDIX F: INSTRUMENTS AND HANDOUTS

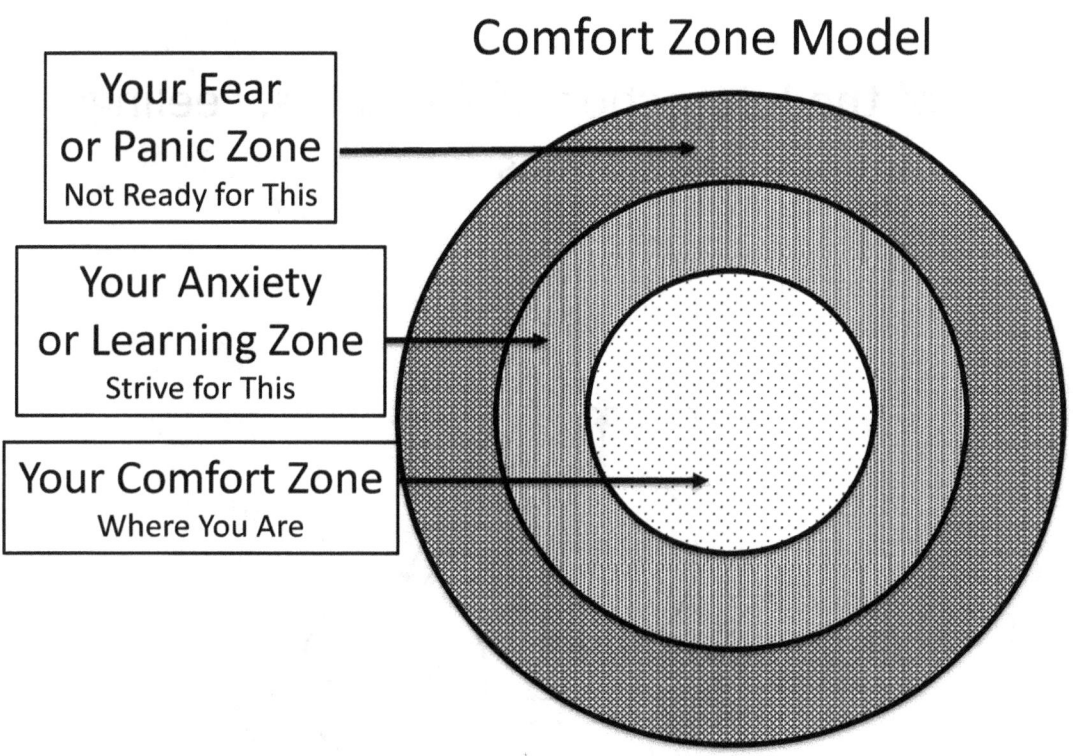

A Model of the Interaction of Thoughts, Feelings, & Actions

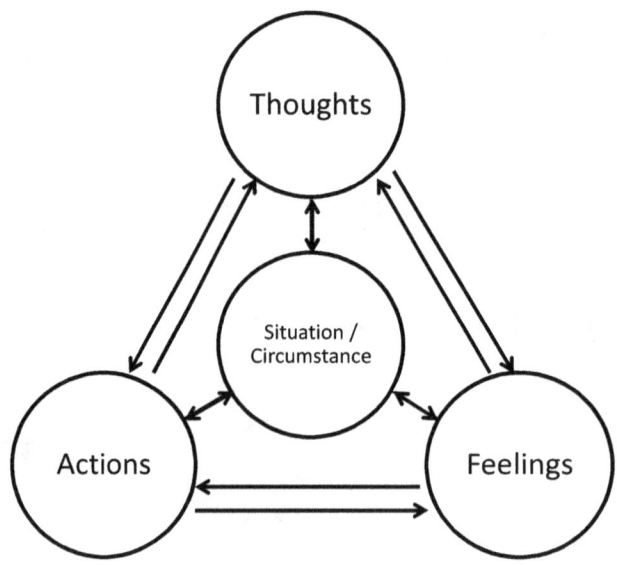

MY LIFE JOURNEY

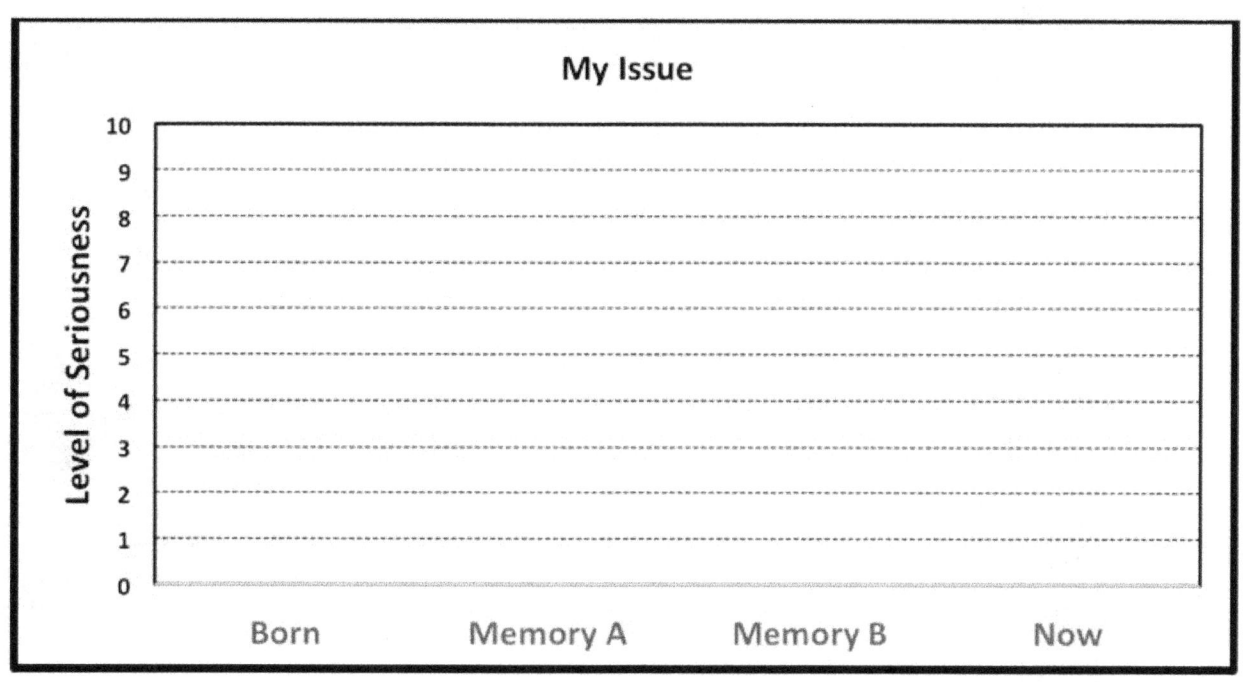

Personal Appraisal of Support for Stuttering–Adult (PASS–Ad)
Kenneth O. St. Louis

Name _____ Age ___ Sex (M/F/Other) Years of formal education ___ Years of speech therapy ___

Supporting others with difficult life circumstances means many things. It also varies for different circumstances and for different people. This questionnaire asks what **you feel** about **support for you now** as a person who stutters or who stuttered in the past.

****

How supportive <u>for me</u> would it be if a person were to…?	Not supportive at all		Neither support nor lack of support		Very supportive	Not sure
Leave me alone	-2	-1	0	+1	+2	u
Interact with me but never mention or react to my stuttering	-2	-1	0	+1	+2	u
Ask me how he/she could help me with my stuttering	-2	-1	0	+1	+2	u
Appear to be concerned or express concern about my stuttering	-2	-1	0	+1	+2	u
Help me by trying to finish words I stutter on	-2	-1	0	+1	+2	u
Stutter for real himself/herself when we talk	-2	-1	0	+1	+2	u
Put some "faked" stuttering into his/her own speech when we talk	-2	-1	0	+1	+2	u
Use the term "stutterer" when commenting about me and my speech	-2	-1	0	+1	+2	u
Make a joke about stuttering to try to reduce the awkwardness surrounding stuttering	-2	-1	0	+1	+2	u
Wait to let me say what I want	-2	-1	0	+1	+2	u
Ask me questions about stuttering	-2	-1	0	+1	+2	u
Ask me to help him/her with his/her own stuttering	-2	-1	0	+1	+2	u
Tell me where I can get information about stuttering	-2	-1	0	+1	+2	u
Tell me how I should feel about stuttering	-2	-1	0	+1	+2	u
Tell me what I should do when I stutter	-2	-1	0	+1	+2	u
Tell me his/her own story of stuttering	-2	-1	0	+1	+2	u
Offer to refer me to someone whom he/she believes could help me cope with—but not change—my stuttering	-2	-1	0	+1	+2	u
Offer to refer me to someone whom he/she believes could help me stop or greatly reduce my stuttering	-2	-1	0	+1	+2	u
Use the term "person who stutters" or "PWS" when commenting about me and my speech	-2	-1	0	+1	+2	u
Invite me to a self-help or support group for stuttering persons	-2	-1	0	+1	+2	u
Invite me to his/her party	-2	-1	0	+1	+2	u

Copyright, 2021, Populore Publishing Company. All rights reserved.

Downloads of the *PASS–Ad* are available for a fee at www.teacherspayteachers.com.

Arrange for me to talk with someone else who stutters	-2	-1	0	+1	+2	u
Maintain normal eye contact with me while we talk	-2	-1	0	+1	+2	u
Give me a brochure, book, video, etc. about stuttering	-2	-1	0	+1	+2	u

Overall the degree or amount of support for my stuttering that...	None		Average		A lot	Not sure
I have experienced from other people in my life	-2	-1	0	+1	+2	u
I have wanted from other people	-2	-1	0	+1	+2	u
I have personally tried to get from others	-2	-1	0	+1	+2	u

Overall the degree or amount of support that...	None		Average		A great deal	Not sure
I have provided for other people who stutter	-2	-1	0	+1	+2	u
I want to provide for other people who stutter	-2	-1	0	+1	+2	u

The support I have experienced up to now for my stuttering from the following persons or groups is...	Not applicable	No support		Neither support nor lack of support		A great deal of support	Not sure
My mother	n/a	-2	-1	0	+1	+2	u
My father	n/a	-2	-1	0	+1	+2	u
My sibling(s)	n/a	-2	-1	0	+1	+2	u
My other relatives	n/a	-2	-1	0	+1	+2	u
One of my closest friends	n/a	-2	-1	0	+1	+2	u
Another of my closest friends	n/a	-2	-1	0	+1	+2	u
My social media friends (e.g., Facebook)	n/a	-2	-1	0	+1	+2	u
My elementary school teachers	n/a	-2	-1	0	+1	+2	u
My elementary school classmates	n/a	-2	-1	0	+1	+2	u
My middle (junior high) school teachers	n/a	-2	-1	0	+1	+2	u
My middle (junior high) school classmates	n/a	-2	-1	0	+1	+2	u
My high school teachers	n/a	-2	-1	0	+1	+2	u
My high school classmates	n/a	-2	-1	0	+1	+2	u
My university teachers	n/a	-2	-1	0	+1	+2	u
My university classmates	n/a	-2	-1	0	+1	+2	u
My current work boss	n/a	-2	-1	0	+1	+2	u
My current coworkers	n/a	-2	-1	0	+1	+2	u
My work boss in a past job	n/a	-2	-1	0	+1	+2	u
My coworkers in a past job	n/a	-2	-1	0	+1	+2	u

One of my speech-language therapists	n/a	-2	-1	0	+1	+2	u
Another of my speech-language therapists	n/a	-2	-1	0	+1	+2	u
A self-help or support group for people who stutter	n/a	-2	-1	0	+1	+2	u
People talking about their stuttering on television, YouTube, social media, the Internet, etc.	n/a	-2	-1	0	+1	+2	u
Famous people who stutter	n/a	-2	-1	0	+1	+2	u
Actors/actresses portraying people who stutter in films	n/a	-2	-1	0	+1	+2	u

What are the five (or fewer) important things a non-stuttering person could do or demonstrate that he/she supports me as a person who stutters?

1)
2)
3)
4)
5)

How supportive would the following activities be for people who stutter?	Not supportive at all		Neither supportive nor not supportive		Very supportive	Not sure
Reading a brochure or watching a video that summarizes recent information on the problem of stuttering	-2	-1	0	+1	+2	u
Talking face-to-face with a person who stutters	-2	-1	0	+1	+2	u
Reading, watching, or listening to personal stories of a few people who stutter	-2	-1	0	+1	+2	u
Attending a self-help or support group for people who stutter	-2	-1	0	+1	+2	u
Walking around with a nonstuttering person who "fakes" stuttering in several social situations without disclosing that he/she really does not stutter	-2	-1	0	+1	+2	u
Other? _____	-2	-1	0	+1	+2	u

Personal Priorities Checklist
Kenneth O. St. Louis

Today, the importance of each of these aspects in my life is…	Never important		Usually not important		Equally important or not important		Usually important		Always important	I Don't Know
being safe and secure	1	2	3	4	5	6	7	8	9	u
being free to do what I want	1	2	3	4	5	6	7	8	9	u
spending quiet time alone	1	2	3	4	5	6	7	8	9	u
attending parties or social events	1	2	3	4	5	6	7	8	9	u
imagining new things	1	2	3	4	5	6	7	8	9	u
helping the less fortunate	1	2	3	4	5	6	7	8	9	u
having exciting but potentially "dangerous" experiences	1	2	3	4	5	6	7	8	9	u
practicing my religion	1	2	3	4	5	6	7	8	9	u
earning money	1	2	3	4	5	6	7	8	9	u
doing my jobs or my duty	1	2	3	4	5	6	7	8	9	u
getting things finished	1	2	3	4	5	6	7	8	9	u
figuring out how to solve important problems	1	2	3	4	5	6	7	8	9	u

In 5 years, I want the importance of each of these aspects in my life to be …	Never important		Usually not important		Equally important or not important		Usually important		Always important	I Don't Know
being safe and secure	1	2	3	4	5	6	7	8	9	u
being free to do what I want	1	2	3	4	5	6	7	8	9	u
spending quiet time alone	1	2	3	4	5	6	7	8	9	u
attending parties or social events	1	2	3	4	5	6	7	8	9	u
imagining new things	1	2	3	4	5	6	7	8	9	u
helping the less fortunate	1	2	3	4	5	6	7	8	9	u
having exciting but potentially "dangerous" experiences	1	2	3	4	5	6	7	8	9	u
practicing my religion	1	2	3	4	5	6	7	8	9	u
earning money	1	2	3	4	5	6	7	8	9	u
doing my jobs or my duty	1	2	3	4	5	6	7	8	9	u
getting things finished	1	2	3	4	5	6	7	8	9	u
figuring out how to solve important problems	1	2	3	4	5	6	7	8	9	u

Copyright, 2021, Populore Publishing Company. All rights reserved except permission to copy and use by the purchaser only.

Downloads of the *Personal Priorities Checklist* are available for a fee at www.teacherspayteachers.com.

APPENDIX G. SESSION GOALS FOR PARTICIPANTS

FOR STUTTERERS

- Maintaining better eye contact
- Speaking more slowly
- Resisting a tendency to avoid words or substitute words
- Resisting a tendency to use any particular accessory (secondary) behavior, such as hand movements, eye blinks, looking away from the speaker, etc.
- Voluntary stuttering or faking stuttering in any particular way
- Practicing any fluency shaping target, such as light contact, easy vocal onset, slow rate
- Practicing any stuttering modification voluntary control, such as cancellations, pull-outs, or preparatory sets
- Holding on to stutters longer than necessary
- Changing the form of any stutter, i.e., the usual repetitions, prolongations, or blocks
- Being more accepting of your stuttering
- Noticing and monitoring an accessory behavior that is virtually automatic
- Deliberately using a feared word throughout the session as often as possible

FOR CLUTTERERS OR STUTTERERS WHO ALSO CLUTTER

- Concentrating on speech more than usual
- Speaking more slowly
- Speaking more clearly
- Thinking about the message of what to say before starting to say it
- Pausing between sentences for 1–2 seconds
- Pronouncing all the syllables of long words

FOR NONSTUTTERING GUESTS

- Learning something new about stuttering
- Getting to know some new people
- Learning everyone's names

- Being willing to move out of your comfort zone

FOR ANYONE
- Improving small talk
- Volunteering to participate more readily than usual
- Being an active listener
- Reducing fillers such as "um," "uh," "like," "you know," "well," "and," and "so"
- Speaking with a full, clear voice
- Speaking as clearly as possible
- Speaking louder than usual
- Using a more pleasant voice
- Making your points more succinctly
- Waiting to respond and not interrupting others
- Being as supportive of others as possible
- Practicing appropriate assertiveness
- Being fully "present" for the entire session

APPENDIX H. GLOSSARY OF STUTTERING WORDS

Anticipation: Anticipation refers to the ability that many stutterers have to predict in advance when they are going to stutter. (See also *expectancy*.)

Blocks: Blocks in stuttering are when the speech flow stops unexpectedly and longer than normal either within a word (e.g., "I fff [3-second silent pause] orgot your name.") or between words (e.g., "Tomorrow is the my little [4-second pause] sister's birthday.")

Cancellation: This is a stuttering modification approach wherein the speaker stutters through a word in the typical way, then rehearses (first out loud but later mentally) (1) a shortened version of the primary tension or abnormality, (2) a shortened version of an easier (but not necessarily fluent) form of the word, and (3) a repeat of the stuttered word in a modified way if possible. It is important that the cancelled word not be said immediately after the original stuttered word, but only after a pause of at least 2–3 seconds wherein the abnormality and revised versions are rehearsed. Cancellation is the first voluntary control learned. It will later be a backup procedure to follow a failed pull-out. (See also *stuttering modification, pull-out, preparatory set*.)

Cluttering: Cluttering is a fluency disorder wherein conversational speech rate in one's native language is typically and frequently too fast overall, too irregular, or both. The fast and/or irregular (i.e., jerky) speech rate must further be accompanied by one or more of the following: (a) excessive non-stuttering disfluencies; (b) abnormal or excessive collapsing or deletion of syllables; and/or (c) abnormal pauses, juncture, or syllable stress.

Comfort Zone: Comfort zone refers to the place or situation where one feels the most comfortable. Moving or going beyond that zone typically induces discomfort, uncertainty, anxiety, or stronger emotions.

"Continuous Phonation": "Continuous phonation" (or voicing) is often the last fluency shaping target learned in speech therapy. It involves keeping the voice on and prolonging most syllables slightly more than usual. While the voice is not technically kept on all the time (e.g., during voiceless sounds), the speaker thinks about "continuing" or prolonging voicing of sounds and words. Easy voice onset helps the speaker get started; "continuous phonation" maintains a similar change in voicing throughout the utterance. (See also *fluency shaping, easy voice onset*.)

CWS: As a "person-first" labelling strategy, CWS is used by some for "child who stutters."

Delayed Auditory Feedback (DAF): This is the phenomenon of hearing what one just said up to 1/5 of a second later in addition to or rather than what one is currently hearing. It is generated by devices designed to hear speech at pre-determined delays. Listening to one's delayed speech often results in a slower, more prolonged pattern of speech, with less or no typical stuttering, similar to fluency shaping. Sometimes, under DAF, speakers repeat syllables that occur later in multisyllabic words, even people who don't stutter. (See also *SpeechEasy®*.)

Desensitization: Desensitization typically refers to a wide variety of techniques that are designed to reduce the learned, negative emotions (anxiety or fear, embarrassment, shame, guilt, frustration, or anger) associated with stuttering. Desensitization is a goal of many of the plans in this book.

Disfluency: Disfluency is any break in the speech flow that is not a normal production of speech sounds or the normal pauses that occur. They can be normal disfluencies or abnormal disfluencies. Normal disfluencies consist of unforced word repetitions (e.g., "Let's-let's all take a break."), phrase repetitions (e.g., "If you find-if you find the correct answer, tell us."), fillers (e.g., "Like when you reach First Street, you um turn right."), or other normal breaks such as rewording (e.g., "Please help me a [short pause] Help us to get this right.") Abnormal disfluencies, or dysfluencies, are the same as stuttering. Some speech-language pathologists or people who stutter use *disfluencies* to mean the same thing as *stuttering*, although that is not the correct usage.

Easy Voice Onset: Easy voice onset involves learning to begin utterances with a breathy voice, or with vocal folds that do not completely close before a sound emerges. It sounds like a very small /h/ sound precedes a beginning sound that is voiced, such as in the word, "apple." The word should not sound like "happle," but a little air should precede the beginning of the "a." (See also *fluency shaping*.)

Expectancy: Expectancy refers to the ability that many stutterers have to predict in advance when they are going to stutter. (See also *anticipation*.)

Faking: This is the same as voluntary stuttering.

Fluency: For a stuttering person, fluency is regarded as the opposite of stuttering, or when he or she is not stuttering. In linguistics, it describes the flow of speech, including normal pauses.

Fluency Disorder: A fluency disorder is a term speech-language pathologists use to include stuttering, cluttering, and sometimes other related problems. Some speech-language pathologists use *fluency disorder* and *stuttering* interchangeably although this is not the most accurate use of the term.

Fluency Shaping: Fluency shaping has come to refer to a large group of speech therapy strategies to treat stuttering. Also referred to as a "speak more fluently" approach, fluency shaping involves learning to talk in a semi-artificial way by focusing attention on specific speech "targets" all the time while one talks. Common targets include slowing one's speaking rate (slow rate), beginning voicing or phonation gradually (easy voice onset), pronouncing speech sounds with minimal effort or in an almost-but-not-quite slur (light contact), and shortening pauses between words such that they almost run together ("continuous phonation"). If one can do this continually, stuttering typically drops out or greatly diminishes. The approach is relatively easy to learn but requires a great deal of ongoing concentration, which can be difficult to achieve. Also, without careful coaching and considerable practice, the resulting speech can sound extremely artificial, almost robotic. (See also *slow rate, easy voice onset, light contact, and "continuous phonation."*)

Frequency Altered Feedback (FAF): This is the phenomenon of hearing what one is saying, either as a much higher voice (e.g., "Mickey Mouse voice") or a much lower voice (e.g., "Darth Vader voice"). It is generated by devices designed to hear speech at pre-determined vocal frequencies by filtering out low or high frequencies. Listening to one's frequency altered feedback often results in little or no stuttering. (See also *SpeechEasy®.*)

Insight: Insight refers to the understanding one acquires about something. In the case of stuttering, it includes both understanding one's own thoughts and feelings related to stuttering as well as the thoughts and feelings of others (such as beliefs, reactions, and symptoms). The optimal insight is knowledge that is consistent with facts or theories of stuttering derived from careful research. Better insight is a goal of many of the plans in this book.

Light Contact: Light contact involves pronouncing speech sounds with minimal effort or in an almost-but-not-quite-slurred fashion. For example, in the word, "popcorn," the lips don't come quite together to build up normal pressure on the /p/ sounds but let a small amount of air escape as the pressure in the mouth increases. (See also *fluency shaping.*)

Preparatory Set: This is a stuttering modification approach, learned after one is able and willing to do pull-outs effectively with typical stutters. In this case, the speaker, rather than beginning with a typical tense or unusual posture or "set," in a slow, controlled, and highly voluntary way, eases into the stuttered word and progresses slowly through it. If unsuccessful, they should do a pull-out on the word. And if unsuccessful with that, they should do a Cancellation of the stuttered word. (See also *stuttering modification, pull-out.*)

Prolongations: Prolongations in stuttering involve stretching individual speech sounds longer than normal (e.g., "mmmmmmmmmmmmmine") or stretching syllables longer than normal (e.g., "geeeeeeeennnnnerally").

Prolonged Speech: This is another name given to the speech that typically results from fluency shaping. (See also *fluency shaping*.)

Pull-Out: This is a stuttering modification approach, learned after one is able and willing to do cancellations after typical stutters. In this case, the speaker begins with a tense, uncontrolled stutter as usual but then, while continuing to stutter, slows it down, reduces the tension, and continues in the stutter until they believe that they can say the word more easily than normal. The word should be finished in an unhurried, highly voluntary way. If successful, the speaker continues. If not, he or she should do a cancellation on that word. (See also *stuttering modification, cancellation, preparatory set*.)

PWS: As a "person-first" labeling strategy, PWS means "person who stutters." It has been variously advocated for addressing a stuttering individual instead of using the direct label *stutterer*. Some who stutter prefer to be addressed as a "person who stutters." Some prefer the abbreviation PWS. Some, like this book's author, prefer the term *stutterer*, because in several research studies there has been no evidence that the term *stutterer* is pejorative.

Repetitions: Repetitions in stuttering typically focus on individual sounds (e.g., "f-f-f-f-f-fun") or syllables (e.g., "co-co-co-co-coming"). Sometimes it includes repetitions of whole words (e.g., "We-we-we-we-we can help out."), especially in stuttering children. Repetitions of entire phrases can, but do not have to be, symptoms of stuttering (e.g., "I want-I want-I want an-I want an ice cream cone.").

Role Play: Role play involves assuming the role of oneself or someone else in a make-believe situation. Typically, role playing is done in order to practice, try out, or gain experience in a potentially difficult situation in a safe environment.

Slow Rate: Slow rate involves learning to slow one's speaking rate while maintaining otherwise normal-sounding pronunciation, loudness, pitch, and vocal intonation. Typically, a person is taught at a highly exaggerated slow rate, e.g., one syllable per second, and as the skill is learned, the speaking rate is increased by steps until a "slow normal" rate is achieved. (See also *fluency shaping*.)

SpeechEasy®: SpeechEasy® is a commercial device, developed with hearing aid technology that provides programmable levels of delayed and frequency altered feedback. Some who stutter become more or completely fluent using the SpeechEasy© device.

Stammering: Stammering is synonymous with stuttering. In the United Kingdom, India, and in other places, stammering is still used in some regions instead of stuttering. In the last century, stammering was differentiated from stuttering, but that no longer is the case.

Stuttering: Stuttering has more than one meaning, depending on who is defining. Following are four definitions:

Stuttering is a speech disorder characterized mainly by any combination of abnormal repetitions, prolongations, or blocking while trying to say sounds or syllables. Speech-language pathologists typically prefer this definition. (See also *repetitions, prolongations, blocks.*)

Stuttering is what people consider to be stuttering, even if they cannot clearly identify specific symptoms. Researchers often prefer this definition.

Stuttering is the feeling of being out of control or "blocked." People who stutter typically prefer this definition.

Stuttering is a symptom of a physiological or psychological problem that is regarded as its cause. Examples include genetic differences, neurological or movement deficiencies, social anxiety, etc. Researchers and clinicians seeking the cause of stuttering usually have their own preferred, causal definitions.

Stuttering Modification: Stuttering modification refers to a group of approaches to stuttering therapy that involve the speaker learning to voluntarily change his or her typical stutters to an easier, more relaxed form of stuttering. Also referred to as a "stutter more fluently" approach, the goal is "fluent stuttering." Stuttering modification was popularized by the late Charles Van Riper; hence, it is also sometimes called the Van Riper approach. The common "voluntary controls" involved are cancellations, pull-outs, and preparatory sets. (See also *cancellation, pull-out, preparatory set.*)

Voluntary Stuttering: This is a desensitization technique in which a stuttering speaker stutters on purpose on various words. Typically, the speaker plans which word(s) in advance that they will stutter on, as well as the type of stutter to be attempted. In most cases, when a stutterer can do voluntary stuttering, he or she finds that the temptation to avoid or struggle is reduced. It is impossible to avoid something and, at the same time, seek to do it. (See also *faking.*)

APPENDIX I. OTHER IDEAS FOR SUPPORT GROUP SESSIONS

- Arrange for a guest speaker who is well-known in the self-help community to speak to the group, followed by questions. This can be arranged through Zoom, Skype, or another type of electronic meeting.

- Contact another National Stuttering Association (NSA) chapter and arrange to have their group join your group remotely, e.g., through Zoom.

- Following the Dallas NSA tradition, arrange to meet sometimes for a "Chat and Chew" session at a local restaurant with no agenda but to socialize and enjoy one another.

- Begin some meetings with short agendas with an open-ended opportunity for all the stutterers present to simply talk about "what's going on" with them.

- Have a holiday party at someone's house.

- Arrange to publicize the group by setting up a booth at a local health fair, university student union, or some other venue and have it staffed by veteran support group members.

- Invite local speech-language pathologists to attend a meeting. Inform such visitors that the meeting is not a place for them to recommend therapy strategies for members but to discover a place where they can send their own stuttering clients as a place to interact with other stutterers or practice their own speaking techniques.

- If a university training program for speech-language pathologists is nearby, contact the instructor of the course for stuttering or fluency disorders and invite the entire class to a special meeting where they will have an opportunity to learn from real stutterers and ask questions.

APPENDIX J: SAMPLE DESCRIPTIONS OF ACTUAL GROUP MEETINGS

National Stuttering Association Morgantown Chapter Support Group

Location: 802B Allen Hall, WVU
Date: xx/xx/xx
Time: 6:00–7:00 PM
People Who Stutter or Clutter: Jill, Juan, & Dennis

Facilitator: Rita
Co-Facilitator: Brenda
Chapter Leader: Ken
Visitors: Lindsey & Anne

THEME

- Managing and Understanding Listener Reactions

MEETING GOALS:

1. To foster desensitization to listener reactions

2. To foster insight into stuttering by exploring...

    » How to positively change the reaction of a listener to help ensure that you are being heard in the way that you would like to be.

    » How those who stutter can affect listener reactions with most people.

    » How some listeners' reactions cannot be changed.

WELCOMING WORDS: Read by Jill

INDIVIDUAL GOALS: (See below, Individual Goal Evaluation.)

ICEBREAKER

I (Rita) announced to the group that we would be playing a guessing game. "Everyone will be given a face of a well-known person or character. When given the character, we will display it for other players to see, though we will not know what character we are. We will take turns asking yes/no questions to guess the character that we are."

ACTIVITY

1. First, I said to the participants, **"I am going to ask everyone to pair up. Each team will include one speaking role and one listening role. Everyone will get to try out both roles, so it doesn't matter which you are initially. Speakers are encouraged to act naturally as they normally would while given their speaking role. Listeners are encouraged to do their best to portray the listening trait that they have been given while carrying on the conversation. Brenda and I will go first to give everyone an idea of what they will be doing."**

    - Rita: pet store topic (speaker) & Brenda: listener (absent, zoned-out)
    - Jill: hotel topic (speaker) & Lindsey: listener (uncomfortable eye contact)
    - Ken: lost in Toronto without a working phone (speaker) & Dennis: listener (make no eye contact)
    - Juan: looking for the train conductor (speaker) & Anne: listener (act as though you have more important things to do; constantly check your watch)

2. After everyone participated in one role play session, I said to everyone, **"Now we will all switch roles and partners. I'd like to ask everyone to come up in no particular order and take turns playing the opposite role that you played the first time."**

    - Brenda: wanted to return a shirt to a department store (speaker) & Jill: listener (really intense eye contact)
    - Lindsey: went to IKEA to look for a desk (speaker) & Juan: listener (laugh at inappropriate times and make everything seem like a joke)
    - Anne: I left my Mac in my car (speaker) & Rita: listener (constantly interrupt the speaker)
    - Dennis: new student at WVU trying to find their class (speaker) & Ken: listener (very intense eye contact)

3. Once everyone had played both a speaking role and a listening role, I asked the group, **"Now that we have seen many examples of these different listening traits, what are some strategies that we can use to handle a listener that acts in such a way? We can break it down and talk about each listening trait at a time."**

    - Jill: I've talked a lot about this in the past, but when you're having an issue with a bad listener I've learned over the years that it's how I interact with the listener that affects how they listen to me for most cases. Say I'm talking to Ken, and he is trying to give me eye contact but I'm not reciprocating eye contact because I'm too focused on my speech. In the past, I would get really emotional because I would think the listener was mean or rude. But then I realized that they were reacting to me not giving them eye contact. So once I learned to maintain eye contact, even when I stuttered, then the listener also maintained eye contact. For the most part, I feel like we can shape how others will listen to us.

- Rita: I'd say, "Kill them with kindness."
- Jill: If someone is being rude and filling in my words with their words, I'll just keep trying to get my word out and even get louder if I have to.
- Dennis: When people are not good listeners, I will raise my voice when they interrupt me. That seems to be the most common problem that I have. I have difficulty maintaining eye contact myself when I'm talking. When I realize people aren't listening to me anymore, I just give up. I'm not really sure what to do in those situations.
- Juan: I just try to kill bad listeners with kindness. And if they still don't listen, I just continue and kill them with more kindness. If that doesn't work then I might give up, but sometimes I will change how I'm delivering the topic so they might be more apt to listen.
- Ken: I might not be the best listener myself because I tend to interrupt people. I always look for the gap in conversation to get my point in. Maybe because I'm fairly self-assured I often really don't care if someone is a good listener or not. It's not going to stop me, and I'll just go ahead and say what I was going to say. Maybe that's not very effective. It's like giving a lecture; I talked for an hour but did anybody hear me? I like Jill's answer. If people would interrupt me when I was stuttering, then I would just keep on stuttering. If you keep on stuttering through their interruptions then they will realize that they aren't helping, and they will just stop doing it. I think we men can learn something from women; most women, when they are listening, are nodding. It's a female thing; guys tend not to do anything. I've learned that if I do that (nodding) then I have a better conversation.
- Lindsey: It sounds bad, but I would give up easily. I would move on to someone else who could help me, but, if I really needed to talk to a specific person, then I would, "kill them with kindness."
- Anne: I feel like I give up a lot. I'm thinking of a specific co-worker who always talks over me, and I just feel like no matter what I do they will just keep talking over me.

TAKEAWAY LESSONS

I asked, **"Would anyone like to share how they think they can use these strategies to sway listeners into becoming better listeners in real life?"**

- Jill: I find too that a casual disclosure will sometimes make a world of difference. I don't say, "Hi, I stutter, how are you?" but I will say that sometimes it takes me longer to get my words out. And then I will quickly change the subject, which usually works well. For example, if someone walks into the room with one arm, you as a listener will mentally say to yourself, "I'm going to look them in the eye. I'm going to make good eye contact and not stare at their arm." But if you've never met someone who stutters then you have no way of predicting how that conversation is going to turn out. You have no way of knowing that we stutter until we open our mouths, and so you guys are completely caught off guard. So you only have a split second to think about what you will do: "Do I ignore/acknowledge the stutter? Do I make good eye contact?" As the listener who does not stutter, you have no way of preparing yourself for a conversation with a stranger who stutters.

- Juan: I try to be really nice, and at some point I might give up. But usually being nice works well.

- Dennis: In terms of trying to get a class to listen, I do find that sometimes they have trouble remembering what I've said for an assignment. So, then I'll repeat a lot which drives home what I want them to learn or understand. I try to listen to them to the best that I can to try to foster an environment where they feel comfortable and open in class. I reward them for good comments. I also am not sure who among the 40 students is listening and who is not.

- Juan: There are times when I ask a patient, "Do you have any questions?" And that's my way of seeing if they are getting what I'm saying. I think that might help them engage better, and then I can make sure they were listening.

- Dennis: The most obvious way to tell if someone is not listening is if they are looking at their phones. So sometimes I will just glare at someone or get their attention in some way to try not to interrupt the entire class.

INDIVIDUAL GOAL EVALUATION

- Jill: to try and complete each thought (7)
- Dennis: eye contact (8.5)
- Brenda: appropriate loudness level (10)
- Rita: speaking slowly (6)
- Lindsey: good body language/posture when speaking (8)
- Ken: good & bad pull-outs (3)
- Juan: easy onsets (5)
- Anne: appropriate loudness level (7)

CLOSING WORDS: Read by Juan

LISTENING AND SPEAKING ROLES USED

1. Listening Roles:

    - Use a vacant expression while the speaker is talking. Look zoned out. Take long pauses before you talk.
    - Make no eye contact with the speaker. Look behind one of their shoulders, not down. Talk to them as you usually might, but avoid any eye contact.
    - Constantly interrupt the speaker.
    - Act as though you have more important things to do. Constantly check your watch, rush the conversation, and give short answers.
    - Laugh at inappropriate times at things that are not intended to be funny, as if you actually think that they are.
    - Hold strong and uncomfortable eye contact as if you are peering into the soul of the speaker.
    - You're tired and distracted. Yawn frequently and act both bored. Find it hard to have anything to say.

2. Speaking Roles:

    - You're at a department store to return a shirt and you're trying to convince the sale clerk that you bought it from them, but you seem to have lost the receipt.
    - You're at a pet store asking for help to find the perfect toy for your new dog that destroys everything it touches.
    - You're staying at a hotel in NYC and cramming four extra people into your room. You need to go to the lobby to ask for extra towels and blankets as inconspicuously as you can.
    - You're new to WVU and have a class at the downtown campus, though you are on Evansdale campus. You stop a nearby person to explain your situation and ask for help.
    - You're at the Apple store to inquire about why your Mac laptop won't turn on after you left it in your car all day.
    - You're on a train from Pittsburgh to Boston and realize you purchased a ticket for the wrong day, though the train is already moving and the train is full, so you don't have a seat. You find a conductor and explain your story, asking what you should do.

- You need a new desk for your office and go to IKEA to inquire about desk designs and prices. You explain what you like to a sales attendant and ask about what they have at IKEA.
- You're lost in Toronto, Canada. You ask a nearby person for directions on how to find the famous aquarium. You explain that your phone doesn't have a signal since you are not in the states, so you need thorough directions.

National Stuttering Association Morgantown Chapter Support Group

Location: 802B Allen Hall, WVU
Date: xx/xx/xx
Time: 6:00–7:00 PM
People Who Stutter or Clutter: Lucia, Zane, Mia, Robert, Ahmet, Jill, Kevin

Facilitator: Nora
Co-Facilitator: Isabelle
Chapter Leader: Ken
Visitors: Avery, Brooke, Grace, Nicole

THEME

- What Motivates You to Change?

MEETING GOALS

1. To foster insight into stuttering by exploring...

    » Personal major changes made in life

    » Determining what motivates personal changes

    » Change as a process

WELCOMING WORDS: Read by Mia

INDIVIDUAL GOALS: (See below, Individual Goal Evaluation.)

ICEBREAKER

I (Nora) described the negative outcome of not buying the product while Isabelle described the positive benefits of it. I explained that without the Coca-Cola you would be sleepy, dull, distracted, bored, lethargic, sluggish, etc. Isabelle talked about how alert, full of energy, productive, etc. the Coca-Cola would make you feel. In no particular order, I asked participants to choose between purchasing caffeinated Coca-Cola from either Isabelle or me, based on which advertising technique appealed to them the most.

ACTIVITY

I began by stating, "Every time you make a choice and do something, you do so because you want to avoid/remedy a negative or achieve/experience an outcome." I challenged everyone to think of a personal significant change they had made in their life or were currently making. It should not be something small, but something that was a big deal." I gave examples such as moving away from home and beginning or ending a relationship. Then I gave participants the opportunity to share their major change with the group.

- Jill: "Going to buy my first vehicle"
- Lucia: "Study for the Boards coming up"
- Ahmet: "Trying to leave my country"
- Ken: "Divorce"
- Avery: "Transition from undergrad to graduate school"
- Brooke: "Transition from undergrad to graduate school"
- Grace: "Moving from living with a boyfriend to living with a best friend"
- Mia: "Transferred schools after sophomore year"
- Zane: "Coming to college"
- Robert: "Leaving Morgantown after graduation"
- Nicole: "Gaining independence from my parents"
- Isabelle: "Getting my license and driving"
- Nora: "My eating habits"

2. I asked participants, **"What important factors came into play that made you make your change?"** I explained that, when preparation meets opportunity, you are going to change something. I talked about the importance of being ready when it comes to making a change.

- Jill: "Embarrassment in the car I drive now, especially when pulling into parking lots"
- Lucia: "Booked the date and everyone is studying and trying to manage time between studying and working"
- Ahmet: "Had enough of living over there, and I have a strong belief in freedom and over there I can't have that"
- Ken: "Extreme difficulty in going against what I had always said I would do, one of the most agonizing decisions"
- Avery: "Time management and letting go of the 'free time' I had in undergrad"
- Brooke: "Application deadlines and GRE, unsure of decision if WVU was the right school to choose"
- Grace: "Transition of learning to live with a friend"
- Mia: "Went to a really small school with about 2,000 people and wanted away from the high school scene...wanted to go somewhere I loved not just something that was easy"
- Zane: "College was the next step for a job"
- Robert: "Next step that is necessary to take, just have to do it"

- Nicole: "Work in progress, I'm trying to find a balance between pushing away and gaining independence without hurting feelings"
- Isabelle: "Laziness? Part was not having my own car and didn't want to borrow from my mom or have friends to take me places"
- Nora: "Change from living at home and having my mom cook for me to having the freedom to cook and experiment with recipes and flavors on my own"

3. I drew a scale on the board from A–Z, with A representing something not even being on your mind, and Z representing something that has been achieved. I asked participants to plot on the scale where they thought they were with respect to their issues.

    - Jill: "In the process right now, biggest struggle is how much of a monthly payment can I afford? Never having a car payment before is nerve wracking. It feels like I have to have approval from too many outside influences"
    - Lucia: "Can't get around to putting the thoughts into actions"
    - Ahmet: "I have to go back in 2 weeks so I am starting from 0"
    - Ken: "98%...I don't think I'll ever get past all the regret but 25 years have passed so, I am through it"
    - Avery: "Lowest rating possible, bad week to be asked about this topic!"
    - Brooke: "Chugging on, but on the struggle bus right now"
    - Grace: "Haven't quite moved just yet, but I do think about it a lot"
    - Mia: "Transferred schools after sophomore year, so I'm here"
    - Zane: "Z...I'm here"
    - Robert: "Very middle of the spectrum. I know that is something that I have to do, but it just can't happen yet"
    - Nicole: "Middle, working on it, but I haven't achieved it yet"
    - Isabelle: "Achieved it, because I got my license and am driving"
    - Nora: "Happy with where I am, but it is not where I want to be just yet"

4. I moved the focus to the stuttering group. I asked participants, **"Reflect back to the first time you attended this group. Why did you come? and What did you hope to plan or achieve?"**

    - Jill: "Spring 2004, I'd only been stuttering for a month. I didn't have time to react when it started, because a doctor told me about it and started individual and group therapy immediately."
    - Lucia: "Last week was the first time. I'd never had formal speech therapy before, stressful events in life was causing the stuttering episodes to get much worse. I found Ken on the internet and that brought me here."

- Ahmet: "September 2012…It is hard to remember exactly, but I know stuttering was having a big impact on my life and got in touch with someone from NSA who put me in touch with Ken."
- Mia: "My family initiated conversation about therapy, and I took the initiative to look into it and found Ken on the internet. I was really nervous at first, but now I feel thankful to be here."
- Zane: "Dad brought me, and now I come more consistently because I didn't want the stuttering to impact my life in a negative way."
- Robert: "Started coming 3 ½ years ago when I was a freshman in college. I realized I needed to make a change with my speech. The help of my dad gave me the push I needed to come join the group."

5. On the same A–Z scale in another color, I asked participants (with stuttering in mind as their change) to plot on the scale where they thought they were when they first came to group. I then asked participants to explain why they put themselves where they did on the scale.

    - Jill: "I didn't know what I wanted to achieve at the time…just trying to understand what it entailed. I just wanted to learn why I couldn't talk. My stuttering changed me from an introvert to an extrovert. Work on yourself and accept what makes you who you are as a person."
    - Lucia: "Wanted to learn to speak fluently regardless of emotional influences and find out how to get more support. Find comfort in knowing that I am not the only one. It is a part of me, and if I hate that, it is not going to improve anything. I don't want to hate any part of me."
    - Ahmet: "I never know why I come every week, but I know I am way more comfortable now than when I first came. I always hate my stuttering, but since I came here, I am more confident and because of group I can feel that inside of me. It's part of Ahmet."
    - Mia: "My stutter itself hasn't changed as much, but I feel more comfortable with myself. It's been a mental growth process."
    - Zane: "Reduce my stuttering all that I can."
    - Robert: "Be completely fluent, which I quickly learned was probably not going to happen. So it ended up, wanting to be more comfortable."

6. I then asked participants to plot on the scale where they think they are now. I gave them the option of also putting where they think they will be down the road. I again asked them to explain why they put themselves where they did on the scale. (Overall, everyone has furthered his or her process to some capacity!)

    - Jill: Almost all the way to Z on the spectrum

- Lucia: Knew a little coming in and has moved through the process of change a bit, but since it has only been two weeks, still has room to grow
- Ahmet: About letter S on the A-Z spectrum
- Mia: About letter P on the A-Z spectrum
- Zane: About letter E on the A-Z spectrum
- Robert: Almost all the way to Z on the spectrum

7. I proposed the idea of looking at the A–Z scale as a process and briefly described Manning's stages of change [below] as possibly what this process might entail. I had everyone reflect on how far they have come and asked that everyone think about whether this is where they are comfortable being or not.

- Pre-contemplation Stage: Person is generally unaware of the problem and does not recognize the need for change
- Contemplation Stage: Awareness is increasing and the individual begins to actively consider the possibility of change
- Preparation Stage: Individuals begin to identify goals and priorities and may begin making small changes and seek information
- Action Stage: Make and modify changes
- Maintenance Stage: Begin to stabilize their changes

TAKE-AWAY LESSONS

- Change is a process and everyone has their own journey.
- People have to be ready for change.
- Moving targets: you might start out with a change in mind, but upon realizing things about that change you might move back or forward in the process.
- Nobody is going to make a change until they are ready to do it.
- Every time we make a significant change, we are avoiding a negative and/or trying to achieve a positive.
- Sometimes seeking help can help you realize the importance of the other things that make you who you are.
- Change happens when preparation meets opportunity.

INDIVIDUAL GOAL EVALUATION

- Isabelle: Concentrate on listening rather than thinking about what I'm going to say (8)

- Nora: Not type so loudly (8)
- Ken: Use voluntary stuttering to practice (9)
- Ahmet: Concentrate on listening rather than thinking about what I'm going to say (5)
- Avery: Not to get flustered about things out of my control and not use any fillers (6)
- Nicole: To listen and learn (8)
- Jill: Good eye contact (6)
- Brooke: Not fidget (8)
- Zane: To learn (6)
- Grace: To use less fillers and not talk so quickly (7)
- Robert: Use pull-outs if I do stutter (8)
- Mia: Say everything that I want to say and not use replacement words (7)
- Lucia: Speak less than last time (4)
- Kevin (First-time visitor to group): "It was fine."

APPENDIX K: BENEFITS FOR VISITORS

Following are excerpts from written reactions of Communication Sciences and Disorders graduate students who visited the Morgantown NSA Support Group or the nearly identical group therapy over the past years. Their comments speak for themselves.

Kristen: The meeting had a friendly, welcoming atmosphere, which made it easy to speak honestly and be an active participant. I found this to be a positive experience for learning more about stuttering's impact on a person's life as well as identifying and sharing areas of my own life that need support.

Alyssa: Over the course of my past three visits to stuttering group, I have learned so much. I was shocked at the first meeting, because I never expected to gain so much from the group. I learned so much about stuttering and how much it varies from person to person.

Carolyn: My favorite part of the group was how laid back the whole thing is. It was neat to see Ken [professor] in a different setting as well. I am so glad that I was able to attend the group to see stuttering through the eyes of my peers. It was an excellent learning tool for the course.

Cairna: I was surprised at how quickly the time went by during the group. It was very enjoyable and fun. Moreover, it was a very healing, meaningful experience for me. Although I went into group feeling stressed and negative, I felt very joyful on my way home. The group caused me to recognize the positive things in my life, and it gave me the good feeling of having shared life experiences with others.

Casey: Facilitating the stuttering group has been more interesting, educational, and fun than I ever imagined it could be. Not only have I met and gotten to know many different people, I've also learned so much about myself. Even though I don't stutter, I often face the same challenges the stutterers in our group do....The stutterers taught me how to be a better conversational partner, and if I come in contact with others in the future, I will be able to make them comfortable and portray that I am more interested in them as who they are as a person, not what they do as a stutterer. Even though Benjamin and I were the facilitators of the group discussions, the stutterers in the group were definitely the teachers.

Allegra: At this meeting, I had expected to find a fairly somber occasion where techniques on dealing with stuttering were divulged and discussed, and repetitions and prolongations were acknowledged and cancelled. I was pleased to find that the meeting mostly consisted of cheery conversation and humorous individuals who were happy to discuss what stuttering means to their lives, but were much happier just discussing life.

Katie: As someone who is not a stutterer, I was intrigued by the comment Megan made to me, "Now you know what it feels like to be a stutterer!" when I brought up the fact that I often feel panic and don't know what to say when in an uncomfortable situation. When I look back on some of those terrifying moments, I realize that not once during those times did I ever think about how others might feel, like a stutterer, in a similar situation. I believe now when I begin to feel those moments, I will recall her comment, and realize some people have to deal with those feelings all the time.

Hannah: In regards to the activity regarding risks and gains, I think that Ken perfectly summed up the point toward the end, asking, "Is it possible to have the gains without the risks?" In my personal opinion, you have to risk some amount to gain something. Like Tim whispered to me, "No pain, no gain."

LeAnn: One aspect that was very interesting for me was listening to the stutterers in spontaneous conversation. At first, their overt behaviors were very noticeable to me, and a little shocking initially. However, it wasn't long before I hardly noticed or paid attention to the stuttering characteristics. That was one important thing that I learned, that stutterers are just like people who don't stutter. They have unique personalities, and when you get to know them for the people that they are, you don't see the stuttering, but instead, you see their personalities.

Melyssa: I think one important thing to take from the group would be that talking helps. It doesn't matter if you are a stutterer or not, it feels good just to let your feelings be heard. I think Megan said it best by saying that if you hold your feelings in, you're like a can of soda that has been shaken up, you need to let it all out and then the pressure will be released. I think if we all took that advice then we may not have as much ridicule. Everyone has something strange or different about them and if we all could learn to talk and accept each difference I think life's "pressure" would be released.

Isabella: The main activity was so much fun! We were assigned to disclose or not disclose a stutter or other problem while giving a sales pitch. An assortment of ridiculous items were available to "sell" including a dancing Elmo, a plastic orange diamond ring, a cup full of water, and miniature golf clubs. My assignment was to disclose the fact that I sweat profusely after it began happening. So, during my sales pitch on the beautiful plastic ring, I apologized for being a profuse sweater and had to wipe my face several times. Several of the other participants had silly situations like these, while others asked the participant to disclose that they stutter even before they begin their sales pitch. This opened up a rather intense conversation debating whether a stutterer should disclose that they stutter and at what point in a conversation they should do this.

Phil: I really enjoyed the hour that I spent in the stuttering group. I met some fantastic people and heard some really interesting stories about their experiences living with stuttering. This was a great opportunity for me as a student, and as an individual, to get several new aspects of how people cope and live their lives with stuttering. In turn, their ideas and methods of how they deal and overcome certain situations with their stuttering will give me ideas about how to overcome my situational fears.

Jenny: I tend to have a shy and quiet disposition that is often overlooked or overwhelmed in a large group of stronger louder personalities. I've often received the question, "Why are you so quiet?" in a tone that clearly said there's something wrong with you. I used to see this as a flawed trait that I needed to overcome. Over the years I've realized that on some level "being quiet" is a part of who I am, just as "being a stutterer" may be part of who someone is. ... I think the big take away from the stuttering group tonight for both stutterers and nonstutterers is to find the balance between working to overcome what you can control and learning to accept and embrace the things you can't.

Natalie: Tonight, I had such a wonderful time and it was a great experience. After I walked out of that room, I had one big smile on my face. It was very optimistic, and the atmosphere from within the group was so—well—comfortable.

Molly: I learned that group therapy sessions are a great opportunity for expanding social boundaries, learning new techniques, and they are a great way to get to know new people with the same speech disorder. I also think that since the atmosphere was laid back and inviting it helps those who are shy to open up and express themselves. I can personally say that I felt included and not once did I feel out of place. I thoroughly enjoyed the group therapy session and would love to be involved in one in the future!

Meredith: I don't want to sound like a cliché, but I had absolutely no idea what to expect from the support group. I walked in thinking I would not have anything in common with the other members of the group. I left feeling like I had just hung out with my friends. With snacks and casual outfits, I soon became comfortable and casually chatted with other group members about weather and their jobs.

Tori: My goal of learning something new was achieved and far surpassed. Not only did I learn about how important posture, facial expressions and attitudes are, but also that people are unique. Most of the time, just talking to someone does not indicate their true personality and what they stand for. What is more important is what lies beneath the words. The individuals I met in the meeting were truly wonderful and I will, without a doubt, use the lessons I learned there throughout my life.

Blake: I cannot completely express how important this experience was; the take away message I gained was "I can't change anyone's reaction to my struggles, but I can control my reaction." I believe that epiphany will truly help me be a better person. I came expecting to learn all about stuttering and how people who stutter feel; however, I also learned a great deal about myself and my classmates. Stuttering group was a night well spent—full of laughs and insights. Stuttering group is more than just for stutterers, it is for all walks of life. Finally, the closing words were perfect, ending with "share the music of our voices." Truly inspirational.

Whitney: This meeting truly became the highlight of my day. It was also nice that I got to see an old familiar face in Tony. We both attended the same elementary, middle, and high school together. He was a year younger than me, but it was nice to see someone I hadn't seen since I graduated high school. That made this experience even better. After attending the stuttering group, I can truly see how something like group therapy can be extremely helpful for those who stutter. In the future as a speech pathologist, I would like to set up a group similar to this one for stutterers and maybe even for those suffering from other speech and language impairments.

Megan: I found Ryan's goal very interesting and thought provoking. She said she would like to feel more comfortable in a place where there are very few African Americans like herself. Being a minority is something you rarely think about unless you are in fact part of a minority. I have never experienced this so hearing it was very fascinating and frustrating at the same time because I know that I will probably never understand her feelings. I feel that it definitely drew the group closer together because she was able to relate to the members that stuttered. Though most of us weren't directly able to relate, we can all remember a time when we felt like an outsider....I also found it amazing when Megan said that the stuttering group had changed her life for the better. Something that seems small to some, just an hour-long meeting once a week, has had a profound impact on people's lives. Her statement made me want to continue working with clients with fluency disorders in the future, especially involving support groups.

Kaitlyn: I learned a life lesson after attending the group therapy session. What I learned was to take chances in life, to simply live, and to not let anything get in the way of doing something we want to do. After missing an opportunity most of us feel bad about it, so it is important that we take chances. Also, it is important not to worry about what others think because, chances are, they're worrying about what we're thinking of them.

Lauren: The group members were open and honest, the clinicians were fun and easy going, and Ken [group leader] was relaxed, yet daring, when he and Tim struck up a bet that Tim would not stutter, if Ken would.

Brittany: I will definitely take the opinions that were shared in group with me when I am treating an adult or child stutterer. All the research and books in the world will not be as powerful as experiencing the ideas first-hand....Above all, I believe it was thoroughly enjoyable, and we could all use a dose of group therapy once in a while!

Paula: The theme of the group therapy session I attended was "support." I was really touched by how much support each regular group member said they received from the regular stuttering group therapy, as well as how open everyone was with the amount of support they needed and how appreciative each person was of the role the stuttering group played in their lives. From attending only one session, I truly realized how effective the stuttering group therapy is. Although there was a structure and theme to the evening's session, the simple fact of each other's presence and acceptance of each other was the most powerful component.

ABOUT THE AUTHOR

Kenneth O. St. Louis is an emeritus professor of speech-language pathology at West Virginia University (WVU). Ken's primary focus for nearly 50 years has been to improve the lives of people with fluency disorders. His career as a speech-language pathologist, college professor, and scientist involved teaching classes to more than 4500 undergraduate and graduate students, supervising or treating hundreds of adults and children who stutter, presenting to more than 400 professional audiences, and publishing more than 200 peer-reviewed journal articles, chapters, or books. He has been recognized as a Fellow of the American Speech-Language-Hearing Association and was awarded the Lifetime Achievement Award by the International Fluency Association. Other awards include the Deso Weiss Award for Excellence in Cluttering, the Dave Rowley Award for International Initiatives, WVU's Benedum Distinguished Scholar Award, and WVU's Heebink Award for Outstanding Service to the State of West Virginia. He led efforts to found the International Fluency Association, the International Cluttering Association, and the first specialty recognition program for fluency and fluency disorders. Twenty years ago, he inaugurated the International Project of Attitudes Toward Human Attributes with the mission of measuring and improving public attitudes toward stuttering around the world. In this still ongoing effort, Ken has collaborated with hundreds of colleagues internationally.

Ken struggled with stuttering as a child and young adult, but, with excellent therapy, since college has been mostly recovered. The exception was a two-year stint in the US Peace Corps in Turkey, where his stuttering returned while speaking Turkish. Ken has visited Turkey many times, and still collaborates with numerous colleagues there.

www.ingramcontent.com/pod-product-compliance
Lightning Source LLC
Chambersburg PA
CBHW080437170426
43195CB00017B/2808